Psychology Revivals

Applications of Conditioning Theory

The area of applied psychology known as behaviour modification or behaviour therapy had progressed remarkably in the ten years, prior to publication. Illustrative of this progress is the variety of therapeutic and behaviour management techniques now available to the applied psychologist. This volume, originally published in 1981, describes some of the important characteristics of this development, and in particular, the relationship between behaviour change techniques and the principles of conditioning theory that generated them.

This brief gives rise to three main themes. First, the book describes some of the reasons underlying the adoption of the conditioning paradigm and the epistemological advantages of the paradigm for behaviour modification. Second, a number of chapters discuss the current trends in specific areas of applied psychology where conditioning principles play an important heuristic role. These chapters deal with the uses made of conditioning theory in the areas of mental handicap, psychiatric therapy, work organizations, and the treatment of brain injury. Third, later chapters discuss some of the more recent theoretical developments in the field of behaviour modification/therapy, in particular the drift from strict behaviouristic applications of conditioning principles to more cognitive ones.

Applications of Conditioning Theory

Edited by
Graham Davey

LONDON AND NEW YORK

First published in 1981
by Methuen & Co. Ltd.

This edition first published in 2018 by Routledge
2 Park Square, Milton Park, Abingdon, Oxon OX14 4RN

and by Routledge
711 Third Avenue, New York, NY 10017

Routledge is an imprint of the Taylor & Francis Group, an informa business

© 1981 This collection; Methuen & Co. Ltd
© 1981 Individual chapters; the respective authors

All rights reserved. No part of this book may be reprinted or reproduced or utilised in any form or by any electronic, mechanical, or other means, now known or hereafter invented, including photocopying and recording, or in any information storage or retrieval system, without permission in writing from the publishers.

Publisher's Note
The publisher has gone to great lengths to ensure the quality of this reprint but points out that some imperfections in the original copies may be apparent.

Disclaimer
The publisher has made every effort to trace copyright holders and welcomes correspondence from those they have been unable to contact.

A Library of Congress record exists under ISBN: 0416735606

ISBN: 978-1-138-57485-4 (hbk)
ISBN: 978-1-351-27308-4 (ebk)
ISBN: 978-1-138-57494-6 (pbk)

Applications of Conditioning Theory

edited by
GRAHAM DAVEY

METHUEN
LONDON AND NEW YORK

*First published in 1981 by
Methuen & Co. Ltd.
11 New Fetter Lane, London EC4P 4EE
Published in the USA by
Methuen & Co.
in association with Methuen, Inc.
733 Third Avenue, New York, NY 10017
This collection © Methuen and Co. Ltd 1981
Individual chapters © the respective authors 1981
Typeset by Inforum Ltd, Portsmouth
All rights reserved. No part of this book may be reprinted
or reproduced or utilized in any form or by any electronic,
mechanical or other means, now known or hereafter
invented, including photocopying and recording, or in
any information storage or retrieval system, without
permission in writing from the publishers.*

British Library Cataloguing in Publication Data

Applications of conditioning theory. –
(Psychology in progress)
1. Behavior modification
I. Davey, Graham   II. Series
153.8'5   BF637.B4   80-42230

ISBN 0-416-73560-6
ISBN 0-416-73570-3 Pbk

Contents

Notes on the Contributors	vii
Editor's introduction	xi
1 The experimental analysis of behaviour and its relevance to applied psychology *Derek Blackman*	1
2 Applied behaviour analysis: intervention with retarded people *Laurence Tennant, Chris Cullen and John Hattersley*	29
3 The token economy *Alan Kazdin*	59
4 Application of behaviour modification in the treatment of traumatically brain-injured adults *Rodger Wood and Peter Eames*	81
5 Behaviour modification in organizations *Graham Davey*	102
6 Pavlovian principles and behaviour therapy *Glyn Thomas and Mark O'Callaghan*	129
7 Establishing behaviour: the constructional approach *Chris Cullen, John Hattersley and Laurence Tennant*	149

8 Self-instructional training and cognitive behaviour 162
modification: a behavioural analysis
Fergus Lowe and Peter Higson

9 Conditioning principles, behaviourism and 190
behaviour therapy
Graham Davey

Name index 215
Subject index 221

Notes on the contributors

Derek Blackman is Professor and Head of the Department of Psychology at University College, Cardiff. He wrote *Operant Conditioning: An Experimental Analysis of Behaviour* (Methuen, 1974), and with Dr. D.J. Sanger edited *Contemporary Research in Behavioral Pharmacology* (Plenum, 1978). He has served on the Editorial Board of the *Journal of the Experimental Analysis of Behavior*. His research interests have centred on operant conditioning in animals, especially in recent years with respect to the effects of drugs on behaviour. However, he also has interests in general aspects of contemporary behaviourism.

Chris Cullen is currently director of a research project on facilitating residents' development in mental handicap hospitals, based at the Hester Adrian Research Centre, University of Manchester. His Ph.D was gained in 1975 for work on complex schedules or reinforcement and he later went on to qualify as a clinical psychologist. His research interests primarily concern applications of the philosophy of radical behaviourism to human affairs, both clinical and social, and his published work reflects this orientation.

Graham Davey is a lecturer in psychology at The City University, London and has published articles on animal learning and human behaviour modification. Recently he has written *Animal*

Learning and Conditioning (Macmillan, 1981) and is currently editing a book on animal models and human behavior (John Wiley forthcoming). His research activities are centred around Pavlovian and instrumental conditioning in animals, but also include an interest in Pavlovian conditioning in humans and behavioural self-control techniques.

Alan E. Kazdin is Professor of Psychiatry and Program Director of the Children's Psychiatric Intensive Care Service of Western Psychiatric Institute and Clinic, University of Pittsburgh School of Medicine. His interests include evaluation of behavioural techniques primarily with children, and assessment of child psychopathology. His most recent books include *History of Behavior Modification* (University Park, 1978); *The Token Economy* (ed., Plenum, 1977) and *Research Design in Clinical Psychology*.

C. Fergus Lowe is a Lecturer in Psychology at the University College of North Wales, Bangor. He has published numerous articles and book chapters dealing with human and animal learning. He has edited (with C. Bradshaw and E. Szabadi) *The Quantification of Steady-State Operant Behaviour* (Elsevier/North Holland, 1981) and is a member of the Editorial Boards of: *Journal of the Experimental Analysis of Behaviour*, *Behaviour Analysis Letters* and *The Behaviour Analyst*. Presently, he organizes the Experimental Analysis of Behaviour Group in the UK. His research interests include the development of verbal control of behaviour in children, self-instructional therapies, and temporal psychophysics in animals and humans.

Mark O'Callaghan is currently Clinical Psychologist for Solihull Area Health Authority with special responsibilities for rehabilitation services, and a community-based residential service. Current research interests concern the relevance of behavioural principles to the neuropsychological and neurophysiological approaches to schizophrenia and stuttering. He is co-author with Dr Douglas Carroll of *Psychosurgery: A scientific analysis* to be published shortly by Charles C. Thomas.

Peter Eames is Consultant Neuropsychiatrist at St. Andrew's Hospital, Northampton. His specialist training, acquired mainly in the Royal Air Force, was in neurology and psychiatry, but his clinical practice over the past ten years has focused mainly on the 'no-man's land' between these two disciplines, neuropsychiatry. Two years ago, he was involved in setting up The Kemsley Unit, a special unit for the management of behaviour disorders in head-injured adults, and for their concomitant rehabilitation. In addition to the study of this novel area of application of behavioural treatment methods, his research interests concern brain mechanisms as revealed by clinical and clinical-neurophysiological experience and study, and the development of treatment methods arising from this.

John Hattersley is Principal Clinical Psychologist based at Coldeast Hospital, Southampton. He obtained his M.Sc in clinical Psychology at Birmingham University and has since specialized in work with mentally retarded people and their families. His interests are based upon the application of a radical behaviourist orientation to clinical work. His research interests include support groups for parents with retarded children, teaching methods for use with retarded individuals and the stimulus control of behaviour.

Peter J. Higson is a Clinical Psychologist at the North Wales Hospital, Denbigh. He has published articles on animal and human learning processes. Currently he is a member of the national committee of the British Association for Behavioural Psychotherapy and is one of the editors of the Association's Newsletter. His clinical/research interests include behavioural approaches to the rehabilitation of psychiatric patients, the nature of verbal control over in psychotic individuals, and self-instructional therapies.

Laurence Tennant is currently District Principal Psychologist in the Northern District of Warwickshire Area Health Authority, where he is responsible for the Clinical Psychology Service. His research activities have centred on the application of radical behaviourism in a variety of clinical settings. In recent years, through an honorary appointment to the University of Birmingham, his teaching interests have included a post graduate course on radical behaviourism in clinical psychology.

x   Applications of conditioning theory

Glyn Thomas is currently Lecturer in the Department of Psychology, University of Birmingham. His early research work concerned temporal discrimination and schedule control of operant behaviour for which he was awarded the degree of PhD by the University of Nottingham. His published work includes studies of basic learning processes in animals and applications of learning theory to clinical psychology and to the training of mentally handicapped children.

Rodger Wood is Consultant Neuropsychologist at St. Andrew's Hospital, Northampton. Part of his work has been the organization of a behaviour management programme to facilitate the retraining and rehabilitation of severely brain-injured patients. His research interests include the management of acquired behaviour disorders after head-injury, and the effects of attentional impairment on behavioural learning. He has published research papers on the relationship of attentional disturbance to early schizophrenic illness, and on a comparison of psychological and neuro-radiological indices of brain damage.

Editor's introduction

All undergraduate psychology students know that our knowledge of conditioning stems from the work of such people as E.L. Thorndike and J.B. Watson in the United States, and the physiological studies of the Russian Nobel Prizewinner Ivan Pavlov, and yet, although they are familiarized with the jargon, the principles and the details of those clumsy prototypical experiments, they are rarely taught – and almost certainly fail to appreciate – the hopes that these scientists held for a better world as a result of their discoveries. For the reader possessing only the layman's knowledge of conditioning, the links between a salivating dog, rats running mazes and hopes and aspirations for a 'better world' must seem tenuous if not entirely puzzling. Even so, perhaps more remarkable is the fact that these scientists working at the turn of the century, and apparently tinkering with the physiology and behaviour of animals, could foresee the potential of the principles they were uncovering. Ivan Petrovich Pavlov was arguably the most influential of these figures, and he is important in the historical development of conditioning for two major reasons. Firstly, he was the person who initially developed the idea of the adaptive nature of physiological phenomena, and characterized this by bringing together the doctrines of associationism and reflexology – a combination which was to provide the basis for nearly all future principles of conditioning. Secondly, and perhaps most important, to all intents and purposes he demystified the phenomena of learning. Those before him – and even his close contemporaries – were content to interpret learning as the manifestations of the learner's 'psychical' activity: for instance, secretion from the dog's salivary gland during conditioning seemed merely to reflect a certain inner state of the organism which was inaccessible to investigation by scientific methods. However, Pavlov spurned these 'psychical' interpretations and remained faithful to his materialistic upbringing by explaining his findings in terms of environmental-behaviour interactions, and by purposely disregarding the thoughts, desires and emotions of the animal undergoing the experiment.

These principles, as all informed readers will know, eventually helped to give rise to the influential American school of psychology known as Behaviourism. J.B. Watson, often considered to be the founder of behaviourism, based much of his writings on the concepts of conditioning outlined by Pavlov, and even took them to their logical extreme by claiming that practically all meaningful human behaviour was the result of environmental contingencies operating through the principles of conditioning. However, both Watson and Pavlov were well aware of the possible affront to human dignity that would be sparked by the denigration of free will inherent in the conditioning approach to behaviour. A man's destiny was apparently removed from his own control and placed in the unsympathetic hands of the environment. Pavlov, clearly, preferred to contend that his materialistic analysis of behaviour had changed nothing: the notion of free will still remained, even in his own mind. In 1932 he wrote:

> is not man at the summit of nature?.... Is not this sufficient to maintain the dignity of man, to fill him with highest satisfaction? And there still remains in life all that is also embraced by the idea of freedom of will with its personal, social, and civic responsibility; for me these still remain and hence also the obligation for me to know myself and constantly using this information, to maintain myself at the utmost height of my capabilities. Are not the social and civic duties and requirements situations which present themselves to my system, and which must lead to appropriate reactions that will promote the integrity and perfection of the system?

Watson, on the other hand, believed that although the classical notion of free will had been devalued within a conditioning framework, this analysis did allow the individual greater understanding of why he did the things he did, and in that fact his dignity could be maintained and his position in nature set apart from other animals.

It is at this point in time that we see the first glimmerings of a behavioural technology based on learning principles. In the most complete statement of his psychological position, *Psychology from the Standpoint of a Behaviourist* (1919), Watson ultimately emphasized that psychology – be it behaviourist or any other persuasion – should exist to help man and, although he rarely discussed the ethical issues that a technology of behaviour might raise, he nevertheless conveyed a crusading attitude to applying his psychology, Indeed, he believed that it was largely on an individual level that a behaviourist analysis could be most useful. In a biography of Watson, David Cohen (1979) writes:

> Armed, with what Watson termed 'the balance sheet of the self', you can set about developing that strength, combating that foible, getting rid of that irrational fear, working on yourself as if you were a piece of clay to mould. The interesting thing about this idea is that, for Watson, it was the individual who could usually choose how and where to improve himself. His ideal society was one of self-shapers. People could use psychology to make themselves better, more 'efficient' than they were. Many of the questions that he asked individuals to confront themselves with are precisely the kinds of questions that occur in encounter groups or other forms of therapy. Each individual should exploit psychology. The science of psychology, like the other sciences, was there to enhance the perfectibility of man.

Even Watson, it seems, advocated the use of conditioning principles for self-control, an aspiration which was not to be realized until the advent of behavioural self-control and cognitive behaviour modification techniques during the 1970s.

As it turned out, conditioning principles were applied only sporadically to human problems during the forty or so years following 1919, and most time was taken up between 1930-50 constructing elaborate, but often unwieldy, theories of animal learning. Surprisingly enough, although Watson and Rayner's classic study of conditioning in Little Albert is regularly cited as one of the cornerstones of the conditioning approach to psychotherapy, it sparked little activity in its immediate wake. Indeed, rather than being an impetus for the immediate application of conditioning theory, it appeared to drift into folklore, with few of the references that subsequently cited it providing anything like an accurate account of the original study (Harris, 1979)!

In fact, the aspirations of Pavlov and Watson had to wait until the late 1950s before a conditioning theory analysis of human problems was reborn. Applications of conditioning theory appeared first of all in clinical settings, as rather crude adaptations of simple Pavlovian principles to neuroses and emotional problems, or as the application of operant reinforcement theory to behavioural disorders in psychiatric patients (see Chapter 9). These divergent roots led to two broad areas of application. Firstly, behaviour therapy, which relied for its theoretical support on Pavlovian principles and often consisted of therapies which contained an uneasy mix of conditioning principles and psychodynamic assumptions that many therapists were unwilling to completely abandon. Secondly, there was behaviour modification, which derived its *raison d'être* not so much from specific conditioning principles as from a general functional approach to the explanation of behaviour. This group of therapies relied heavily on the radical behaviourist writings of B.F. Skinner and the central tenet that behaviour was controlled by the nature of its environmental consequences. Because of their inherent nature (e.g. dealing primarily with emotional problems of a one-to-one client-therapist basis), behaviour therapy techniques have tended to be restricted to the clinical settings for which they were initially devised. This was not so with behaviour modification: because these techniques were based more on a commitment to an explanatory paradigm than on specific principles, their usage has expanded to cover a huge variety of situations where behaviour change is required. In a review for the United States Department of Health, Education and Welfare in 1975, Brown, Wienckowski and Stolz (1975, pp. 3-4) catalogued the many situations in which behaviour modification techniques had been used (see also Chapter 3, and Davey, 1981). These included

Editor's introduction xv

(1) their use with autistic children, who might otherwise have to be continually restrained because of their self-destructive behaviour,

(2) the teaching of relatively advanced linguistic and self-help skills to severely mentally handicapped children, who were previously considered incapable of acquiring anything but the most fundamental responses (see Chapter 2),

(3) the use of behaviour modification techniques to improve teaching methods and classroom management,

(4) their use in teaching social skills and helping with marriage guidance problems, and

(5) apart from their now accepted use in clinical and therapeutic settings, such techniques have been extended to social problems such as 'the facilitation of cooperative living in a public housing project, decreasing littering, encouraging the use of public transportation and enabling unemployed persons to find jobs'.

Apart from this explosive expansion in the problems considered relevant to a technology based on conditioning principles, the techniques derived from conditioning theory have themselves undergone significant diversification in the 1970s. Many therapies (e.g. overcorrection, generalized imitation, behavioural rehearsal) involve principles which are not readily reducible to traditional principles found in any conditioning theory (Chapter 9). Other therapies have disposed of the modifier-modified relationship by teaching the individual to arrange his own contingencies of reinforcement (e.g. behavioural self-control). Finally, perhaps the most radical change has involved the mixing of two paradigms which classical theorists such as Watson would have probably found intolerable: the creation of cognitive behaviour modification techniques by applying conditioning principles to change what are essentially 'cognitive' attributes. This latter category is continually expanding, but currently includes such techniques as covert conditioning, coping-skill therapies and self-instructional training (see Chapter 8).

Thus, we have reached the point in the history of applications of conditioning theory at which this volume appears. After a faltering start, and in a climate that was largely hostile to what was called this 'crude slot-machine model' of the mind (Koestler,

xvi Applications of conditioning theory

1967), conditioning theory has finally given birth to a spectrum of therapeutic and management techniques of which Watson and Pavlov surely could not have conceived.

This volume was designed to bring together a number of authors who have worked for some years with conditioning theory, either in the laboratory or in the applied field. The chapters they have contributed address three major questions related to recent progress in applied conditioning theory:

(1) What kinds of technique are available to a clinician within a particular applied field?
(2) Conversely, what is the range of problems in which particular techniques have been successfully used?
(3) Are many modern behaviour therapy or behaviour modification techniques faithful to, or consistent with, their conditioning theory heritage?

The first five chapters explore the first two themes. In Chapter 1, Derek Blackman introduces the assumptions of the approach on which much behaviour modification is based – the experimental analysis of behaviour. Chapters 2, 4 and 5 critically discuss the analysis and behaviour change techniques currently available in three areas of application: mental handicap (Laurence Tennant, Chris Cullen and John Hattersley), the rehabilitation of brain-injured patients (Rodger Wood and Peter Eames), and work organizations (Graham Davey). In Chapter 3, Alan Kazdin reviews the diversity of situations to which Allyon and Azrin's Token Economy system has been successfully applied.

The later chapters deal largely with more theoretical issues and the relationship between behaviour change techniques and modern conditioning theory. Recent developments in our knowledge of the associative mechanisms underlying Pavlovian conditioning in animals suggest that a critical reappraisal of therapies based on Pavlovian principles should be attempted. In Chapter 6, Glyn Thomas and Mark O'Callaghan come to the conclusion that although one might be uneasy about the original rationale for many of these therapies, recent findings may help to guide the therapist in his choice of techniques for particular behavioural-emotional problems. In Chapter 7, Chris Cullen, John Hattersley and Laurence Tennant elaborate the virtues of Goldiamond's constructional approach to behavioural problems. It is certainly

Editor's introduction xvii

the case that in its early days many behaviour therapists saw applied conditioning theory simply as a means of irradicating undesirable behaviours rather than as a method of constructing new and adaptive behavioural repertoires. This was a misconception whose results probably fuelled the rather sterile debate on the existence of symptom substitution following the use of behavioural therapeutic techniques. In Chapter 8, Fergus Lowe and Peter Higson move on to discuss some of the attributes of that relatively new branch of applied conditioning theory – cognitive behaviour modification. In particular, they discuss the utility of self-instructional training, emphasizing the relative neglect by behaviour theorists of the verbal control of behaviour, and how this analysis might be integrated within a radical behaviourist framework.

Finally, we might ask 'how does the contemporary state of applied conditioning theory stand in relation to its origins in Watsonian behaviourism and Pavlovian and Thorndikian conditioning theory?' Behaviour modification and behaviour therapy techniques of one kind or another are used frequently in the majority of clinical psychology settings in the United Kingdom and the United States – usually successfully. But had Watson and Pavlov been bestowed with eternal youth and an endless enthusiasm to pursue their academic and social aspirations, would these techniques have been the end-products of their work? I sincerely doubt it. They almost certainly provided a broad philosophical base for the explanation of behaviour which behaviour therapists and behaviour modifiers still tacitly adhere to; and probably they also provided some of the first statements advocating a technology based on a scientific, experimentally oriented psychology. Nevertheless, they may have unwittingly done applied conditioning theory a disservice by discovering their principles with non-human animals. As Bandura (1974) has pointed out:

> The capacity to learn from correlated experiences reflects sensitivity, but because Pavlov first demonstrated the phenomenon with a dog, it has come to be regarded as a base animalistic process. Had he chosen to study physiological hyperactivity in humans to cues associated with stress, or the development of empathetic reactions to expressions of suffering, conditioning would have been treated in a more enlightened way.

Cognitive behaviour modification has gone some way to incorporating these 'base animalistic processes' into a framework more acceptable to those who consider cognitive variables to be of necessary importance in mediating human behaviour. But, like all technologies, it is eventually practical effectiveness that overrides theoretical dogma, and many present-day behaviour change techniques can probably be best described as playing only lip-service to their behaviourist origins and, in many cases, the conditioning principles on which they purport to be based. These are my conclusions in Chapter 9. However, this is not to denigrate the heuristic value of conditioning theory – either in the past or at the present time. Conditioning theory still provides an effective analytical framework for identifying the variables controlling behaviour, and recent advances in conditioning theory – even with non-human animals – can still provide insights into what manipulations will be effective for which problems. What the final therapeutic product will look like, however, will be determined by the desire to achieve specific goals rather than the faith one holds in particular theoretical tenets.

GRAHAM DAVEY

References

Bandura, A. (1974) Behavior theory and models of man. *American Psychologist* 29: 859–69.

Brown, B.S., Wienckowski, L.A., and Stolz, S.B. (1975) *Behavior Modification: Perspective on a Current Issue*. US Dept. of Health, Education and Welfare: Publication No. (ADM) 75-202.

Cohen, D. (1979) *J.B. Watson: The founder of Behaviourism*. London: Routledge & Kegan Paul.

Davey, G.C.L. (1981) How Skinner's theories work: Behaviour analysis and environmental problems. *Bulletin of the British Psychological Society*.

Harris, B. (1979) Whatever happened to little Albert? *American Psychologist* 34: 151–60.

Koestler, A. (1967) *The Ghost in the Machine*. London: Hutchinson.

1 The experimental analysis of behaviour and its relevance to applied psychology

D. E. Blackman

This chapter discusses in a general way the relationships beteen one systematic approach to experimental psychology and an orientation to problems confronted by applied psychologists. It is often asserted that 'the experimental analysis of behaviour' has provided the scientific foundation for 'applied behaviour analysis' and for the techniques of 'behaviour modification'. However, the links between basic and applied research in these fields have also sometimes appeared to be strained. To what extent, then, do they share common assumptions, aims and methods? In what respects do they diverge?

In order to consider such questions, it is necessary to define our terms carefully and resist being sucked into a loose use of words which has allowed them, particularly 'behaviour modification', to mean different things to different people. In doing this, it is not of course possible to claim to be an arbiter of *correct* language, for the meaning of a word is in its usage and the usage of words evolves over time. Nevertheless, it can at least be asserted immediately that the contemporary movement within psychology known as *'the* experimental analysis of behaviour' is merely *one* approach to investigating behaviour experimentally, that the term 'applied behaviour analysis' is but one system of analysing and interpreting behaviour in applied settings, and that not all methods (not even all effective methods) of changing behaviour

2 Applications of conditioning theory

are to be subsumed under the rubric of 'behaviour modification'. Perhaps these bald statements made at the outset may serve to assuage to some extent any expectation that by embarking on this discussion we are engaging in an imperialistic crusade which seeks to define psychology, both pure and applied, in a particular way, insensitive to the aspirations and achievements of psychologists of different persuasions.

The experimental analysis of behaviour

First then, what are the distinctive characteristics of 'the' experimental analysis of behaviour? It has been suggested previously (Blackman, 1974) that there are three identifiable and logically separate aspects of this approach. These are: (i) the use of the experimental techniques of operant conditioning; (ii) the search for empirical statements about behaviour which are valid and reliable but which relate to individuals rather than to differences between groups; (ii) the broad philosophical position within psychology known as radical behaviourism. When these three elements are combined together, they result in a coherent and effective strategy in experimental psychology. However, since the three strands are logically distinct, each deserves careful consideration in its own right.

Operant conditioning

The experimental methods of operant conditioning have developed from Skinner's pioneering investigations (1938). He defined operant behaviour as that which organisms emit and which is affected by its consequences, intending thereby to distinguish it from the more stereotyped and limited reflexes which are simply elicited by antecedent stimuli and which formed the basis of earlier experimental studies in classical, or Pavlovian, conditioning. Operant conditioning is the empirical study of how such emitted and potentially variable behaviour may nevertheless adjust to different arrangements of environmental circumstances and consequences. The prototypical experiment certainly requires little exposition here, so well-known has it become in psychology. In general, laboratory animals such as rats or pigeons are exposed to consistent arrangements of environmental events which are carefully controlled by the investigator. This can be achieved by testing the animals in constrained chambers (Skinner boxes) in which extraneous and uncontrolled environmental variations can be kept to a minimum, and in which the animals can remain for substantial periods of time without being disturbed by the experimenter. Within such environments, a limited number of readily controlled events can be introduced by the experimenters. These generally take the form of lights or noises (either of which may be sustained or relatively brief), the delivery of small amounts of food or water, and in some experiments the occasional delivery of brief electric shocks. Within these limited arrangements, the animal is free to behave in a variety of ways at any time. However, there is usually some device in the test chamber which can be readily operated by the animal, such as a key at which a pigeon may peck or a lever which a rat may press. If such patterns of behaviour occur, they can be easily recorded in a consistent and objective manner, usually by the automatic sensing of the closure of a microswitch or contact relay, though more sophisticated recording systems have also been used. Normally these patterns of behaviour, which are arbitrarily selected on the basis of their convenience to both the experimenter and the animal, provide the examples of operant behaviour whose occurrence is studied in the different conditions provided by different arrangements of lights, noises, food-presentations, etc.

These examples of operant behaviour are usually called responses, though it must be emphasized that this term defines the unit of behaviour studied and should not be taken to imply that the behaviour, which the animal is normally free to emit or not at any time during an experimental session, is bound to some eliciting stimulus as are the reflexes studied in classical conditioning. A good deal of unnecessary confusion might have been avoided if the units of operant behaviour had been termed 'bits' or 'acts', but the use of the term operant responses has become entrenched over time. A similar point might be made with respect to the environmental events such as the noises or lights normally employed in operant conditioning experiments. These have been termed stimuli although they rarely elicit an 'automatic' reaction on the part of the animals and they therefore do not have the properties of a goad which characterize the stimuli used in classical conditioning experiments.

The highly controlled experimental arrangements used by

4 Applications of conditioning theory

operant conditioners have made it possible to study effectively the ways in which simple patterns of behaviour are influenced by different arrangements of environmental events. At the most basic level, of course, it can be shown that the lever-pressing of rats becomes more frequent if it is followed by certain events; for example by the presentation of food, especially if the experimental animal has been deprived of food for a short time. It is required by the definition of operant behaviour that it should be affected by its consequences, and when the frequency of lever-pressing (operant responding) increases in this way, the consequence is defined as a reinforcer and the strengthening of behaviour is termed reinforcement.

Operant conditioners have investigated the ways in which different rules for delivering reinforcers affect behaviour. They have demonstrated (some might say ad nauseam!) that the intermittent delivery of reinforcers can exert very powerful effects and that characteristic patterns of operant behaviour over time emerge as a function of different schedules of reinforcement to which an animal is exposed. The early work of Ferster and Skinner (1957) showed, for example, that when the number of reinforcers to be delivered is expressed as a proportion of the number of responses emitted (ratio schedules) high rates of responding are typical, whereas when the availability of reinforcers is determined by the passage of time (interval schedules) lower rates of operant responding occur. Similarly, rates of responding are more consistent over time when reinforcement is unpredictable (variable schedules) then when it occurs after a specified number of responses or becomes available after a specified period (fixed schedules). One enduring interest in operant conditioning has been to identify exactly the important aspects of schedules of reinforcement which lead to these characteristic patterns of schedule-controlled behaviour in experiments with animals (for a recent set of such experimental and theoretical analyses, see Zeiler and Harzem, 1979).

Another important interest has been in discovering the circumstances in which events will serve as reinforcers. Since a reinforcer is defined in terms of its effects on behaviour, it is an empirical matter to specify when such events as the delivery of food or the delivery of other stimuli such as noises or lights or even electric shocks will serve to increase the frequency of the behaviour to which they are related (see Gollub, 1977; and Morse and Kelleher, 1977, for recent reviews of these topics). Operant conditioners have also investigated the effects on established behaviour of withholding reinforcers (extinction: see Ferster and Skinner, 1957) and of delivering response-dependent events which lead to a decrease in the frequency of that behaviour (punishment: see Azrin and Holz, 1966). They have also studied the effects on behaviour of schedules which maintain behaviour by reducing the frequency with which an event is delivered ('avoidance' schedules: see Hineline, 1977). The details of such work are not relevant here, except in so far as it is possible to claim that operant conditioners have done a great deal of experimental work to investigate and identify the effects on behaviour of different forms of consequences and different arrangements for their delivery. Their experiments have taken psychologists a very long way from a simple awareness that some patterns of behaviour can be affected by their consequences.

A parallel, but sometimes less emphasized, interest in operant conditioning has been the experimental investigation of the discriminative control of behaviour. At its simplest, this develops from the observation that aspects of the environment which accompany specified schedules of reinforcement may come to set the occasion for patterns of behaviour appropriate to that schedule. For example, if a pecking key is illuminated with a green light whenever a variable-interval schedule of reinforcement is in operation but is lit with a red light when no reinforcers are scheduled, pigeons will begin to peck at the key at a moderate sustained rate whenever the green light is present but will cease responding in the presence of the red light. In such a situation, the experimenter finds himself in a position to turn on or off at will the key pecking behaviour of the pigeon simply by presenting the green or red light on the key. Once again, a great deal of experimental work has been conducted to identify the circumstances in which an event (a discriminative stimulus) may acquire such facilitatory or inhibitory control over operant behaviour (see Terrace, 1966).

Operant conditioning has been a particularly active part of experimental psychology for more than two decades. Like other fields of experimental endeavour, it has become increasingly technical and doubtless ever more intimidating to the newcomer.

6 Applications of conditioning theory

Current work in this area is characterized by investigations of increasingly complex patterns of behaviour. For example, the ways in which animals allocate responses between alternative schedules which are simultaneously available have provided a method of studying 'choice' in experimental animals. The field is also marked by the use of increasingly complex mathematical expressions as operant conditioners attempt to improve the precision in their ability to quantify behaviour in relation to measurable aspects of the environment in which it occurs (see Bradshaw, Szabadi and Lowe, 1980; Zeiler and Harzem, 1979). Furthermore the experimental work of operant conditioners has in recent years become better integrated with the theoretical and experimental concerns of other psychologists, as for example with species-differences in behaviour (e.g. Seligman and Hager, 1972) and varying theoretical interpretations of learning (e.g. Mackintosh, 1974), and for this reason operant conditioning has become more diffuse from a theoretical point of view. However, for the purpose of the present chapter enough has perhaps been said to identify the principal features of operant conditioning as a component in the experimental analysis of behaviour: its principle concern is the empirical investigation of the relationships between emitted behaviour and the environmental milieu in which it occurs. It has demonstrated the power of consequences and setting conditions to exert characteristic control over patterns of behaviour which are free to occur at any time. To this extent, operant conditioners have provided empirical evidence that the behaviour of animals in controlled experiments is a delicate function of the environmental conditions to which they are exposed, and they have therefore made a significant (but not all-embracing) contribution to experimental psychology in general.

Single subject vs. group studies

The second element in 'the' experimental analysis of behaviour concerns the logical nature of the statements which psychologists working within this tradition seek to make. All empirical psychologists, of course, aspire to knowledge about behaviour which is valid and reliable, and which has some degree of generality. That is to say, their data should be correct and should support the interpretations which are placed on them, they should be

The experimental analysis of behaviour 7

likely to emerge once more if a direct replication of a study is carried out, and they should normally have some general significance rather than being limited to the particular subjects used or to the specific situation investigated. Beyond such common goals, however, Bakan (1967) has distinguished two different kinds of statement. He describes these as aggregate propositions and general propositions. The former assert something which is presumed to be true of samples of subjects considered *as* aggregates, while the latter assert something which is presumed to be true of each and every member of a designable class of subjects. Either kind of statement can emerge from appropriate experimental investigations, but workers in 'the' experimental analysis of behaviour overtly aim for general propositions through their studies of limited numbers of individual subjects.

The distinction between these two kinds of statements may appear vague and can sometimes be overlooked. It is therefore worth considering a hypothetical example. Suppose, for example, we wish to examine the proposition that people are happier in Italy than in Norway. We could aim to check the validity of this statement as an aggregage proposition by asking random samples of people who live in Italy and in Norway to complete our well-constructed questionnaire on happiness which leads to a valid and reliable 'happiness quotient'. Having collected our data, we might compare the means and standard deviations of the happiness quotients from the two samples, using the established techniques of inferential statistics to guide us to a decision as to whether the distributions of the scores are significantly different from discrepancies which we might expect between the scores of two random samples by chance alone. If a significant difference can be established, then we have supported our hypothesis expressed as an aggregate proposition, one which refers to the difference between samples as aggregates. Of course, there may very well be some people in Norway who have higher happiness quotients than some in Italy, but *overall* it is possible to detect a difference between the two samples taken as wholes: the happiness quotients are higher in Italy *on average*. However, we may also legitimately interpret the hypothesis that people are happier in Italy than in Norway in terms of what Bakan describes as a *general* proposition, one which is presumed to be true of each and every member of a designable class (in this case, 'people'). Now we

8 Applications of conditioning theory

would need a random sample of people and it would be necessary to expose each of them to Italy and to Norway, administering happiness tests to them in each country. Our question is now whether persons A to Z have higher happiness quotients in Italy than in Norway. To the extent that all these subjects do have higher scores in Italy, we have established empirical support for our hypothesis as a general proposition. Before leaving this facetious example, it is worth noting that there is no logical reason why the truth of the statement as an aggregate proposition should necessarily imply its truth as a general proposition (or vice versa). For example, our test of the aggregate proposition might quite reasonably be based on samples consisting almost entirely of Italians in Italy and Norwegians in Norway, and the differences might perhaps be the outcome of genetic differences between these groups. On the other hand, our sample for testing the general proposition might, for example, consist of one arbitrary member of every nationality in the world, and it is quite conceivable that in this case they might be happier in Norway than they are in Italy. If so, this does not contradict the validity of the aggregate proposition that people are happier in Italy.

There is no need here to discuss which of Bakan's two types of propositions is the more important in psychology: it is surely the case that psychology has need of both. However, it is a little disconcerting to realize how much of our psychological knowledge arises from studies which by their very nature can lead only to aggregate propositions and which therefore relate to groups, rather than to individuals. Thus a great deal of experimental psychology is based on group designs in which subjects are allocated to experimental conditions and control conditions at random and inferential statistics are used to compare the scores of the groups. It is also disconcerting to note Bakan's (1967) suggestion that psychologists sometimes slide inadvertently from studies of groups to statements about individuals.

The movement known as 'the' experimental analysis of behaviour is one area of experimental psychology (but not the only one) which is overtly directed towards uncovering propositions which are true of individual members of a designable class. Indeed, its principal organ, *Journal of the Experimental Analysis of Behavior*, was set up in 1958 'primarily for the original publication of experiments relevant to the behavior of individual organisms', and not for reports of operant conditioning experiments as such. However, operant conditioning is one of the relatively few experimental techniques (at least with animals) which lend themselves to research with individual subjects. This is a result of the unusual degree of experimental control exerted by operant conditioning experiments over the behaviour of individual subjects. As discussed above, animals are exposed for long periods of time to carefully controlled experimental conditions until the behaviour reflects a sustained adjustment to the environmental contingencies: 'steady states' of behaviour emerge as a function of the reinforcement schedules which are programmed in the experiment. Such experimental, as opposed to statistical, control of chance factors opens up the possibility of within-subject research designs in search of general propositions. The reversal or ABA design is the most basic. Here, individual animals are exposed for long periods of time to an initial experimental condition (A) until their behaviour becomes predictable. This steady state of behaviour is then used as the control condition against which the effects of changing an experimental variable may be assessed. Once more, each subject's behaviour is allowed over time to become consistent from one experimental session to the next. The differences between the steady state of behaviour achieved in this second condition of the experiment (B) and the behaviour observed in the initial condition are assessed with each subject. This assessment is wholly by means of a direct and overt judgement by the researcher, often being based on simple inspection of the data over the experimental sessions in conditions A and B. If the repeated measurements of the stable behaviour in condition B are outside the limits of variability observed in A, it would seem that the experimental manipulation from A to B had an effect on behaviour. However, in order to ensure that any differences are not spurious (perhaps due to the continued testing of the same subject, for example), the original condition A is reinstated in order to check that the reversal of the experimental conditions will lead to a recovery of the original baseline of behaviour. In such an event, the differences between the behaviour of an individual subject observed in condition B (experimental) and the two phases of condition A (control) can be safely attributed to the differences in the experimental conditions. In a controlled experiment, these behavioural differences

10 Applications of conditioning theory

can be said to be a true reflection of the differences in experimental conditions for the individual subject. In order to build up a more general statement which can be seen to apply to subjects in such conditions rather than merely to one subject, further subjects can be investigated in the same experimental design and an inductive argument can be developed: the more subjects show similar differences between conditions A and B, the greater is the probability that the phenomenon is a general one. Such an experimental strategy is based on the logic of Bakan's general propositions, and the findings may or may not be mirrored by experiments using group designs and inferential statistics leading to aggregate propositions of a broadly similar kind.

Sidman (1960) has reviewed in detail some of the quite complex variations in the basic single-subject research design which can be used in operant conditioning research. All are based on the experimental control exerted over the behaviour of individuals in more than one condition. For example, two different conditions can be arranged to alternate within sessions, each associated with a different discriminative stimulus or cue (multiple baseline). With such an arrangement, two different patterns of behaviour can be 'switched on and off' repeatedly, each reflecting the control of environmental contingencies but each emitted by the same subject acting, as it were both as experimental and control subject, i.e. as its own control. Traditional multiple schedules of reinforcement, where one cue is associated with one schedule and a second cue with another, are an example of this experimental strategy. Another strategy has been described as the B-probe procedure: here relatively short periods of an 'experimental' condition are arranged to occur occasionally against a controlled and sustained behavioural baseline. The study of the acute effects of drugs on operant behaviour provides an example here, where the disrupting effects of a drug are assessed intermittently against the sustained 'control' condition of a schedule of reinforcement with saline injections, the repeated probing with the drug leading to an inductive generalization about the effects of the drug on the behaviour of the individual subject. The multiple baseline and B-probe designs can be readily combined, for example to assess the acute effects of a drug on two different patterns of behaviour in individual subjects, each acting as their own controls (see Thompson and Boren, 1977). Sidman's account (1960), though written some twenty years ago, still offers readers the exciting challenge of devising procedures which make it possible to exert experimental rather than statistical control to build up psychological statements which have scientific rigour but which apply to individuals rather than to differences between groups. Although Sidman uses the experimental field of operant conditioning as the foundation for his arguments, this research strategy is separable from the experimental techniques of operant conditioning and it is relevant to any experimental science seeking statements about the behaviour of individuals.

Radical behaviourism

The final aspect of 'the' experimental analysis of behaviour to be considered here is provided by the philosophical stance offered by radical behaviourism. This approach seems still to give rise to much misunderstanding. It is often thought to be a system in psychology which is applicable largely to rats or pigeons, which interprets their behaviour within a mechanistic stimulus-response framework, and which has no place for events within an organism at a physiological or cognitive level. However, Skinner's book *About Behaviorism* (1974) presents a coherent argument for interpreting the empirical science of behaviour in general by means of this system. One major theme in this approach is certainly that behaviour can be understood in a real sense by relating it to the environmental circumstances in which it occurs, particularly to the differential consequences that patterns of behaviour may give rise to in specified conditions. To this extent it is natural that radical behaviourism as a philosophical system should find much of its empirical support from the scientific investigations of such relationships in the operant conditioning laboratory. Even in this context, however, we have seen that the terms stimulus and response can be misleading. Radical behaviourism is most certainly not confined to experimental investigations with rats or pigeons, but is extended to the analysis of all aspects of human behaviour, too. Thus radical behaviourists seek to understand human behaviour in terms of the functional significance of the pay-offs for what we do in specifiable settings, and they argue that such an account provides a real but often systematically overlooked explanation of behaviour. It makes scientific sense to

12 Applications of conditioning theory

assert that a pattern of behaviour occurs *because* of the environmental setting conditions and/or because of the consequences for such behaviour in those conditions in the past. When consequences can be identified which have selective effects on behaviour, they are again defined as reinforcers, and it is important to recognize that in this system, as in the operant conditioning laboratory, reinforcers are defined in this functional way: there is no expectation that any single event will necessarily serve as a reinforcer in all situations or to every individual.

The theory of reinforcement as couched in this way is similar in its conceptual status to the theory of evolution in biology. Both provide ways of organizing our attempts to understand natural phenomena. The simple organizational principle in Darwin's theory was of course revolutionary and controversial in its day, but has now been established by its usefulness despite the fact that the survival value of certain variations in species is defined functionally and not *a priori*. It is important to recognize, however, that in biology nobody claims that evolutionary theory provides the only way of understanding living creatures. Explanations at other levels such as the physiological, genetic or biochemical are of course important too, but where the principle of selective survival value can operate it will. The same is true of reinforcement theory in radical behaviourism: explanations of behaviour in other ways are surely important too, but it is an empirical matter that some consequence or other may affect behaviour in all situations regardless of what may be happening at different levels. Skinner argues that psychologists have shown an undue preference for explanations of behaviour expressed in terms of physiological or cognitive events. Such accounts draw attention away from the important relationships between behaviour and the environment which are open to public scrutiny. While physiological events are in principle open to public observation, they must in practice be the domain of skilled physiologists. Cognitive events on the other hand, can in principle never be directly open to public scrutiny for they are by their nature private. Despite such limitations, there is a tendency for us to accept as 'good' explanations of behaviour accounts which emphasize either unobserved physiological processes or private and unobservable cognitive events, although such accounts may often provide us with no more than untested paraphrases of the behaviour which is to be explained.

It should not be assumed from this emphasis on the functional relationships between behaviour and environmental events that radical behaviourism has no place for any events at other levels or that it denies that they have any reality. To deny the existence of physiological or cognitive events would certainly be foolish. The task of incorporating them appropriately in our analysis of behaviour is a general problem confronted by psychologists, however. Behaviourists do deny, though, that mental or physiological events should be regarded as somehow the autonomous prime movers of behaviour or the special causes of behaviour. Instead, these events are themselves conceptualized in terms of possible environmental influences on them. This point can be illustrated in the context of the vexed problem for psychologists of cognitive events or 'mental life'. To accept as an explanation for what a person does simply his report that he wanted to do it, felt like doing it or chose to do it, for example, can have a stultifying effect in preventing us from asking further important questions. What exactly made that person want, feel or choose in that way? Radical behaviourists argue that these mental elements can themselves be seen as constructed by or functions of past environmental contingencies, just as is overt behaviour. In this process verbal behaviour and interactions with other people play an important role.

It is possible for external observers to judge that a person sees a particular colour by detecting any differential relationships between behaviour and lights of physically specified wavelengths. Take as an illustrative example parents who may try to reward a child by expressing pleasure if he utters the word 'green' in circumstances which they judge to be appropriate. Their reaction may be either deliberate (as when teaching) or 'natural' (as in everyday interaction), but in both cases they are providing consequences which will increase the probability of the word being used by the child again in the same or similar circumstances. The parents cannot, of course, share the *experience* of green which they assume to be perceived by the child when he utters the word in appropriate circumstances. So if the child *tells* them that he can *see* a green light they are confronted by a problem in knowing how to treat the validity of this self-directed statement. They are therefore again forced to look to the environmental circumstances to

14 Applications of conditioning theory

decide whether they can regard the statement as appropriate or inappropriate and therefore to be followed by certain consequences on their part. So the parents have to make their best efforts to establish the private event *within* the child (his experience) as a setting condition for a self-directed verbal statement, by reference to aspects of his environment which they can themselves observe. Thus the external world can be used as a check for the authenticity of the statement about a private event in as far as this is possible. In this way, consciousness or awareness of inner events is the outcome of interactions with others – consciousness is seen to be the construction of social interactions (Skinner, 1969).

This process inevitably becomes more tenuous as it becomes more difficult to find external authentications against which a self-directed statement can be checked. If a child says he feels a headache, for example, it will probably be difficult to find an obvious source of inflammation. So only an indirect judgement is possible by others, based on general debility, lethargy or perhaps the paleness of the child, and the authenticity of previous statements about pain made by the child and which would be more readily related to observable aspects of the environment, as with pain in a finger which is visibly damaged by a sharp blow. With more personal statements about such private experiences as joy, gloom or depression, however, it is even more difficult to find a standard against which the reported experience can be calibrated by other people: the language and the experience therefore become more diffuse, for the external community cannot act so effectively in relating the self-report to the experience of which only the person making the report can in principle be aware.

It should be remembered that the functional analyses offered by radical behaviourism are not based on a unidirectional model. Although the above exposition has been forced to use a fairly static example, in which parents are shaping a child to report his experiences and thereby to appreciate or become aware of them, the behaviour of the parents too is a function of environmental influences which have impinged upon them. Thus their behaviour is as much a function of the child's behaviour and the behaviour of others as the child's is a function of theirs.

Radical behaviourism provides, then, an analysis not simply of the reactions of rats to controlled experimental contingencies, but also of the interactions of people in unstructured situations.

This approach to psychology has been discussed elsewhere in much greater detail than is possible here (see Skinner, 1974; Blackman, 1980). Contemporary behaviourists adopt a philosophical position which does not commit them to the assertion that people are no more than puppets, pushed and pulled by forces beyond their control and unable to enjoy or suffer private experiences. Instead, they adopt a way of looking at behavioural phenomena which emphasizes the functional importance of environmental influences on what we do, which seeks to find an appropriate way of incorporating private experiences, and which sets these elements within a dynamic and interactive system.

It can be seen from the above discussion that the three strands of 'the' experimental analysis that have been identified fit together very easily to form a coherent approach to psychology. Operant conditioning experiments reveal the subtle effects of environmental influences on behaviour. The strong experimental control exerted in such experiments makes it possible to investigate the behaviour of individual subjects in different conditions and thus to seek general laws which relate to individuals. The philosophy of radical behaviourism provides a context within which explanations of behaviour in terms of environmental influences can be considered, with empirical support from the findings of operant conditioning. However, as emphasized earlier, the three elements are logically distinguishable. There is, for example, no reason why operant conditioning procedures should not be employed within a group design which aims for aggregate propositions by means of statistical comparisons. The tight experimental control of operant conditioning experiments with individual subjects can also be used to identify physiological or biochemical influences on behaviour. The philosophical stance of radical behaviourism is certainly not relevant only to experimental psychology. Finally it is worth emphasizing that one should not claim that 'the' experimental analysis of behaviour is more (or less) scientifically respectable than other approaches in psychology. It is unfortunate that the strong combination of three distinctive features in the literature of 'the' experimental analysis of behaviour may have contributed to its relative isolation within psychology (Krantz, 1971). It would be unwise to dismiss the empirical data of operant conditioning because one is not in favour of the philosophy of radical behaviourism, for example.

16 Applications of conditioning theory

Applied behaviour analysis

We may now turn to consider applied behaviour analysis and behaviour modification in relation to the experimental analysis of behaviour. Applied behaviour analysis is simply the extension of the philosophy of radical behaviourism to behavioural problems in applied settings. Applied behaviour analysts put their primary emphasis, therefore, on observable behaviour and observable environmental events which may be related to the behaviour and which may influence it. Such essentially *descriptive* accounts of behaviour have not formed a prominent part of psychology over the years, and the contemporary growth of interest in direct observations of human behaviour resulting from ethology and ecological psychology has provided a more sensitive awareness of the complexities of producing valid and reliable descriptions of what people do (e.g. Blurton-Jones, 1972). However, workers in applied behavioural analysis also try to identify and describe any environmental events which might stand in specifiable relationships with particular patterns of behaviour. Such events might provide the setting conditions for behaviour (discriminative stimuli) or might serve as functionally significant consequences. With respect to the latter, of course, operant conditioning has demonstrated that events might serve to develop control over behaviour even if they are presented only occasionally. Such control may reflect the reinforcing effects of events (where they serve to maintain the behaviour to which they are related more frequently than in their absence) or their punishing effects (where they lead to a lower frequency of occurrence of the behaviour). Without a deliberate manipulation of their occurrence, such reinforcing or punishing effects can only be surmised, however, bearing in mind that both reinforcers and punishers are defined functionally in terms of their demonstrable effects on behaviour rather than in terms of any intrinsic hedonic quality which they might possess.

The impact of functional analyses in applied contexts has been more striking than one might have imagined, particularly in the field of clinical psychology. As was mentioned earlier, we seem to favour explanations of behaviour couched in terms other than environmental influences. Conventional psychiatry, for example, has long been permeated by diagnostic classifications which can sometimes have the effect merely of directing attention away from the relationships between behaviour and environment. The diagnosis of 'minimal brain damage' to explain the limited behavioural repertoire of developmentally retarded children may be a case in point, since often no sign of such damage can be detected other than in the behaviour which it purports to explain. The apparently medical diagnosis can direct attention away from the fact that the behaviour of these children *can* be affected by environmental events, even if perhaps not as readily as with normal children. Applied analyses of behaviour favour direct descriptions of problem behaviours in relation to their setting conditions and consequences rather than recourse to hypothetical explanations couched in terms of underlying diseases or malfunction. In seeking to understand or explain behaviour in terms of its dynamic interactions with environmental events (some of them, of course, provided by the behaviour of other people with whom the person is interacting), applied behaviour analysis stands in marked contrast to most predominant modes of explanation of abnormal and normal behaviour. In particular, it tends to break down the sharp division between so-called normal and abnormal behaviour which can arise from models of pathology, although this is certainly not to deny that pathological processes within a person might contribute to unusual interactions between his behaviour and the environment.

Good examples of functional analyses of behaviour in applied contexts are provided by Bijou (1976) with respect to child development from the age of two to five years, by Ferster (1973) with respect to the clinical problem of depression, and by Skinner (1972) with respect to psychotic behaviour. All of these authors provide clear examples of the approach of radical behaviourists to the analysis of practical problems of behaviour, and all place the burden of explaining behaviour (whether described as abnormal or normal) on the influences of environmental events on the behaving organism.

It is perhaps inevitable that a systematic approach to psychology which puts so much emphasis on the relationship between behaviour and observable environmental events should have led to attempts to *change* behaviour. The events which serve functionally as discriminative stimuli and as reinforcers or punishers may sometimes be quite easily manipulated, and as a result different patterns of behaviour may emerge. Applied behaviour

18 Applications of conditioning theory

analysis therefore gave rise naturally to the clinical intervention known as behaviour modification.

Behaviour modification

As noted earlier, the term behaviour modification has come to be used in a casual manner. Initially it labelled the distinctive approach to clinical practice which emerged from radical behaviourism in applied contexts. It used operant conditioning techniques to change problem behaviour by manipulating the environmental events which were functionally significant in controlling that behaviour. Since the clinical problems it confronted were usually problems of individuals, behaviour modification was inevitably concerned to change the behaviour of individuals rather than of groups labelled by different diagnoses. In short, behaviour modification was the extension to the practice of clinical psychology of what we have here discussed as the experimental analysis of behaviour. Early workers such as Bijou, and Ullmann and Krasner were all well versed in the interpretation of human behaviour in functional and environmentalistic terms (see for example Bijou and Baer, 1961). They were also aware of the empirical science of behaviour developing at that time in operant conditioning laboratories. These studies suggested a number of techniques for producing changes in behaviour, for example conditioning 'appropriate' behaviour by means of reinforcement programmes, extinguishing 'inappropriate' behaviour by withholding the reinforcers which sustained it, using techniques to change the discriminative control of behaviour and so on (see Ullmann and Krasner, 1965).

Initially attempts were made to restrict the term behaviour modification to the use of conditioning techniques derived from the laboratory within a broadly behaviouristic perspective. For example, Krasner and Ullmann (1965) distinguished behaviour modification from other attempts to influence behaviour such as psychotherapy, psychosurgery, and the use of drugs and hypnotism. Their attempts to contain the term behaviour modification were certainly not successful, however. Because behaviour modification in its original sense offered an unusually direct and effective role for clinical psychologists, more and more practitioners have been prepared to jump on the bandwagon, at least

The experimental analysis of behaviour 19

in terms of the label they have given themselves. As a result the theoretical bases and the empirical techniques which are now discussed as examples of behaviour modification have become increasingly diffuse (see Chapter 9 of this volume). At the same time, the term has seemed in danger of becoming a pejorative phrase used by commentators who are opposed to any form of behaviour influence. The recent flurry of litigation about behaviour modification in the United States (see Blackman, 1979) has been marked by great confusion. Ethical concern about irreversible procedures such as psychosurgery have been mixed up with legitimate concerns about some programmes which are perhaps more appropriately described as behaviour modification in its original sense, to the inevitable detriment of rational debate and the making of clear policy.

Other chapters in the present book reveal in more detail than is appropriate here the variety of techniques which are now commonly regarded as being examples of behaviour modification. As noted before, we cannot legislate for the appropriate use of words. However, it is legitimate to consider the extent to which the three strands of the experimental analysis of behaviour can still be traced in the contemporary literature of behaviour modification. No attempt can be made here to provide a comprehensive review of such a large and diffuse field as behaviour modification: this can readily be found in the authoritative recent books by Catania and Brigham (1978) and Garfield and Bergin (1978), as well as in Kazdin's (1975) more introductory review of basic principles and in other chapters of the present book. The following short discussion will therefore be centred on general issues.

First, there can be little doubt that the general principles which have been demonstrated experimentally in the operant conditioning laboratory continue to be exploited effectively in applied settings, though the current emphasis in the experimental field on quantifying operant behaviour and choice, for example, has reached a degree of technical sophistication which is hardly relevant to applied practice (but see McDowell, 1980). Thus the simple findings that behaviour can be increased in frequency by making reinforcers dependent on it and that behaviour can be decreased by withholding reinforcers or by presenting punishing consequences, or by reinforcing incompatible behaviours, continue to form the core of the techniques used in behaviour modification (see Kazdin, 1975). These techniques are often described as contingency management. Such gross manipulations are of course used to increase 'desired' behaviour and to decrease 'inappropriate' behaviour (see Chapter 3 of this volume for examples). They are often considerably refined by using techniques of successive approximation to 'shape' new patterns of behaviour initially, by using intermittent reinforcement contingencies to sustain behaviour and to make it more resistant to extinction, and by using generalized conditioned reinforcers such as tokens rather than primary reinforcers (again, see Chapter 3 for a fuller discussion). There is also some emphasis, though perhaps less than there might be, on planning for the appropriate circumstances for schedule-controlled behaviour to be marked by distinguishing events which might serve as discriminative stimuli and thereby set the occasion for the desired behaviour to occur, or alternatively on designing programmes carefully so that such tight discriminative control does not channel behaviour excessively when some degree of generalization is sought.

In one sense at least, it is difficult to see how operant conditioning could ever not be the basis of behaviour modification, or indeed any form of behaviour influence. As we have seen, operant behaviour is defined as behaviour which is emitted and which is affected by its consequences, and most human behaviour can be conceptualized as examples of operant behaviour. This includes of course what people say (see Skinner, 1957), and so even traditional psychotherapy can be considered as operant conditioning, even if the therapist does not interpret the situation in that way (Salzinger, 1969). Moreover, the apparent extension of operant conditioning principles to the modification of autonomic responses in animals (Miller, 1969) has led to the enthusiastic adoption of operant conditioning principles in the applied field of biofeedback, as in the treatment of 'psychosomatic' disorders for example (Schneiderman, Weiss and Engel, 1979). If operant behaviour can indeed be seen as dependent on its environmental antecedents and consequences, any programme which changes these aspects of the environment in the hope of producing a change in behaviour can be conceptualized as an example of operant conditioning. This point is true whatever explanation for such changes may be offered by the therapist.

The use of research designs with single subjects, as in the experimental analysis of behaviour, is also still very much a part of contemporary behaviour modification, and again it is almost inevitable that this should be so, given that applied psychologists are often faced with the task of changing the behaviour of individuals. In fact, the recent contributions to the development and analysis of research designs which use individual subjects as their own controls have been centred on applied programmes of behaviour modification (e.g. Hersen and Barlow, 1976). However, the simple ABA or reversal design which has proved so effective in the experimental analysis of behaviour has sometimes been strained in applied fields. For example, the initial phase of a study may be provided by repeated measurement of a patient's behaviour before a programme is introduced as the second phase (B). Practical pressures may lead to a desire to keep such an initial observation period as short as possible, but there is also a marked degree of variability within the behaviour of individual patients from one period of observation to the next. This variability no doubt reflects the fact that aspects of the environment which influence the patient's behaviour cannot be as well controlled in applied settings as in the artificial world of the Skinner box. This uncontrolled variability can lead to problems when the therapist seeks to evaluate the effects of a programme introduced in phase B. These problems are yet further exacerbated by the fact that there may be moral objections to returning a patient to the original unstructured condition in order to check that any changes in behaviour from the original observation phase to the clinical intervention phase are not merely sequence effects, for such a procedure amounts to an attempt to re-establish the 'problem' behaviour in each individual patient. The behaviour modifier may therefore find himself driven towards an AB design rather than an ABA design, with a pressure for a short initial A phase and the probability of having to evaluate 'noisy' data. It is surely no accident, therefore, that discussion about the use of statistical methods to evaluate differences in repeated measures of the behaviour of individual subjects when they are tested in different conditions should have broken out in the context of applied studies (e.g. Kazdin, 1976).

Behaviour modifiers have developed some additional powerful techniques for identifying the effects of their clinical interventions with individual clients. One such technique is provided by

22   Applications of conditioning theory

the use of multiple baselines of behaviour, in which several different aspects of behaviour may be studied in terms of their relationship with the independent variable to be manipulated in a programme. The intervention is introduced for each of these aspects of behaviour in turn, being sustained with that behaviour or in that setting once it has been introduced. Thus any effects of the intervention can be shown by changes in each part of the behavioural repertoire as the clinical intervention is related to that part, all in individual subjects (see Hersen and Barlow, 1976, Ch. 7). However, it remains true even with these more sophisticated techniques of intervention that incisive interpretation of any effects remains at the mercy of potential uncontrolled variability in behaviour, as discussed above. So the development of appropriate methods for evaluating differences in the behaviour of individuals remains a controversial issue in behaviour modification.

Of course, some behaviour modification programmes have been designed to produce general changes in the behaviour of a group of patients considered as a whole, by encouraging greater use of facilities provided to the patients or by controlling general problems of an organizational kind. Although such general changes depend on changes in the behaviour of at least some individuals in the group, such programmes are sometimes evaluated in global terms. Some token economies designed to implement systems of ward management provide examples here (see Chapter 3). Nevertheless, the contemporary literature certainly reveals that the analysis of interventions with individual subjects remains a predominant concern in behaviour modification. This element continues therefore to be a distinguishing characteristic of the approach in comparison with other contributions to clinical practice which depend more markedly on comparisons between experimental and control *groups* of subjects.

The final aspect of the experimental analysis of behaviour discussed earlier was described as the philosophical stance of radical behaviourism. There is scope for considerable discussion about the role of such a philosophy within contemporary behaviour modification. In fact the argument could readily be developed that the functional analysis of behaviour characteristic of radical behaviourism has proved to be a hard task master, especially in applied fields. As a result behaviour modification as a movement in applied psychology is in danger of losing a valuable link with an analytical system, the appropriate use of which might make its interventions more likely to be effective. In fact, some clinical psychologists have advocated the use of operant conditioning techniques without the general attempt to understand and analyse behaviour in functional terms (e.g. Davison, 1969). This view is supported by the increasing tendency for authors to present behaviour modification in a practical 'cookbook' (e.g. Watson, 1973).

It is of course true that the *'techniques'* of operant conditioning which have proved effective in many behaviour modification programmes can be used without any reliance on functional analyses of behaviour, just as it was suggested earlier that experimental research in operant conditioning is not necessarily dependent on the philosophy of radical behaviourism. However, it was also suggested earlier that the impact of 'the' experimental analysis of behaviour in contemporary academic psychology in part results from the weaving together of three logically distinct strands. The same case could be argued in the case of applied psychology. Operant conditioning techniques will be more effectively and more sensitively used in applied contexts if they continue to be embedded in a functional analysis of behaviour. To encourage the 'cookbook' approach may for example foster the view that some events should be used to strenghten the probability of 'desired' behaviour, regardless of the nature of the environmental events which hitherto have controlled it. The sad parade of ineffective programmes of behaviour modification using 'Smarties' as 'reinforcers' in situations which have not been appropriately analysed in environmental terms and which may still conspire to provide functionally effective pay-offs for inappropriate behaviour provides some support for this suggestion. Far worse would be any tendency for 'behaviour modifiers' to contemplate the use of painful stimuli as 'punishers' without analysing the context in which they are to be used. Operant conditioning experiments with animals have indeed shown that shocks *may* reduce the probability of the behaviour to which they are applied, but they have also shown that they may not have such an effect or may even strengthen behaviour (see Morse and Kelleher, 1977). It is an advantage of functional analysis that such an apparent paradox is not in any sense an embarrassment, for the approach directs our attention to identifying the circumstances in which any event may acquire functional control over behaviour. Such a strength should not be lightly abandoned. Appropriate functional analyses of problem behaviour are more likely to prompt effective interventions based on manipulations of environmental events. They direct attention to the possible effects of consequences for behaviour which may serve to maintain the behavioural problem, and in turn they suggest that it is the manipulation of these events which will be most likely to produce a desired change in behaviour, perhaps by breaking the link between the 'problem' behaviour and functionally effective pay-offs, or perhaps by relating those pay-offs to other more appropriate patterns of behaviour.

The relatively recent incorporation of private events in behaviour modification also deserves brief mention here, though it is discussed in more detail by Lowe and Higson (see Chapter 8). It has been argued above that the functional analyses of radical behaviourism do have a place for such private events, although they are not afforded a role as the autonomous causes of behaviour. To this extent, behaviour modification programmes can (indeed should) seek to incorporate such events in their schemes, and by doing so behaviour modifiers need not deprive themselves of their initial base in functional analysis. The early challenges taken up by behaviour modifiers were to be found in the previously intractable behavioural problems of the patients in back-wards of mental hospitals. Such patients usually had extremely limited behavioural repertoires and often were not able to talk about their private experiences or desires. This may have led to the caricature of behaviour modifiers which I have mentioned before (Blackman, 1980) – confident but furtive technicians who manipulate events in the environment of their clients or patients without discussing their programmes with them. However, it is certainly not cheating on behaviourism to interact with clients. The introduction of 'contingency bargaining' or 'contracting' with more verbal clients shows that in many cases it may simply be common sense to interact with and engage the active participation of clients or patients within the programmes which are set up for them. What a person thinks or says may certainly be a good predictor of what he will do, and so full knowledge by the client (after appropriate discussions) of the environmental contingencies to which he will be exposed provides a hopeful prognosis for an effective treatment programme. To make such an assertion is not thereby to accept that private events are to be regarded as autonomous. Nor does it contradict the earlier suggestion that what a person feels or wants is constructed as a function of his past interactions with the environmental contingencies provided by other people.

The general approach of behaviour modification is being extended to more and more challenging and 'normal' situations, in schools, with the problems confronted by social workers, and in community planning (see Nietzel et al., 1977). It has also been advocated with respect to self-control, where we may attempt to control the environmental contingencies influencing our own behaviour (Watson and Tharp, 1972). Even such an essentially private experience as that of chronic pain has provided the focus for a scientific management programme based on functional analysis and contingency management (Fordyce, 1976). It is in areas such as these that we may expect the approach of behaviour modification to be developed most effectively in the future. However, the problem of finding the most appropriate ways to incorporate the private events which form such a prominent feature in all these areas must be carefully evaluated if the foundations of functional analysis are to be sustained. Some programmes of 'cognitive behaviour modification' appear not to have such foundations (see Lowe and Higson above, Chapter 8).

Summary

The argument developed in this chapter can be briefly summarized. The experimental analysis of behaviour has three related but separable features: an empirical interest in the relationships which can be demonstrated between operant behaviour and the environmental conditions in which it occurs; the goal of developing scientifically respectable statements which are relevant to the behaviour of individuals rather than to the differences between groups of subjects; and a philosophical orientation which seeks to understand behaviour in terms of its functional interactions with observable environmental events. These three features are not logically dependent on each other, but when combined they form a coherent approach to the study of behaviour. Each of the three aspects can be extended separately to psychological problems of an applied nature, and indeed it is possible to identify approaches to such problems which have adopted only some of the characteristic features of the experimental analysis of behaviour. However, the coherence of the three-fold approach suggests that the fruitful interaction between operant conditioning, single-subject research designs and radical behaviourism should not readily be allowed to lapse in relation to our attempts to understand and ameliorate problems in the applied field.

It would have been pleasant if the phrase behaviour modification had continued to imply a commitment to the three elements of the experimental analysis of behaviour. It has not done so however. There is therefore a need for any programme of so-called behaviour modification to be carefully considered in an effort to identify the concepts on which it is based. Since the requirements of good applied practice are so similar to those of good systematic research (Mittler, 1975), perhaps it would be wise to press for the use of one phrase which captures the three elements of 'the' experimental analysis of behaviour regardless of whether they are applied in the laboratory or used in the real world of practical problems.

References

Azrin, N.H. and Holz, W.C. (1966) Punishment. In Honig, W.K. (ed.) *Operant Behaviour: Areas of Research and Application.* New York: Appleton-Century-Crofts.

Bakan, D. (1967) *On Method.* San Francisco: Jossey-Bass, Inc.

Bijou, S.W. (1976) *Child Development: the Basic Stage of Early Childhood.* Englewood Cliffs, N.J.: Prentice-Hall.

Bijou, S.W. and Baer, D.M. (1961) *Child Development I: a Systematic and Empirical Theory.* New York: Appleton-Century-Crofts.

Blackman, D.E. (1974) *Operant Conditioning: an Experimental Analysis of Behaviour.* London: Methuen.

Blackman, D.E. (1979). Ethical standards for behaviour modification. *British Journal of Criminology 19*: 420–48.

Blackman, D.E. (1980) Images of man in contemporary behaviourism. In Chapman, A.J. and Jones, D.M. (eds) *Models of Man.* Leicester: British Psychological Society, pp. 99–112.

Blurton-Jones, N. (ed.) (1972) *Ethological Studies of Child Behaviour.* London: Cambridge University Press.

Bradshaw, C.M., Szabadi, E. and Lowe, C.F. (eds.) (1980) *Recent Advances in the Quantification of Steady-State Operant Behaviour.* Amsterdam: Elsevier/North Holland Biomedical Press.

Catania, A.C. and Brigham, J.A. (eds.) (1978) *Handbook of Applied Behavior Analysis: Social and Instructional Processes*. New York: Irvington Publishers, Inc.
Davison, G.C. (1969) Appraisal of behaviour modification techniques with adults in institutional settings. In Franks, C.M. (ed.) *Behavior Therapy: Appraisal and Status*. New York: McGraw-Hill, pp. 220–78.
Ferster, C.B. (1973). A functional analysis of depression. *American Psychologist* 28: 857–70.
Ferster, C.B. and Skinner, B.F. (1957) *Schedules of Reinforcement*. New York: Appleton-Century-Crofts.
Fordyce, W.E. (1976) *Behavioral Methods for Chronic Pain and Illness*. Saint Louis: C.V. Mosby Co.
Garfield, S.L. and Bergin, A.E. (eds.) (1978) *Handbook of Psychotherapy and Behavior Change* (2nd edn). New York: Wiley.
Gollub, L.R. (1977) Conditioned reinforcement: schedule effects. In Honig, W.K. and Staddon, J.E.R. (eds) *Handbook of Operant Behavior*. Englewood Cliffs, N.J.: Prentice-Hall, pp. 288–312.
Hersen, M. and Barlow, D.H. (1976) *Single Case Experimental Designs*. New York: Pergamon Press.
Hineline, P.N. (1977) Negative reinforcement and avoidance. In Honig, W.K. and Staddon, J.E.R. (eds) *Handbook of Operant Behavior*. Englewood-Cliffs, N.J.: Prentice-Hall, pp. 364–414.
Kazdin, A.E. (1975) *Behavior Modification in Applied Settings*. Homewood, Ill.: Dorsey Press,
Kazdin, A.E. (1976) Statistical analyses for single-case experimental designs. In Hersen, M. and Barlow, D.H. *Single Case Experimental Designs*. New York: Pergamon Press, pp. 265–316.
Krantz, D.V. (1971) Schools and systems: the mutual isolation of operant and non-operant psychology as a case study. *Journal of the History of the Behavioral Sciences* 7: 86–102.
Krasner, L. and Ullman, L. (eds) (1965) *Research in Behavior Modification*. New York: Holt, Rinehart and Winston.
McDowell, J.J. (1980) On the validity and utility of Herrnstein's hyperbola in applied behaviour analysis. In Bradshaw, C.M., Szabadi, E. and Lowe, C.F. (eds) *Recent Developments in the Quantification of Steady-state Operant Behaviour*. Amsterdam: Elsevier/North-Holland Biomedical Press.
Mackintosh, N.J. (1974) *The Psychology of Animal Learning*. London: Academic Press.
Miller, N.E. (1969) Learning of visceral and glandular responses. *Science* 163, 434–45.
Mittler, P. (1975) *Research to Practice in the Field of Handicap*. London: Institute for Research into Mental and Multiple Handicap.
Morse, W.H. and Kelleher, R.T. (1977) Determinants of reinforcement and punishment. In Honig, W.K. and Staddon, J.E.R. (eds) *Handbook of Operant Behavior*. Englewood Cliffs, N.J.: Prentice-Hall, pp.174–200.
Nietzel, M.T., Winett, R.A., MacDonald, M.L. and Davidson, W.S.

(1977) *Behavioral Approaches to Community Psychology*. New York: Pergamon.
Salzinger, K. (1969) The place of operant conditioning of verbal behaviour in psychotherapy. In Franks, C.M. (ed.) *Behavior Therapy, Appraisal and Status*. New York: McGraw-Hill, pp. 375–95.
Schneiderman, N., Weiss, T. and Engel B.T. (1979) Modification of psychosomatic behaviors. In Davidson, R.S. (ed.) *Modification of Pathological Behavior*. New York: Gardner Press.
Seligman, M.E.P. and Hager, J.L. (eds) (1972) *Biological Boundaries of Learning*. New York: Appleton-Century-Crofts.
Sidman, M. (1960) *Tactics of Scientific Research*. New York: Basic Books.
Skinner, B.F. (1938) *The Behavior of Organisms*. New York: Appleton-Century-Crofts.
Skinner, B.F. (1957) *Verbal Behavior*. New York: Appleton-Century-Crofts.
Skinner, B.F. (1969) Behaviorism at fifty (and succeeding notes). In Skinner, B.F. *Contingencies of Reinforcement: a Theoretical Analysis*. New York: Appleton-Century-Crofts, pp. 221–68.
Skinner, B.F. (1972) What is psychotic behavior? In Skinner, B.F. *Cumulative Record* (3rd edn). New York: Appleton-Century-Crofts, pp. 257–75.
Skinner, B.F. (1974) *About Behaviorism*. New York: Knopf.
Terrace, H.S. (1966) Stimulus control. In Honig, W.K. (ed.) *Operant Behavior: Areas of Research and Application*. New York: Appleton-Century-Crofts, pp. 271–344.
Thompson, T. and Boren, J.J. (1977) Operant behavioral pharmacology. In Honig, W.K. and Staddon, J.E.R. (eds) *Handbook of Operant Behavior*. Englewood Cliffs, N.J.: Prentice-Hall, pp. 540–69.
Ullmann, L. and Krasner, L. (eds) (1965) *Case Studies in Behavior Modification*. New York: Holt, Rinehart and Winston.
Watson, D.L. and Tharp, R.G. (1972) *Self-Directed Behavior: Self-Modification for Personal Adjustment*. Belmont, Ca.: Brooks/Cole.
Watson, L.S. Jr (1973) *Child Behavior Modification: a Manual for Teachers*. New York: Pergamon.
Zeiler, M.D. and Harzem, P. (eds) (1979) *Reinforcement and the Organization of Behaviour*. Chichester: John Wiley & Sons.

2 Applied behaviour analysis: intervention with retarded people

Laurence Tennant, Chris Cullen and John Hattersley

Introduction

We wish to argue that, while the mentally handicapped may have some special characteristics as a population (e.g. they learn many things slowly), a behavioural approach with the handicapped has the same basic elements as it does with any other population. Consequently most of what we say here might well apply to other populations. Similar procedures for the identification and manipulation of functional relationships between behaviour and its determinants apply in all cases. The same point has been made recently about behaviour analysis of child development (Bijou, 1979).

Usually, however, applied researchers are interested in variables which have major and important effects on behaviour, rather than small (although identifiable) effects sometimes observed in laboratory settings (Baer, 1977; 1978). We are concerned with socially important repertoires (Wolf, 1978). In so far as we are clinicians, then, we will generally be discussing the effect of major variables on the important behaviour of developmentally retarded people. Applied behaviour analysis may be seen as having the following characteristics (Cullen, Hattersley and Tennant, 1977):

 (a) Observation and data collection,

30 Applications of conditioning theory

(b) interpretation,
(c) intervention,
(d) assessment of the effects of intervention.

The present discussion will be ordered along the lines suggested by these headings. We are not aiming to be comprehensive, but rather to identify some particular aspects of each of the operations which are sometimes neglected in clinical work. Where appropriate, reference is made to fuller discussions which are generally available.

Observation and data collection

The terms 'assessment', 'observation' and 'data gathering' describe behavioural episodes which in turn lead to other actions of the therapist; that is, to interpretation and intervention. There appear to be at least three reasons for making such observations:

(a) choosing target behaviours,
(b) measuring progress,
(c) discovering the determinants of behaviours under consideration.

These differing functions of observation sometimes require different observational methods. Under the first heading come procedures which produce general statements concerning the skills of an individual often in terms of presence or absence rather than more precisely quantified. Examples are formal behaviour rating scales, intelligence tests, measures of linguistic or verbal ability, particular interview procedures such as the constructional questionnaire (Schwartz and Goldiamond, 1975) and so on. These structured prompts for the clinician can lead to comparisons of the individual with a group and they may lead to a formulation of an outline plan for further investigation. For example, the clinician may decide on the basis of statements describing the overall skill pattern of a mentally handicapped person that certain self-help skills such as washing, dressing, self-feeding and so on require attention as opposed to say 'academic' skills.

Often, behavioural data are collected so that progress may be measured once an intervention is in effect. Hopefully, the initial referral will be in terms of a repertoire which the handicapped person lacks (see Chapter 7 of this volume), although often it will be for removal of a problem behaviour. Common examples might be 'how do I teach him to feed/wash/dress himself?' and 'how do we get her to stop banging her head/running away/having tantrums?' The problem for the therapist is to be able to specify exactly what the client is doing or not doing, so that he will be able to tell if the intervention has been successful by comparing the situation before and after therapy.

There are several different levels of complexity at which this exercise might be undertaken. The first is simply to ask the care staff or parents to describe, as well as they can, how things are now. While this is arguably the most common form of observation and data-collection currently used in clinical work, taking all the multivarious types of intervention into account, it is of limited usefulness, unless the changes made are very dramatic. If, in an ideal world, there was a procedure for completely eliminating head-banging, regardless of its form or determinants, then it would probably be enough to have an answer to the question 'does it occur?' However, in practice, such situations are rare, at least in psychology (they may be more common in some fields of medicine), and the simple verbal report is usually too unreliable to be of much use. It is worth reiterating, though, that this is the form of observation and data collection which is often relied upon in making psychological and psychiatric decisions with mentally handicapped people.

At a slightly higher level of complexity we might use a formal global assessment of the handicapped person. An advantage of doing this exercise is that one is able to see in what areas the person is deficient, and what he or she can already do. An intervention can be instituted, and the same (or an equivalent) assessment procedure may be used later to judge success. There are many such assessment tools available for use with the mentally handicapped, ranging from traditional intelligence tests to behaviour checklists (devised for particular instances).

A typical exercise might run as follows. After initial assessment, the client is found to be competent in all self-help skills such as washing, dressing and feeding but lacks the ability to deal with money. Procedures might then be instituted to teach these skills, and sometime later an equivalent battery of tests (or perhaps the same ones) might show an improvement in ability to use money. Obviously, this is a different, and in some ways, a preferable exercise to simply asking care staff if there has been some improvement, but even here there are serious drawbacks. If the handicapped client was found to be deficient in *communication skills*, for example, this usually includes a very wide range of behaviour. True, it does not include independent toileting or digital manipulation but there are very many behaviours referred to as 'communication skills'. If we take our non-communicative client, we still have to choose which of many possible skills to teach, and how to assess our teaching, since the global assessment is likely to be too 'coarse'. We will need more specific detail and this leads us on to the form of data-collection and observation which appears to characterize applied behaviour analysis. There are many topics one might discuss here, such as how to sample behaviour and how to choose a research design, but it is not our intention to review this area in any depth. (A.E. Kazdin has written a great deal on this subject and the interested reader is referred to Kazdin 1975; 1978.) We will discuss, however, one issue which is of some importance to methodology, that of the operational definition of response class. Put simply, the issue is this – in order to evaluate the effectiveness of any intervention, it is necessary to have an objective measure of pre-intervention behaviour which may then be compared with an objective post-intervention measure. It is crucial, therefore, that behaviour is recorded in such a way that observer X can agree with observer Y whether the behaviour has or has not occurred. We might be interested, for example, in teaching a mentally handicapped child to point correctly to colours when asked. Four different coloured blocks are placed on the table and the question is asked 'which one is red?' If the child points briefly in the general direction of the blocks, it would be easy for two observers to differ over which one he was 'actually' pointing to. If, however, the required response was physically to touch one and only one block within five seconds of the question being asked, then there would be little room for disagreement between observers on the occurrence or non-occurrence of the response. It is this specification of responses in observable and measurable terms which, to many, is a major characteristic of applied behaviour analysis.

There are many advantages to such an approach. For example, it becomes possible to quantify how successful an intervention has been. Jane has wet pants five times a day on average, over a period of two weeks. This is the baseline or operant level. For the next six weeks, an intensive toilet training programme is in force and each day she is regularly checked for wet pants. After six weeks, she is wet on average only twice a day. Clearly, the procedure has been partly successful even though she is not completely dry. If we were simply asking staff to say whether she was more or less wet after the programme, clinical experience tells us that there would be a wide range of responses from 'she's definitely much better' through 'I think she's improved but still wets herself' to 'I can't really see much difference'. If we had completed some kind of global behavioural assessment such as the Adaptive Behaviour Scale (AAMD, 1974) before and after the intervention then it would be open to doubt whether she had changed from 'frequently has toilet accidents during the day' to 'occasionally has toilet accidents during the day'.

Once a response class has been operationally defined, there are many measures which might potentially be useful to measure change, and it is incumbent on the therapist to be imaginative and practical in the choice of dependent variables. For increasing responses such as sentence production (e.g. Broden, Copeland, Beasley and Hall, 1977) or for decreasing disruptive acts such as stealing (e.g. Azrin and Wesolowski, 1974) frequency measures might be used. These are the nearest parallel to rate of responding which is often used as a basic datum in the operant laboratory (cf. Skinner, 1966) although Wolf (1973) has argued that this response measure is not as useful for applied research as might seem to be the case.

Variations on the theme of counting responses, such as interval recording and time sampling (cf. Kazdin, 1975) are also relatively common. Many other measures, for example response duration and latency or various behavioural products such as the weight of soiled linen for a ward-wide toilet training programme (Tierney, 1973) have also been used, and while choosing response measures is an important exercise, we do not intend to discuss it in any more detail here. We do want to emphasize, however, that it has been seen as essential that measures of responding are carefully operationally defined.

The practice of operationally defining response classes for assessment and observation purposes gives rise to two major issues of concern. The first is the reliability of the procedure and the second is the relationship of operationalism to a functional analysis of behaviour.

Reliability

One of the reasons for operationally defining a response class in terms of clear observable structures is to enable different observers to agree on the occurrence or non-occurrence of instances of the response class – a necessary exercise in any scientific endeavour. Generally speaking, the question of reliability arises whenever there is no mechanical recording or permanent products; that is, when data are collected by human observers. Kelly (1977) reports that 76 per cent of the research reports published in the *Journal of Applied Behaviour Analysis* prior to 1976 employed this method of data collection and 94 per cent of this population reported assessment of the reliability of the data collected. Assessment of reliability is necessary since experience has shown that, even though response classes may be well defined there are still varying amounts of disagreement between observers as to the occurrence or non-occurrence of responses. (It is also important to remember that *reliability* and *accuracy* are not the same thing. Reliability may be low even when one observer correctly identifies all behavioural instances, or high when both observers are inaccurate in the same way. However, reliability and not accuracy is our concern here.)

Kazdin (1977) has reviewed some of the variables which affect reliability and has shown that many extraneous factors can influence the reliability of recording. For example, reliability tends to be higher when observers believe they are being assessed and lower as the diversity of behaviours being assessed is increased. Observer reliability tends also to decrease with time, unless 'refresher' courses in observation are given.

There are other possible influences upon the behaviour of therapists and experimenters, and it is clear that operational definition of the *subject's* behaviour will not resolve these difficulties since the assessment of reliability is *experimenter* behaviour. These problems are, however, largely technical, and may often be resolved with due attention to careful procedures. The second difficulty associated with operational definitions of behaviour is more fundamental, and possibly more important to the analysis of behaviour.

Operationalism

In the operant laboratory, the response, be it a key-peck or lever-press, is usually taken to be well-defined (operationally) but closer consideration reveals that this is often unlike definitions of behaviour in applied settings. All observers in the laboratory agree when there is an instance of key-pecking or lever-pressing because a microswitch or relay is closed, a counter turns over, a cumulative recorder pen moves, and so on. However, the *form* of the response is usually unimportant. The rat may press the lever or the pigeon peck the key using any part of its anatomy – in general, in any way possible, so long as the microswitch is closed. *It is the effect of the response on the environment in particular settings which tends to be of interest to the experimenter.* This is a part of functional analysis and is the hallmark of the Skinnerian system (Skinner, 1953).

However, when we operationally define the aggressive acts of a mentally handicapped person as 'any contact between his body and that of another person', this is more akin to a *structural* than a *functional* definition and we appear more concerned with the form of the response. Although both structure and function are relevant to a full understanding of behaviour (Catania, 1973) it is important to be aware which exercise one is engaged in. Mary has been referred because she is 'aggressive' and the psychologist initially, after consultation with care staff, decides to obtain a baseline for the problem behaviour, which is operationally defined as above. There are several aspects which may now complicate any measurement. What of the occasion when Mary hugs someone? The definition obviously will have to be changed to include the consequences of her act – i.e. 'hurting someone' but this will probably make observation less reliable, since this is less clear than the act itself. There will be times when Mary slaps a resident, but the resident shows no signs of 'being hurt', and there will be other times when the merest touch sets someone crying. What now if Mary stumbles and falls against someone? This would not be called 'aggression' by the man in the street. To exclude instances of this sort, some reference has to be made to the antecedents of her action to somehow include Mary's 'intent'. (Interestingly, Skinner (1974) has described operant psychology or functional analysis as the psychology of 'purpose'.) There may be occasions when the *form* of the response is not useful at all, as when Mary hits out with a chair or goads another resident into hitting someone.

This is the dilemma of response definition within applied behaviour analysis. Functional definition, which must include reference to determinants (antecedents and consequences) is important – but very difficult to apply. Structural definitions are less useful in a radical behaviourist account (Skinner, 1957) but relatively easy to apply. The problem is present in all areas of clinical psychology – we talk of therapy for sexual dysfunction, phobias, obsessions, etc., all of which are structurally defined response classes.

Goldiamond (1974) has argued that we might more profitably group problems together into functional classes. An agoraphobic woman and an impotent man might well be classed together if their problem behaviours are maintained by spouse attention, for example. We make the same mistake in mental handicap when we class all self-stimulatory behaviour together, or imagine that self-help skills may be taught in the same way or will be maintained by the same factors for all retarded people, regardless of the circumstances in which the person lives.

Is there a solution to this paradox? It is not within the competence of the present authors to resolve such a complex issue at the present stage of our science, but we might suggest a direction in which to look. Functional analysis is the whole exercise of observation, interpretation and manipulation. Until one has interpreted, and made some manipulations to check the validity of the interpretation, then the exercise is incomplete, and one cannot claim to have made a functional analysis (cf. Schnaitter, 1978). Interpretation is the next of our characteristics of applied behaviour analysis.

Interpretation

A central part of any behavioural analysis is *interpretation*. This term describes the behaviour of the clinician as determined by both his training and the data which he has gathered concerning a particular client. The task of the behaviour change agent in a mental retardation setting (as in many others) is either to increase or decrease some aspect of a client's behavioural repertoire and also to set the environment in such a way that the change effected is maintained. Thus, when interpreting, the clinician guesses at the causes of observed high and low frequency[1] behaviours and his intervention is then based upon this operation – that is, upon the data combined with his estimate as to the manipulations which will bring about or strengthen previously agreed target operants or weaken problematic operants.

It is worth re-emphasizing that it is the relative strength of some dimensions of an *operant* rather than of a response which is of interest. This is a relevant distinction: the former denotes a relationship between events as opposed to events in isolation denoted by the latter. That is, an operant is more than the description of a response class. Skinner, of course, describes relationships between antecedents (discriminative stimuli), behaviour and consequences (typically reinforcers) (cf. Skinner, 1969). However, he most commonly stresses the production of similar consequences as the defining characteristic of the response class called 'operant'. In our view this has led to an overemphasis on the importance of consequences as determinants of behaviour in applied behaviour analysis. Antecedents have become simply 'stimuli in the presence of which responses are reinforced'. Certainly in a functional account consequences play a major part by defining the response class. However, we are rarely interested solely, or even primarily, in this aspect of the three-term contingency. The reinforcement procedure *defines* the operant – i.e. a relationship between *antecedent(s) and some aspect(s) of behaviour*, and it is this part of the analysis which is vital in any intervention. It is becoming more widely accepted that we must move on from the traditional view of antecedents or discriminative stimuli with its implication that stimuli become effective as a result of being coterminous with reinforcement. Indeed, it has been suggested (cf. Ray and Sidman 1970) that reinforcement can only operate on an existing antecedent-behaviour relationship, an observation with considerable implications for a technology of behaviour change as we shall see in a later section.

In summary, then, the applied behaviour analyst is concerned with operants and particularly with the way in which consequences of behaviour modify antecedent-behaviour relations.

Interpretation: some potential hazards

Experimental studies have shown that a range of curious and

perplexing behavioural end points can be reached as a result of various scheduling operations. Perplexing, that is, to the observer witnessing the end point but not the experimental history. The clinician is very often in an analogous position to such an observer and thus it may be informative to consider some examples of experimental phenomena and to compare these with parallels in applied settings.

Extinction phenomena It is well known that extinction (here defined as a procedure by means of which a response-consequence relation is broken, the response thus having no scheduled consequence) produces differing effects depending upon the nature of the preceding schedule. Consider, for example, a situation in which some activity appears to be increasing. Our usual assumption is that some consequence is being added, thereby strengthening the operant. This is not, however, the only possible interpretation. A mother in a parent support group once described for us an increasing problem behaviour. Together with the child's teacher, this mother had been attempting to toilet train her child. It was not a typical toilet training problem although the details need not concern us here. In short, her child had learned to sit on a toilet for a reasonable period but was not yet used to urinating appropriately. He had a history of extreme retention (12 hours or more) and of urinating in secret. However, she reported that her son was now on occasion coming to her and *wetting in front of her* and this she viewed as an increasing problem behaviour. Clearly in this instance one would not account for the behaviour by pointing to a new reinforcement contingency and certainly none had been scheduled. In our view a major factor was, in fact, the removal of a punishment contingency. Mother had been instructed to pay no attention to her child's tendency to urinate in various parts of the house and this appeared to have removed the necessity for secrecy. In this instance then, an increase in behaviour followed from an extinction procedure,[2] the punishment contingency being no longer in effect. The mother had been confused in her interpretation of the phenomenon because she had not paid sufficient attention to the history effect (Hattersley, 1978).

A more widely cited extinction phenomenon which can confuse behaviour analysts arises from the possibility of either continuous or intermittent reinforcement. In the simplest view extinction following continuous reinforcement produces more rapid decreases in responding than when it follows intermittent reinforcement. Unfortunately this produces a practical problem: How long should extinction be continued before one decides that the wrong analysis may have been made? For example, it may seem fairly clear that the attention of care staff is a major factor in maintaining a problem behaviour. Staff are advised to ignore this particular response but find that in the early days little decline takes place. But why? Several possibilities remain:

(a) staff attention may not have been a significant determinant,
(b) some reinforcement may be occurring, albeit at a low level,
(c) the previous maintenance schedule usually produces this effect in extinction.

Further, in the absence of a more detailed knowledge of the previous history it is difficult to know when to discount the third possibility.

Behaviour maintained or produced by aversive events The observation that behaviour can persist in circumstances where it produces consequences which would normally punish is now fairly well documented (cf. Hutchinson, 1978). Barrett and Glowa (1977), for example, reported a procedure in which responding was both maintained and suppressed by the same electric shock scheduled under differing antecedents. It is these kinds of finding which have led to wider acceptance of the functional view that different behavioural effects are not functions of stimulus *properties* alone but are a result of different scheduling operations. In the clinical field this has been less readily accepted. Bachman (1972) reviewed self-injurious behaviours (SIB) (a structurally defined class of problems) and the various related management or change procedures described in the literature. He described four therapeutic procedures: differential reinforcement of other behaviour, wherein *any* response other then the self-injurious behaviour is reinforced; extinction, when the behaviour produces no consequences (i.e. it is effectively ignored); time out, where the self-injurious behaviour results in the person being removed from the potentially reinforcing environment for a period of time; and punishment, which is the process of reducing the frequency of the behaviour by the contingent presentation of an environmental event (usually one which people label as 'aversive'). These procedures imply that self-injurious behaviour may be maintained by some schedule of positive reinforcement, typically by social consequences. As Bachman points out, however, this is not always the case and he cites an example of self-injurious behaviour in which prior physical abuse by parents was the context in which the behaviour came to be maintained by periods of isolation or withdrawal of social contact – analogues to an experimental 'escape' procedure.

Clearly the arrangement of a time-out contingency in this instance might well be expected to increase rather than decrease the incidence of self-injurious behaviour, since being in the presence of the parents is likely to be less 'desirable'than being isolated (Green, 1968). Bachman, in concluding his section on etiology, comments on:

> the importance of close observation of a self-injurious child when attempting to analyse the variables that are maintaining his SIB. It is possible that what a therapist considers reinforcing (or punishing) for a child might actually be just the opposite for the child. Treatment methods for SIB should, if possible take into account the reinforcement history of that behaviour. (p. 223)

Self-injurious behaviour, in common with other behaviours, can be discriminatively controlled and maintained by apparently unpleasant events or even by events which in other circumstances would reduce behaviour and this possibility must be retained when making an analysis.

Multiple determination Goldiamond (1975) has suggested that much operant experimentation upon which interpretation in applied behaviour analysis is based is unilinear, considering only the effect of manipulating a single variable on a single response class. Some authors, however, have attempted to extend analyses developed in the laboratory to more complex repertoires and have emphasized the importance of multiple determination (cf. Skinner, 1957; 1969).

Unfortunately clinical interpretations are often made in oversimplified terms paying little attention to the possibility that actions may be a result of several different interacting factors, or further that a response class may become strong because *the determinants of another class* have changed. Goldiamond (1975) offers a framework for the analysis of behaviour in terms of alternative sets. Here, an attempt is made to show that interpretation, taking account of many response classes and sets of determinants, may introduce important complexities into our understanding of behaviour. An example of this reappraisal can be seen in Goldiamond's handling of the phenomenon of so-called avoidance responding. The issue is basically that behaviour seems to be occurring *without any obvious consequences*, since, by definition, successful avoidance responding is evading a potential consequence. A popular examination question for undergraduate students has always been 'what is the reinforcer for avoidance responding?' The anomaly is emphasized by examining the consequences for the target behaviour (TB) both during maintenance and when the contingencies are no longer in effect, i.e. during extinction.

Maintenance: TB produces no programmed consequences
Extinction: TB produces no programmed consequences

Here, then, is a case where maintenance and extinction *seem* to be identical, yet where behaviour in one condition (maintenance) will continue indefinitely, while in the other (extinction) will eventually disappear.

The traditional view has been that in the maintenance condition the occurrence of the target behaviour reduces some previously existing aversive state, allegedly physiological. This state, it is argued, is the result of a previous learning history in which some aspect of the environment becomes associated with an aversive stimulus. Sometimes this alleged state is referred to as 'conditioned anxiety'. The two-factor theory has not seemed plausible to radical behaviourists (cf. Schoenfeld, 1969) and those theorists committed to a functional account have pointed to the occurrence of shock (or a functionally equivalent event) in relation to responding as the crucial determinant (see, for example, Hernstein, 1969). However, logical difficulties arise from interpretations which describe the animal as responding for a lower as opposed to a higher probability of shock, since one then has to explain how the animal acquired the repertoire described as 'estimating the probability of shock occurrence'. Goldiamond's formulation, by contrast, could be labelled as a competing response account although this is an over-simplification.[3] In addition to a description of relationships between the target behaviour and its determinants he asks for an account of those between at least two other mutually exclusive behaviours and their determinants. He labels these AB (alternative behaviour) and NB (neither behaviour). The resulting framework for avoidance behaviour in maintenance and extinction conditions is shown below and suggests why the target behaviour occurs in one condition but declines in the other:

Maintenance: TB produces no programmed consequences
AB produces shock
NB produces shock

Extinction: TB produces no programmed consequences
AB produces no programmed consequences
NB produces no programmed consequences

As we have indicated above a response class may occur frequently because of factors reducing the likelihood of other behaviours – Goldiamond's approach draws our attention to manipulable functional relationships and moves us away from a view which might be theoretical in Skinner's sense (Skinner, 1950). (Tryon (1978) has also attempted to resolve the avoidance paradox by an analysis of multivariate response contingencies.) In the real world, at any given point for an individual a wide range of responses are possible. The behavioural outcome is likely to be determined both by the consequences for that outcome and by the controlling factors affecting the alternatives. Our analysis must take account of this fact.

High and low frequency behaviours: what are the possibilities?

When a particular behaviour has been observed to be at an unacceptable level (i.e. high frequency, extreme duration, high intensity, etc.) the clinician, in designing a management procedure, must take account of the range of determinants. This is not merely an academic exercise. It is very likely that the effect of the therapy will not be independent of the history of the behaviour in question; indeed, this has been a central part of our discussion. What then are the possibilities? Consider a hypothetical example – a child who is observed to be regularly engaging in a self-injurious activity such as head-banging. We would suggest the following arrangement of environmental events could at least in principle be acting:

(a) *Positive reinforcement* This is a well documented effect. It is often the case that undesirable behaviours are maintained by, for example, social consequences. Head-banging could easily be the occasion upon which a child obtains the attention of care staff in the day room of a unit for the developmentally retarded.

(b) *Differential reinforcement of high rate (DRH)* A refinement (in terms of reinforcement schedules) of the previous example is the circumstance under which only a high rate of self-injury produced staff attention. This is conceivable in a poorly staffed environment where minimal injury might be tolerated and might generate contingencies analogous to DRH schedules described in experimental studies (cf. Ferster and Skinner, 1957, Chapter 9).

(c) *Extinction of a punishment contingency* As noted earlier a response class may increase in strength when a punishment contingency is removed. It is sometimes the case that behaviour problems are kept under control by staff who take a punitive approach. Again in the example under consideration it is possible that head-banging might increase in a period following the departure of a member of the care staff if this person had systematically controlled self-injury by employing some kind of punishment procedure. (There would, of course, probably be another schedule also in effect to maintain the behaviour at a stable level in the absence of the punishment contingency.)

(d) *Avoidance behavioural/differential punishment of other behaviour (DPO)* In a previous section we referred to an alternative view of so-called avoidance repertoires taking account of different behaviour-environment sets. Hence one further possibility in considering a high-frequency response is that it is one form of avoidance response – i.e. that it comes to strength as a by-product of punishment contingencies in effect for other response classes. Although this analysis does not easily fit the hypothetical self-injury example discussed so far, it clearly is possible that some aspect of a person's behaviour may well be determined in this way. Consider the resident in an institutional setting who spends considerable periods sitting still. There may be no scheduled consequences for this behaviour, although many other behaviours involving movement from the chair may have resulted in punishment.

(e) *Negative reinforcement/escape behaviour* Self-injury may under some circumstances be maintained because it reduces or removes some stimulus – as when ward staff reduce the demands on a resident as a consequence of head-banging. This possibility was referred to in the previous section.

(f) *Multiply determined behaviour* This is something of a cover-all category which indicates the possibility, even probability, that any behaviour class may be multiply determined combining a number of the factors indicated above.

Turning now to the circumstances in which low frequency behaviour is identified as problematic we find a similar range of possibilities. Consider the handicapped person who shows little speech – why should this be?

(g) *Punishment* An individual may not speak on many occasions because this behaviour has been punished. In an institutional setting residents who 'bother' staff (or other residents) may suffer this kind of management and come to speak less as a consequence.

(h) *Differential reinforcement of other behaviour (DRO)* As with DPO this is a particular example of multiple determination. A handicapped person may become less likely to speak because other forms of communication – signs, gestures and so on – are accepted or interpreted by those around him or her. It is often thought that this is the case for Down's Syndrome people, and casual observation in hospital settings does indicate that often they manage to communicate without talking. However, in a home setting, this may well not be the case (cf. Buckhalt, Rutherford and Goldberg, 1978).

(i) *Extinction* Obviously a repertoire may decline as a result of an extinction procedure. One may speculate that some so-called institutionalized mutes who have lost vocal speech over a number of years have done so because in their living environment there were no differential consequences for speech.

(j) *Differing stimulus conditions: a stimulus control problem* When stimulus conditions differ dramatically from those found in training, a well-established response class may not appear. Some of the early studies reported in the behaviour modification literature describe attempts to establish language behaviours with a heavy reliance on edible reinforcers (cf. Lovaas, 1966). Unfortunately, as has been argued elsewhere (Ferster, 1974 and Cullen et al., 1977), while strong response classes may have been established, generalization was often limited. In retrospect, it is clear that insufficient attention was paid to the natural determinants of speech. Much verbal behaviour is differentially controlled by very specific antecedent conditions and only a limited portion of verbal repertoires (mands) (Skinner, 1957) are primarily a function of motivational conditions. Hence a child may not speak because the environment in which he/she is observed is significantly different from the one in which he/she acquired a vocal repertoire.

(k) *Differential reinforcement of low rates (DRL)* This rather specific scheduling operation was developed in animal laboratories and realistic analogues in everyday circumstances are hard to find. Nevertheless, it is a possibility which should not be dismissed without consideration.

(l) *The repertoire has not been established* The most obvious possibility in evaluating a low probability response class is that it has never been established and this, of course, is a familiar feature of the repertoires of developmentally retarded people.

Interpreting behaviour is a complex operation in itself, but to the practising clinician it is not an end point. It is intended to allow a more informed and useful intervention.

46   Applications of conditioning theory

Intervention: the practice of changing behaviour

Data gathering and interpretation of behaviour provide the basis for intervention; they are the precursors of that part of the clinician's repertoire. In the context of mental handicap or developmental retardation many of the principles of intervention are derived from, or have parallels in, operant research. There is an irony, however – laboratory experimental analyses of behaviour have concerned themselves primarily with steady states of responding and have generally regarded the phenomena of response acquisition as necessary prerequisites to study rather than of primary interest in themselves. By contrast applied behaviour analysts are usually concerned with the ways in which *transitions* can be brought about. A good example is response shaping, which in the experimental laboratory is usually the preparatory stage of an experiment, whereas for the clinician it is a central technique – an essential part of his repertoire. Similarly, there is a contrast of emphasis in the study of stimulus control. As we noted in an earlier section the clinician is concerned with the problems of establishing and altering stimulus control in its own right rather than arriving at the study of such problems as a by-product of the reinforcement process.

Behaviour change procedures employed with retarded persons have included the following:

(a) *Response shaping*   Here behaviour in a particular setting is gradually changed as a result of alterations in the response requirement for a particular consequence. In general, the setting remains unaltered. The procedure relies on the repeated occurrence of the response class and also upon some variation in the structural dimensions of the response class. As a teaching method response shaping alone has limited applications. This is because considerable amounts of time would be required to establish structurally complex responses from a limited repertoire. However, simple behaviours, such as eye contact, can be effectively strengthened in this way. Furthermore, most teaching programmes contain a response shaping element in which the behaviour requirement is gradually increased or changed.

(b) *Prompting*   In some circumstances a response class rarely or never occurs and thus cannot come into contact with reinforcement. Prompts are changes in the setting which make the response much more likely. Usually they are either physical (taking the person through the movement), gestural (a sign or a model of some kind), or verbal (an instruction). A major problem is that the prompt is often an arbitrary part of the setting but may become part of the operant that is strengthened (a difficulty to which we shall return).

(c) *Fading* When behaviour is well-established under the above arbitrary conditions the clinician fades the prompts. That is, by gradually changing the setting whilst retaining the occurrence of the behaviour an attempt is made to alter the stimulus control of responding to more natural antecedents. For example, the theoretical sequence of events when teaching a handicapped child to put on a coat might be:

	setting conditions	*behaviour*	*consequences*
from	physical guidance + verbal instruction + low temperature + child going outdoors	puts on coat	goes outdoors
through	verbal instruction + low temperature + child going outdoors	puts on coat	goes outdoors
to	low temperature + child going outdoors	puts on coat	goes outdoors

Early studies in this area suggested that critical factors in successful prompting and fading included very gradual stimulus changes and an effort to reduce the number of errors made in training. Here, experimental literature reported under the heading *errorless learning* has often

48 Applications of conditioning theory

been cited along with the view that large numbers of errors decrease the likelihood of continued programme participation. The general procedure has found wide application being employed in teaching a range of skills including self-help, pre-academic and academic repertoires.

(d) *Modelling and imitation learning* A very specific literature has developed here based upon the early research of Bandura and his co-workers. Imitation is undoubtedly a crucial basic ability in the same sense as *attending* and *instruction following*. Imitative repertoires can be seen as particular kinds of prompted behaviours, in which there is a structural identity or similarity between the behaviour of one individual (usually the trainer) functioning as an antecedent for the behaviour of the trainee. Many training programmes rely to a large extent on imitation (Baer and Sherman, 1964).

In addition to the above procedures, which are all oriented towards increasing behaviour, there are a number of techniques having a basis in the experimental literature which result in response attenuation. The majority of these are based either explicitly or implicitly upon the punishment paradigm. The most widely cited procedure is that of *time-out*, a procedure which along with some others in the behaviour modification literature has suffered various shifts in meaning. Thus, in a clinical setting *time-out* can refer to a procedure analogous to the familiar experimental manipulation in which there is a signalled absence or removal of the previous response – consequence relation, or by contrast it may refer to the physical seclusion of an individual for an extended period following a problematic behaviour. This is one area of clinical practice in which terms derived from an experimental background have been imported and on some occasions extended beyond their initial usage.

Recent years have seen the development of techniques of response attenuation which supposedly have rehabilitative components, for example *overcorrection* (cf. Murphy, 1978; Ollendick and Matson, 1978). However, there is very little evidence to support the view that overcorrection is anything more than an effective punishment procedure. Such procedures predate the publication of Goldiamond's proposal for a constructional approach to social problems (see Chapter 7 of this book) and certainly it can be argued that methods which emphasize response attenuation are often ineffective on their own and might be replaced with good effect by a constructional orientation.

The basic principles of intervention with retarded persons, including those listed above, are based in the main on experimental procedures and usually from within the operant tradition. A number of sources describe such applications in detail and the interested reader is referred to Kazdin (1975) and Catania and Brigham (1978) for a wider coverage.

In spite of differences in emphasis, the clinician or behaviour analyst works in a similar way to the laboratory researcher. As noted above, the programme of change procedures are determined by the data gathered and by the clinician's interpretation of that data. Further, intervention typically involves changes in some aspect(s) of behaviour-environment relationships, for example:

(a) establishing new responding in a particular setting, as when teaching self-help skills;
(b) altering stimulus control so that a new setting comes to control behaviour already occurring under other circumstances, as in toilet-training procedures.

The approach to effecting such changes is essentially an experimental one. The intervention strategy is a 'best guess' at the steps necessary to effect the desired change and the outcome strengthens or weakens the confidence of the clinician in his initial interpretation. Intervention is not, as is sometimes assumed, the simple application of a formula producing an entirely predictable outcome. The basic principles of behaviour change remain poorly understood and we wish to conclude this section by describing some recent developments in one area of applied behaviour analysis based on research into errorless procedures for establishing stimulus control.

Stimulus control: some practical difficulties

Many of the training procedures for establishing self-help skills employ some variation of a prompt and fade methodology. In early behaviour modification texts, discussion of such methods included reference to a 'hierarchy of prompts' – verbal, gestural and physical – which were intended to direct the fading procedure. If training was successful, then a repertoire which initially required physical guidance by a trainer would ultimately occur without a prompt. The prompts are, of course, arbitrary aspects of an environment intruded so as to ensure the occurrence and thus reinforcement of a weak repertoire. The task of the trainer is to remove them whilst maintaining the link between the natural antecedents and the behaviour in question. Thus, in a programme designed to teach washing skills, the antecedents for *turning on the tap* may initially include physical guidance by the trainer. Ultimately, however, the natural antecedent for this response ought to be the previous response of *inserting the plug*. Unfortunately it is sometimes the case that control of the new skill is complicated during the course of the fading procedure to the extent that some aspect of the trainer's behaviour becomes part of the operant established – 'He knows how to do it but he won't do it unless I am there.' This is, of course, a stimulus control problem.

Some of the earlier applications of errorless procedures for establishing discriminative control of behaviour were very similar to their experimental precursors. For example, handicapped persons have been taught appropriate responses to colours by means of methods in which the colour to be labelled (S+) is present in each training trial. Initially an alternative stimulus (S−) is introduced at very low intensity and gradually made more prominent over a series of trials (cf. Cullen, 1976). However, in extending this technology, some interesting problems have come to light. Jones and Cullen (in press), for example, reported a series of studies in which control of responding was lost in the latter stages of the training programmes. In establishing appropriate responding to socially significant words, they altered the size of five stimuli (S−), gradually increasing them to equal the size of S+. They reported errorless performance until the stimuli were of equal size, at which point responding returned to a chance level. They encountered similar problems in establishing appropriate naming of number symbols using changes in stimulus intensity.

It seems possible, therefore, to inadvertently establish control by an 'irrelevant' stimulus dimension as a result of the training procedure adopted. In the self-help skill example, perhaps the ultimate desired control is by proprioceptive and visual stimulation – completion of one action sets the occasion for the next. However, the training procedure introduces arbitrary verbal antecedents in order that appropriate responding will become more likely, *but* these antecedents become actual features of the operant. Similarly although the discrimination of words ought to be a function of stimulus *form*, in the example given about some other aspects of the complex of stimuli used in training (e.g. stimulus *intensity*) became a critical part of the operant.

Clearly, control of responding by an inappropriate stimulus dimension must be avoided. Schilmoeller and Etzel (1977) have suggested that an evaluation of the eventual stimulus dimensions controlling responding will allow decisions to be made involving the selection of the most appropriate dimension for training. In one example, the experimenter was trying to establish a discrimination between ⊃ and a series of C s. He rejected the option of stimulus size as the fading dimension in favour of gradually opening a very small hole in the left side of a O to arrive at ⊃ .

Problems in method may arise, however, where dimensions co-vary. In Schilmoeller et al.'s example the first method was unsuccessful probably because S+ and S−, as well as being mirror reflections, were *until the final stage* different in size and thus size differences controlled responding until that final stage, at which point the discrimination was lost. They argue that since the form of the letter was the target dimension, the subsequent manipulation of the gap in a O as S+ was more relevant. Although this was a successful method in this instance the rationale may not be entirely accurate. Even here control might have been irrelevantly acquired. A subject attending to the *relative size of gaps* would also respond appropriately until the final stage when the gaps were of equivalent size. In practice it seems very difficult to identify stimuli which can be varied on one significant dimension alone. Ray and Sidman (1970) cited an instance which amplifies this point. In a simultaneous discrimination task, children were taught a line tilt discrimination selecting a line at 45° (S+) from other horizontal lines. A stimulus shaping method was employed in altering this to a discrimination of a 45° line from seven other lines at 45° in the opposite direction. Thus the S− stimuli were gradually adjusted from horizontal to 45° in gradual steps. Most subjects acquired this discrimination and, one might argue, the dimension chosen for change was the relevant one. One subject, however, did not acquire the final discrimination. As in the examples given earlier, performance was maintained *until the final stimulus change*. In this instance the authors suggest that the controlling dimension was in fact the distance of stimulus lines from the top of the upper border of the displays. This dimension in addition to line direction would distinguish S+ from S− until the final stage.

Schilmoeller and Etzel (1977) have drawn our attention to the probable interaction between training method and the repertoire established. They suggest a view which appears to emphasize a comparison of stimulus properties during and after training. Thus they suggest that an analysis of the ultimate stimulus control required will direct us to the relevant dimensions for change. Unfortunately, this view tends to exclude the dynamic properties brought to the training setting by the subject. It seems more likely that one must also take account of existing operants in the subject's repertoire since 'stimulus shaping adds nothing to the effectiveness of reinforcement in generating new stimulus control unless shaping follows the contours of existing control' (Ray and Sidman, 1970). That is, relevant dimensions must be selected on the basis of both stimulus properties and operants at strength *in the repertoire of that particular subject* prior to training. Catania (1973) has suggested a distinction between *functional* and *descriptive* operants in which he drew attention to circumstances in which the *response* topography described by an experimenter (the descriptive operant) was at variance with the response topography actually determined by the experimental contingencies (the functional operant). Here is an example of that distinction in which the differences are to be found when comparing the description of controlling antecedents offered by the behaviour analyst with those stimuli which subsequently are found to be discriminative for the response class.

In essence the problem appears to be that of ensuring that relevant stimulus dimensions do in practice enter into a relationship with responding. At least two difficulties are possible. As indicated above, an irrelevant aspect of the stimulus array can come to be functional. Alternatively, the control developed may be too narrow, that is, only a small part of the total stimulus complex may enter into the controlling relationship. Jones and Cullen (1980) reported an attempt to teach a retarded woman to copy the letters *b* and *d*. Initially, although successful with the former, she was rarely correct

Applied behaviour analysis: retarded people 53

when asked to copy a *d*. She was then taught to copy a *d* by tracing over a *d* which had a single *d* above it. Gradually the letter used as a guide was made more faint until she was able to write the letter *d* beneath the sample. On re-test however, her ability to copy a *b* had fallen to the chance level; that is, when asked to copy either letter she produced a *d*. The response of writing a *d* was not under the control of the sample stimulus *d* but probably under the control of any instruction to 'copy that letter'.

The sample stimulus was made functional in this case by altering the training procedure to include an observing response. Early in the training which followed the subject was required to observe the sample stimulus which was either a *b* or *d*, below which were both letters. She was thus asked to point to the matching letter before tracing it. Again, over a series of trials the guiding stimulus and instructions to point to the correct letter were faded and successful copying followed. The inclusion of the observing response extended the stimulus control of the whole repertoire.

The importance of control by the whole of a stimulus complex is clearer in the study of conditional discriminations. Schilmoeller, Schilmoeller, Etzel and Leblanc (1979) have suggested that stimulus shaping (i.e. changing the form of the stimuli) is a more effective method than stimulus fading (i.e. changing the 'intensity' of the stimuli) or trial and error methods, where the final repertoire will require a conditional discrimination. They suggest that stimulus shaping offers the subject an opportunity to compare the defining characteristics of the stimuli early in training. An alternative interpretation would suggest that the programmed alteration of the components of the stimulus array is yet another means of 'directing attention', i.e. making control by the whole array more likely.

It seems likely therefore that stimulus control problems may sometimes be avoided by a proper choice of method prior to training (e.g. stimulus-shaping as opposed to fading) or, and this is the more likely case, such problems may require adjustments during training. Only continual monitoring of the range of the subject's stimulus-control variability will provide a basis for successful training and 'when breakdown occurs the experimenter has essentially measured the limits of stimulus control variation' (Ray and Sidman, 1970). Once unwanted control has been identified steps can be taken to alter it. Perhaps the traditional method of fading prompts, used in many training programmes, introduces unwanted control which might be avoided either by fading verbal and physical prompts simultaneously or by omitting verbal prompts altogether.

The practical implications of the above are familiar to many skilled teachers. In teaching self-feeding, for example, the trainer takes account of response variability ('can he now perform the action of loading the spoon?') and stimulus control variation ('will a slight touch control the responses that were previously determined only by constant contact?')

However, our theoretical understanding of the former (response shaping) has been further developed than our knowledge of the role of stimulus change. Hence, to paraphrase Ray and Sidman (1970), the problem of establishing stimulus control may never admit of a solution that is generalizable across different groups of individuals or different stimuli within a given group. All stimuli are compound in the sense that they have more than one element or aspect to which an individual may attend. To ask that a therapist be aware of all the possibilities is already, perhaps, an impossible demand. To ask further that the therapist arrange conditions so that no undesired stimulus-response correlation is ever reinforced sets a truly impossible task. For these reasons we may never have a generalizable formula for forcing individuals to discriminate a specific stimulus aspect. We may have to settle instead for a combination of techniques, each of which is known to encourage stimulus control.

We have suggested here that programmes of behaviour change are essentially experimental in nature – the problems of stimulus control arising from training procedures seem to amply demonstrate this fact.

Conclusion

In the early 1960s there was an atmosphere of great optimism. It was widely hoped that behaviour modification procedures would radically change the lives of retarded people. Certainly the mentally retarded have better lives now than was the case twenty years ago and some of this change is due to behaviour modification procedures. However, the optimism was perhaps premature. As we have progressed in applied behaviour analysis, we have come to realize that behaviour is a complex subject matter, and changing it is not usually straightforward. In this chapter we have concentrated on some aspects of the behaviour of the retarded person, but we have already ignored many other crucial factors such as the behaviour of care staff and administrators.

Although changes over the last two decades have not been as dramatic as people had hoped, perhaps the foundations laid have been more secure than many initially saw the need for. Behaviour modification or applied behaviour analysis is now an established discipline, and we may look forward to a future in which we can begin to understand some of the complexities of behaviour. In 1970, B.L. Hopkins reviewed a decade of behaviour modification in which it was becoming apparent that there were still many problems to be overcome. He looked to the next decade to solve the problems, since 'the first twenty years are the hardest' (Hopkins, 1970). As we write this, the third decade is starting, and we are still looking forward. But we have learned a lot of lessons about the complexities of behaviour, and that gives us great optimism, founded, perhaps, on more secure ground than the optimism of the 1960s.

Notes

1 Frequency is one dependent variable measure, the most typical. Other measures such as duration, intensity, etc. are used and sometimes described as estimates of probability of response. It may be that this concept does not, in fact, unify what are diverse measures.
2 Note that one may expect increases in behaviour both from extinction following reinforcement (Ferster and Skinner, 1957) *and* following punishment.
3 Goldiamond accepts that accounting for TB by referring to 'all other responding' as a single unit – i.e. defining the latter class by exclusion, will be a logically unsatisfactory exercise producing an explanation without predictive force.

References

AAMD (1974) *Adaptive Behaviour Scale for Children and Adults*. 1974 revision. American Association on Mental Deficiency.

Azrin, N.H. and Wesolowski, M.D. (1974) Theft reversal: an overcorrection procedure for eliminating stealing by retarded persons. *Journal of Applied Behaviour Analysis* 7: 577–81.

Bachman, J.A. (1972) Self-injurious behaviour: a behavioural analysis. *Journal of Abnormal Psychology* 80: 211–24.

Baer, D.M. (1977) Perhaps it would be better not to know everything. *Journal of Applied Behaviour Analysis* 10: 167–72.

Baer, D.M. (1978) On the relation between basic and applied research. In A.C. Catania and T.A. Brigham (eds) *Handbook of Applied Behaviour*

56 Applications of conditioning theory

Analysis: Social and Instructional Processes. New York: Irvington Publishers Inc.
Baer, D.M. and Sherman, J.A. (1964) Reinforcement control of generalised imitation in young children. *Journal of Experimental Child Psychology* 1: 37–49.
Barrett, J.E. and Glowa, J.R. (1977) Reinforcement and punishment of behaviour by the same consequent event. *Psychological reports 40*: 1015–21.
Bijou, S.W. (1979) Some clarifications on the meaning of behaviour analysis of child development. *The Psychological Record 29*: 3–13.
Broden, M., Copeland, G., Beasley, A. and Hall, R.V. (1977) Altering student responses through changes in teacher verbal behaviour. *Journal of Applied Behaviour Analysis 10*: 479–87.
Buckhalt, J.A., Rutherford, R.B. and Goldberg, K. (1978) Verbal and non-verbal interaction of mothers with their Down's Syndrome and non-retarded infants. *American Journal of Mental Deficiency 82*: 337–43.
Catania, A.C. (1973) The nature of learning. In J.A. Nevin and G. Reynolds (eds) *The Study of Behaviour: Learning, Motivation, Emotion and Instinct*. Glenview, Ill.: Scott Foreman.
Catania, A.C. and Brigham, T.A. (1978) *Handbook of Applied Behaviour Analysis: Social and Instructional Processes*. New York: Irvington Publishers Inc.
Cullen, C. (1976) Errorless learning with the retarded. *Nursing Times 72*: 45–7. Reprinted in *Journal of Practical Approaches to Developmental Handicap* 1979, 2, (3): 21–4.
Cullen, C., Hattersley, J. and Tennant, L. (1977) Behaviour modification: some implications of a radical behaviourist view. *Bulletin of the British Psychological Society 30*: 65–9.
Ferster, C.B. (1974) The difference between behavioural and conventional psychology. *Journal of Nervous and Mental Diseases 154*: 153–7.
Ferster, C.B. and Skinner, B.F. (1957) *Schedules of Reinforcement*. New York: Appleton-Century-Crofts.
Goldiamond, I. (1974) Towards a constructional approach to social problems. Ethical and constitutional issues raised by applied behaviour analysis. *Behaviourism 2*: 1–84.
Goldiamond, I. (1975) Alternative sets as a framework for behavioural formulations and research. *Behaviourism 3*: 49–86.
Green, A.H. (1968) Self-destructive and behaviour in physically abused schizophrenic children. *Archives of General Psychiatry 19*: 171–9.
Hattersley, J. (1978) A behavioural analysis of the toileting skills of a mentally handicapped child. *Behaviour Analysis 12*: 14–22.
Hernstein, R.J. (1969) Method and theory in the study of avoidance. *Psychological Review 76*: 49–69.
Hopkins, B.L. (1970) The first twenty years are the hardest. In R. Ulrich, T. Stachnik and J. Mabry (eds) *Control of Human Behaviour — Volume 2*. Glenview, Ill.: Scott Foreman.
Hutchinson, R.R. (1978) By-products of aversive control. In W.K. Honig

and J.E.R. Staddon *Handbook of Operant Behaviour*. Englewood Cliffs, N.J.: Prentice-Hall.
Jones, L. and Cullen, C. (1980) Errorless learning with the retarded: some further considerations. *Journal of Practical Approaches to Developmental Handicap* 4, (2): 18–22.
Kazdin, A.E. (1975) *Behaviour Modification in Applied Settings*. Homewood, Ill.: Dorsey.
Kazdin, A.E. (1977) Artifact, bias and complexity of assessment: the ABCs of reliability. *Journal of Applied Behaviour Analysis* 10: 141–50.
Kazdin, A.E. (1978) Methodology of applied behaviour analysis. In A.C. Catania and T.A. Brigham *Handbook of Applied Behaviour Analysis: Social and Instructional Processes*. New York: Irvington Publishers.
Kelly, M.B. (1977) A review of the observational data-collection and reliability procedures reported in *The Journal of Applied Behaviour Analysis*. *Journal of Applied Behaviour Analysis* 10: 97–101.
Lovaas, O.I. (1966) A programme for the establishment of speech in psychotic children. In J.K. Wing (ed.) *Early Childhood Autism: Clinical, Educational, and Social Aspects*. London: Pergamon.
Murphy, G.H. (1978) Overcorrection: a critique. *Journal of Mental Deficiency Research* 22: 161–73.
Ollendick, T.H. and Matson, J.L. (1978) Overcorrection: an overview. *Behaviour Therapy* 9: 1–13.
Ray, B.A. and Sidman, M. (1970) Reinforcement schedules and stimulus control. In W.N. Schoenfeld (ed.) *The Theory of Reinforcement Schedules*. New York: Appleton-Century-Crofts.
Schilmoeller, K.J. and Etzel, B.C. (1977) An experimental analysis of criterion-related and noncriterion-related cues in 'errorless' stimulus control procedures. In B.C. Etzel, J.M. LeBlanc and D.M. Baer *New Developments in Behavioural Research: Theory, Method and Application*. Hillsdale, N.J.: Lawrence Erlbaum Associates.
Schilmoeller, G.L., Schilmoeller, K.J., Etzel, B.C. and LeBlanc, J.M. (1979) Conditional discrimination after errorless and trial-and-error training. *Journal of the Experimental Analysis of Behaviour* 31: 405–20.
Schnaitter, R. (1978) Private causes. *Behaviourism* 6: 1–12.
Schoenfeld, W.N. (1969) 'Avoidance' in behaviour theory. *Journal of the Experimental Analysis of Behaviour* 12: 669–74.
Schwartz, A. and Goldiamond, I. (1975) *Social Casework: A Behavioural Approach*. New York: Columbia University Press.
Skinner, B.F. (1950) Are theories of learning necessary? *Psychological Review* 57: 193–216.
Skinner, B.F. (1953) *Science and Human Behaviour*. New York: Macmillan.
Skinner, B.F. (1957) *Verbal Behaviour*. New York: Appleton-Century-Crofts.
Skinner, B.F. (1966) Operant behaviour. In W.K. Honig (ed.) *Operant Behaviour: Areas of Research and Application*. New York: Appleton-Century-Crofts.
Skinner, B.F. (1969) *Contingencies of Reinforcement: A Theoretical Analysis*. New York: Appleton-Century-Crofts.

58 Applications of conditioning theory

Skinner, B.F. (1974) *About Behaviourism.* New York: Alfred A. Knopf.

Tierney, A.J. (1973) Toilet training. *Nursing Times,* December 20/27: 1740–5.

Tryon, W.W. (1978) An operant explanation of Mowrer's neurotic paradox. *Behaviourism* 6: 203–11.

Wolf, M.M. (1973) Comments by Reviewer A on A.E. Kazdin *Methodological and Assment Considerations in Applied Settings. Journal of Applied Behaviour Analysis* 6: 532–4.

Wolf, M.M. (1978) Social validity: the case for subjective measurement or how applied behaviour analysis is finding its heart. *Journal of Applied Behaviour Analysis* 11: 203–14.

3 The token economy

Alan E. Kazdin

The use of rewarding consequences to influence behavior is a basic feature of social existence. Basic social institutions such as education, child-rearing, government and law, business, and religion illustrate the use of rewarding and punishing consequences with the expressed purpose of altering or managing behavior (see Kazdin, 1978; Skinner, 1953). The application of rewards on a large scale for purposes of treatment, rehabilitation and education is a relatively recent phenomenon. Even so, programmes based upon the administration of rewards developed long before the emergence of behaviour modification.

One of the most extensively applied reward systems was developed in England by Joseph Lancaster (1778–1838) who devised a system to provide free education for large numbers of children (Kazdin and Pulaski, 1977). Classes in Lancaster's school quickly became overcrowded, occasionally including over 1,000 pupils in a classroom. To help teach and monitor progress of the children, Lancaster developed a system in which selected children in class served as monitors and checked the work of others. Both the monitors and their pupils received tokens or conditioned reinforcers (tickets) that could be exchanged for various prizes (e.g. a toy or picture). Indeed, a relatively intricate set of rewards was administered to provide incentives for progress in class to encourage advancement in areas of academic performance.

Applications of conditioning theory

The system pioneered by Lancaster in contemporary terminology would be referred to as a *token economy*. Generalized conditioned reinforcers (tokens) were provided for specified behaviours and these could be exchanged for a variety of rewards, referred to as *back-up reinforcers*. It is especially interesting to note that Lancaster's system was not an isolated application of reward techniques. Indeed, his system spread to a large number of countries throughout the world.

Token economies represent an important development in contemporary behaviour modification. Token economies provide a way of systematically delivering consequences to groups of persons and structuring the living environment to support pro-social behaviour (Ayllon and Azrin, 1968). Thus, treatment and rehabilitation settings for such populations as psychiatric patients, the mentally retarded, and delinquents can profit from reinforcement programmes. Token economies have been widely applied to different settings, populations and age groups (Kazdin, 1977). The purpose of the present chapter is to describe and illustrate the use of token economies and their range of application. In addition, the chapter examines the effectiveness and limitations of token economies.

Characteristics of the token economy

The basic token programme

Implementing a simple token economy requires relatively few ingredients. Essentially three ingredients are needed, including a token or medium of exchange, back-up reinforcers, and a set of rules that describe the interrelationships between behaviours and token earnings and between tokens and back-up reinforcers. Tokens can consist of poker chips, cards, points, marks, stars or any other medium that can be delivered and exchanged. Of course, it is important that the token cannot be easily counterfeited since it serves the same function as money. If a person can make more tokens on his or her own, there will be no reason to earn them. In some programmes, tokens are individualized by using pieces of paper with the name of the client written on each one.

Aside from the token, back-up reinforcers are required. These reinforcers, of course, are purchased by the tokens. Back-up events

The token economy 61

usually include consumables (e.g. food, chewing gum), high probability behaviours (e.g. free time in class, watching television), money, clothes, cosmetics and others. Back-up reinforcers need not necessarily be elaborate or expensive. In many programmes, persons can purchase free time to engage in activities on their own or are allowed to rent on a time-limited basis special equipment such as a radio or record player. The important feature of back-up reinforcers is that persons are provided with a wide range of options. In many ways, the initial and long-term value of the tokens depends upon the range of reinforcing events that back up the tokens. The selection of back-up reinforcers for a given population is based upon identifying available privileges in the setting, observing behaviours and activities the clients perform when provided with free time, and asking client preferences for specific rewards. Although the only basis for evaluating whether an event is a reinforcer is by making it contingent upon behaviour, these other procedures usually provide a list of events which exert this influence.

The rules of the token economy require specifying several details about how and when tokens are earned, lost and spent. It is useful to provide the rules in the clearest possible fashion. Indeed, clear instructions that specify the precise reinforcement contingencies can enhance the effects of reinforcement. To maximize clarity, some programmes specify the contingencies in a written manual or post them conspicuously in the setting so they can be referred to as needed. Of course, the specific population included in the programme and their level of comprehension may dictate the manner in which the programme is presented.

An example of a recently reported token economy will help to illustrate the basic requirements. Token economies have been implemented in many hospitals that provide treatment for psychiatric patients. As an example, Nelson and Cone (1979) used a token economy with sixteen psychiatric patients on a locked ward. Both psychotic and mentally retarded patients were included in the sample. These patients were on a locked ward because of episodes of aggressive behaviour and attempts to escape from the hospital. The purpose of the programme was to alter behaviours in four general categories: general hygiene, personal management, work on the ward and social skills. Within each of these categories, several specific behaviours were identified. For example, social skills included behaviours such as verbally greeting staff, answering

62 Applications of conditioning theory

questions about the current hospital environment and participating in group discussions. Behaviours that were included in each category were observed directly on the ward. Each behaviour was associated with a value in terms of tokens (coloured tickets) that would be delivered contingent upon its performance.

Patients were informed of the programme in a general ward meeting in which the specific behaviours, tokens, back-up events and general rules were discussed. A 'store' was made available in the setting which was opened at three different times throughout the day. Several commodities could be bought with token earnings including hot and cold beverages, fruit, biscuits, sweets, ice-cream, cigarettes, records, wallets and other items.

In addition, patients could occasionally leave on shopping trips outside the hospital and exchange their tokens for small amounts of money to spend at local stores in the community. To keep patients informed of the system posters were placed on the ward that conspicuously indicated the target behaviours, token values, ward rules and a schedule of activities.

The effects of the token reinforcement procedures were marked. Changes were evident for several behaviours within each general category mentioned earlier. In addition to marked changes in specific behaviours, ratings of the patients by the staff indicated improvements in several general areas such as social competence and interest, neatness, and decrements in patient irritability. Thus, general ward behaviour improved as well.

Options and variations

The basic token programme is not particularly complex. However, several procedures and technique options can be added to the programme. The options and variations can be used for several reasons, such as increasing the effectiveness of the contingencies, making the programme more acceptable to the clientele or staff, and making the procedures more convenient to implement. A few of the options that are commonly employed are noted briefly below.

The *type of contingencies* that are used provides several options in a token economy. Typically, reinforcement programmes utilize contingencies based upon an individual client's performance. The client receives consequences for his or her own behaviour. However, several other contingencies may be used in which the group is incorporated. One variation includes a group contingency in which performance of the *group as a whole* determines the consequences (tokens) that are administered to each individual. For example, in one programme for psychiatric patients, a group contingency was used to help patients make decisions about their discharge (Greenberg, Scott, Pisa and Friesen, 1975). Patients were placed in groups that were given the task to present recommendations in the form of proposals to the staff for their own discharge. The recommendations were graded by the staff. Each patient in the group received tokens as a function of how well the group as a whole devised these proposals.

Another type of group contingency of *consequence sharing* which often is used when a token programme is designed for only one or a few persons. In such cases, the tokens earned by one person are delivered to that person as well as his or her peers. That is, the consequences are shared among persons even though these latter persons may not have earned them. For example, Kazdin and Geesey (1977) used consequence sharing in a special education classroom for mentally retarded children. Two children participated in the programme to improve their work on academic tasks. When one of the children earned tokens for himself, he could purchase back-up reinforcers in the usual way. However, the back-up reinforcer he purchased for himself (e.g. little prizes, free time) was also given to the entire class. Sharing consequences with others was found to be markedly more effective than earning the same consequences for oneself.

Several variations of group contingencies and consequence sharing exist. The advantages of incorporating the group into the contingencies is that the group support, encouragement and praise add important prompting and reinforcing consequences to the contingencies. For many populations and in many situations peer group contingencies may be more effective than those contingencies implemented by the staff. Group-based contingencies help take advantage of the important role of the peers to alter behaviour.

In addition to type of contingencies, token programmes often vary in whether they use punishment. In particular, *response cost* has been used in many programmes in the form of fines for engaging in undesirable behaviours. The convenience of response cost in part accounts for its extensive use. If tokens are provided for some behaviours they can be withdrawn for others in the form of fines.

64 Applications of conditioning theory

Thus, a punishment contingency can be added to the programme with little difficulty.

A few programmes in which response cost has been used have evaluated its contribution to the over-all programme. For example, Phillips, Phillips, Fixsen, and Wolf (1971) used a token programme for predelinquent youths who lived in a home-style treatment facility in which several behaviours were reinforced. In this particular study, tokens were used to help increase the boys' knowledge of national and international events in the news. Tokens were provided for recalling information after watching the news on television. Token delivery was shown to improve performance. Interestingly, token reinforcement for correct responses was more effective in altering behaviour when combined with response cost for incorrect answers than when reinforcement was presented alone. Other studies also have suggested that response cost is a valuable adjunct to a token programme.

Another option for a token economy is to utilize *peers* to administer the contingencies. In the usual programme, of course, staff deliver tokens based upon their observations of the clients. However, peers may be used in this function as well. For example, in a classroom programme for children in a psychiatric hospital, a peer manager administered the tokens (Drabman, 1973). The students elected the peer who administered tokens to each student. The peer manager placed poker chips in each child's canister and individually informed each student how many chips had been earned for appropriate behaviour. The peer who administered tokens to the others received tokens from the teacher on the basis of his performance. The programme administered by the peer worked as well in altering classroom deportment as had an alternative programme administered entirely by the teacher.

Occasionally, programmes utilize *self-administered reinforcement* where persons provide their own consequences. For example, in one classroom study, elementary school students administered points to themselves for on-task behaviour (Glynn and Thomas, 1974). Intermittent tape recorded signals (beeps) sounded aloud in class at random intervals. When the sound occurred, each child was instructed to place a checkmark on his card if he considered himself to be attending. At the end of the lesson, free time was earned according to the total number of checks each child had administered. On-task behaviour increased under this self-reinforcement

The token economy 65

programme. Several other programmes, usually conducted in classroom settings, have utilized self-administration of consequences.

The use of group contingencies, consequence sharing, response cost and peer- or self-administered contingencies represent major options for token economies. Variations of these procedures also exist so the basic token economy can be modified in several ways. Indeed, the large number of available options makes the token economy a highly flexible system. Perhaps it is this flexibility that partially accounts for its widespread application to diverse populations and settings.

Overview of accomplishments

Range of applications

The token economy has been extended to many different populations in various treatment, rehabilitation and educational settings. Because of the large number of applications, it would be impossible to detail each area of application thoroughly. However, to convey the range of applications, token programmes will be highlighted across several populations.

Psychiatric patients Programmes have been used extensively in hospitals for psychiatric patients. Part of the reason for applying token economies is to overcome the apathy, withdrawal and institutionalization that often occurs with custodial hospital care. Several programmes have relied upon token reinforcement to improve adaptive behaviours such as self-care, job performance, attendance to and participation in activities and social interaction. Although these behaviours may not seem uniquely relevant for psychiatric patients, increases in adaptive behaviours within the hospital often are associated with reductions in symptoms such as depression or hallucinations and increases in discharge rates from the hospital. Thus, token economies within the hospital have had implications for the patients' final adjustment in the community. In fact, a recent study indicated that patients discharged from a token economy have greater symptom reduction and longer stay in the community than patients discharged after routine hospital care (Paul and Lentz, 1977).

The mentally retarded With mentally retarded persons, programmes have varied widely depending upon the specific age, level of retardation and setting in which the programme has been conducted. For severely and profoundly retarded persons in institutional settings, reinforcement contingencies have emphasized basic self-care skills such as feeding, toileting and grooming. For persons with higher levels of initial performance basic speech and language acquisition or performance on pre-academic tasks are altered.

Social behaviours also have received considerable attention. Tokens are provided for initiating or engaging in play or for conversing or making greeting responses (Knapczyk and Yoppi, 1975). Work behaviours such as completing jobs and coming to work on time have been altered for many persons for whom employment in the community is a viable goal. Perhaps the greatest focus has been on classroom performance (Kazdin, 1977). Mentally retarded persons are usually placed in special education classrooms where more individualized programming of activities is provided. Token economies are commonly used to alter deportment or academic task performance.

Persons in classroom settings The token economy has been applied in classroom settings to several populations ranging from preschool, through high school and college students. The majority of programmes have focused upon classroom discipline. For example, in most programmes elementary school children have received tokens for paying attention to their work, remaining in their seats, asking for permission to speak and so on. Emphasis on deportment, especially in the early years of token economies, probably reflects the concern of teachers and administrators with discipline problems in the classroom.

After years of classroom research, a pattern of results emerged. Improvements in discipline do not necessarily or even usually improve academic performance (Ayllon and Rosenbaum, 1977; Kazdin, 1977). Hence, the emphasis in token economies shifted to alteration of academic performance directly.

In most programmes, academic performance is reinforced directly to promote improvements in such skill areas of reading, arithmetic, handwriting and spelling. The results have been impressive. Across a large number of investigations, academic performance has been accelerated in classrooms with children of normal intelligence and special education populations. Interestingly, classroom deportment, which often is the impetus among teachers in seeking a token economy, improves when academic performance is reinforced directly. Perhaps even more importantly from the standpoint of the child's advancement, improvements evident in academic performance in the classroom often are evident on achievement and intellegence tests. In a few programmes where token economies have been implemented in the classrooms of economically disadvantaged children for several years, the results have been especially impressive (Becker and Carnine, 1980; Bushell, 1978). Years after the programmes had been terminated, long-term gains in areas of academic achievement were still evident.

Delinquents Programmes for delinquent youths often have relied upon tokens. The most well-known programme in the United States is referred to as Achievement Place where a small number of youths reside (Phillips, 1968). The effectiveness of a token economy in altering a variety of behaviours in everyday living (e.g. completing chores, keeping one's room clean, completing homework) has been evaluated in several studies. The youths eventually return home where parents are trained to continue reinforcement contingencies, although these are not as carefully structured and monitored as those implemented in the treatment setting. Interestingly, delinquent youths who complete the programme at Achievement Place have been shown at follow-up two years later to evince better grades at school and fewer contacts with the courts than persons who have received more traditional treatment, e.g. institutionalization, probation (Kirigin, Wolf, Braukmann, Fixsen and Phillips, 1979). Apart from the Achievement Place programme, token economies have been used extensively with delinquent youths. In many programmes emphasis is placed upon classroom performance and academic behaviours, as discussed above.

Additional institutional applications Token economies have been used with several other institutionalized populations such as adult prisoners, drug addicts and alcoholics. Programmes with prisoners usually have focused upon adaptive behaviours within the prison setting such as following rules and participating in activities. In some programmes remedial education and vocational training are also provided (Ayllon, Milan, Roberts and McKee, 1979). With drug addicts and alcoholics, adaptive behaviours within the hospital setting are reinforced. In a few programmes, behaviours related to the problem that served as the basis for hospitalization have been incorporated. For example, for drug addicts, contingencies have been applied for reductions of drug traces in daily urine samples. Similarly, for alcoholics, reinforcement has been provided for reduced consumption of alcohol which is made available on the hospital ward.

Outpatient applications When usually discussed, the token economy refers to a reinforcement programme applied to groups of persons. However, the method can be and often is applied to individuals and used as a basis for outpatient treatment. A frequent use of token programmes on an outpatient basis is in the home to alter child behaviour.

For example, Patterson (1974) has conducted several programmes designed to train parents and teachers to implement behavioural programmes to alter the behaviour of children with severe conduct problems (e.g. stealing, running away, fighting). Parents and teachers usually implement behavioural programmes in the form of token economies with their children. The token economy is merely part of a much larger intervention which attempts to restructure family interaction patterns. In addition to token reinforcement contingencies other procedures are used such as time out from reinforcement and contingency contracting. Parents also learn to monitor the child's changes in behaviour carefully so that programmes can be improved or altered as needed. The behavioural programmes used on an outpatient basis have been effective in modifying severe conduct problems. Token economies in the home have been successful in altering a wide range of behaviours, including cooperative interactions with siblings, compliance with adult demands, school attendance, performance of various chores, idiosyncratic bizarre behaviours and acts of destruction.

With adults, token reinforcement has been used relatively infrequently as an outpatient treatment. A few reports have incorporated token reinforcement as part of treatment designed to alter marital discord (Stuart, 1969). Spouses devised contracts where they received points for various behaviours (e.g. conversing without argument). The token reinforcement procedures helped to structure interactions and to identify and reinforce specific behaviours that promoted positive interactions. Back-up reinforcers included special events that each spouse selects as his or her own rewards (e.g. physical affection). Preliminary reports suggested that marital satisfaction improved with such a regimen, although long-term follow-up has not been reported.

Efficacy of token economies

The effectiveness of token economies can be examined in several different ways. To begin with, the studies highlighted in the overview of applications to different populations reflect hundreds of studies showing that token economies lead to behaviour change (see Kazdin, 1977). Thus, the effectiveness has been well established.

Perhaps of special interest in evaluating the token economy is examination of the relative effectiveness of this technique in comparison with other procedures. Because the token economy has been applied to such a variety of treatment populations, target problems and settings, comparisons of the token economy with most the available alternative treatments have not been completed. However, several comparative studies have been performed and conclusions can be reached about the token economy in relation to selected techniques.

For example, with psychiatric patients, token economies have been compared with routine hospital (and often custodial) care. As expected, patients who participate in a token programmes usually show greater changes in adaptive behaviours and increases in discharge rates than those who do not (e.g Gripp and Magaro, 1971; Shean and Zeidberg, 1971). With hospitalized patients, token reinforcement has been superior to other specific treatments such as individual therapy or milieu therapy (e.g. Hartlage, 1970; Paul and Lentz, 1977).

With other populations such as hyperactive children, token reinforcement has been effective. Some studies have suggested that token reinforcement for behaviours that compete with hyperactivity is superior to drug therapy, although this is not entirely resolved (e.g. Ayllon and Rosenbaum, 1977). In educational settings, the token economy has been compared with other teaching methods in large-scale research conducted over several years. In general, token reinforcement of academic performance has been superior in achieving long-term gains relative to alternate teaching methods, e.g. open classroom (Kazdin, in press; Stallings, 1975).

Although the evidence in support of token economies is generally impressive, actually a relatively small number of comparative studies have been performed. Thus, the token economy has not been contrasted with other techniques for each of the populations to whom treatment has been applied. In addition, few studies using token reinforcement or other procedures have evaluated how durable treatment effects are after the programme has been terminated. A few investigations of token reinforcement have suggested that behaviour changes may be maintained years after the programmes are terminated (e.g. Bushell, 1978; Paul and Lentz, 1977) although much more evidence is needed.

Critical problems and issues

To this point, the discussion of token economies may have inadvertently implied that the procedures are straightforward and even simple to apply. Actually, various problems can be identified that are essential to resolve for the effective application of the procedures. Two issues that warrant special mention include staff training and the development of long-term maintenance of behaviour.

Staff training

Token reinforcement programmes depend upon carefully training staff (psychiatric aides, parents, teachers and other behaviour-change agents) to implement the contingencies correctly. Programmes have demonstrated that if reinforcing consequences are not applied immediately and consistently, very little behaviour change results (e.g. Koegel, Russo and Rincover, 1977). Hence, a major determinant of programme effectiveness is how well those who carry out the procedures are trained. Indeed, without training, studies have shown that hospital staff, parents and teachers often inadvertently reinforce inappropriate behaviours or fail to attend to appropriate behaviours (cf. Kazdin, 1980).

Before implementing a token reinforcement programme, staff need to be trained. Several procedures have been used to train staff. Often, reinforcement programmes are implemented to train staff by rewarding behaviours that staff display in relation to the clients (e.g. giving tokens and attention, ignoring inappropriate behaviour). Praise, tokens and high probability behaviours have been utilized as reinforcers for staff. Usually, it is more difficult to control and deliver reinforcers for behaviour change agents than it is to deliver them to their clientele. For example, it is difficult to provide reinforcers to hospital aides or teachers because some of the events that they highly value (e.g. extra vacations, wages or privileges at work) are not easily applied on a contingent basis because of practical constraints.

However, in many programmes the behaviours of staff have been effectively altered. As might be expected, staff behaviours are not usually maintained unless reinforcing consequences provided for specific behaviours are continued. Hence, after staff are initially trained to perform the desired behaviours in relation to the client, the programme to sustain staff performance must be continued. In general, training staff so that they show the requisite behaviours and maintaining these behaviours at a high level constitute important prerequisites for effective token economies.

Maintenance and transfer of training

The vast majority of token economy programmes have been devoted to showing that behaviour can be changed in a particular setting. Although the demonstrations have been impressive in some ways, they leave the most important questions unanswered. To what extent are behaviours maintained after the programme is withdrawn, and to what extent do the behaviours transfer to new settings in which the programme has not been in effect? These two questions raise issues referred to as *response maintenance* and *transfer of training*, respectively.

Existing evidence suggests that when a token economy is terminated, behaviours revert to pretreatment levels. For example, programmes in hospitals or in the schools show that as soon as reinforcing consequences are no longer forthcoming patient or student behaviour reverts to or near the level evident in baseline. Similarly, when programmes are implemented and restricted to one setting (e.g. the institution, classroom or home), evidence suggests that behaviour changes in these settings do not transfer to other settings where the programme has not been implemented. There are exceptions where behaviours are maintained after the programme is

72 Applications of conditioning theory

terminated and transfer to novel settings where the programme had not been implemented (e.g. Chadwick and Day, 1971; Kazdin, 1973). Unfortunately, however, these are exceptions.

Recently attention has shifted slightly from developing procedures to change behaviour to those procedures that might foster maintenance and transfer of training. Several techniques exist including removing the token economy gradually so that behaviours are maintained with less direct reinforcement; reinforcing behaviours under a variety of situations so that the behaviours are not restricted to a limited range of cues; substituting naturally occurring reinforcers such as praise and activities in place of tokens; altering the schedule and delay of reinforcement to prolong extinction; and utilizing peers and clients themselves as reinforcing agents with the hope that this will sustain long-term performance that extends to a variety of situations (Kazdin, 1980; Marholin, Siegel and Phillips, 1976; Stokes and Baer, 1977).

Current attempts to maintain behaviour usually involve implementing several procedures simultaneously. For example, Ayllon and Kelly (1974) developed speech in an eleven-year-old retarded girl who had not spoken in class for over eight months. Training included reinforcement for components of speech (e.g. opening her mouth, blowing air through her lips, making sounds and eventually responding to questions). To ensure that the behaviours would be maintained and transferred from the sessions in the counsellor's office to the classroom, several techniques were implemented.

First, over the course of training, the schedule of reinforcement was made increasingly intermittent. Second, praise was substituted for primary reinforcement (candy) so that behaviour would come under the control of naturally occurring reinforcers. Third, stimuli associated with the classroom were introduced into the counsellor's office so that the training situation would increasingly resemble the classroom. Other children, a blackboard and desks were added to the training situation. In addition, the trainer stood in front of the children to simulate the teacher's interactions with the students that normally would occur in the classroom. Fourth, to maximize the occurrence of verbalizations in the presence of peers, a group contingency was introduced so that consequences earned by the child were shared among her peers. Finally, training continued briefly in the classroom in which the trainer, and later the teacher, administered reinforcement. Not only did treatment lead to

The token economy 73

increased verbalizations, but a follow-up assessment one year after training had ended indicated that the responses were maintained and had transferred across new teachers and classrooms.

Current research on maintenance and transfer of training is exploring the separate and combined influences of several procedures. In many ways the emphasis has moved away from merely developing a technology of behaviour change to developing a technology of response maintenance and transfer. Preliminary research has identified several procedures which hold promise in achieving long-term intervention effects.

Current trends

The token economy has entered into several areas of research beyond the confines of what traditionally has been the proper domain of the 'mental health' professions. Behaviour change is a goal that pervades many facets of everyday living well beyond the usual interests of treatment, rehabilitation and education. The token economy probably has been widely embraced as a viable behaviour change method for several reasons. The procedures are relatively straightforward, the effects (or lack of effects) can be shown on objective measures, and the procedures are quite flexible so they can be suited to diverse situations. Current research has extended the token economy to a variety of situations, settings and problems, a few of which are illustrated below.

Socially and environmentally relevant extensions

Token reinforcement procedures have been extended to a variety of behaviours that touch upon contemporary social concerns.

Energy conservation Consumption of electricity, gasoline and home fuel oil is a world-wide concern that has major implications for the economies of countries and personal life-styles of many individuals. Demonstration projects usually on a relatively small scale have evaluated whether token economies can be used to curb energy consumption.

For example, programmes have provided small monetary incentives or points backed by various privileges and prizes for reduction of use of energy in one's home or apartment (e.g. Seaver and

Patterson, 1976). In addition, a few demonstrations have provided token reinforcement for using one's car less frequently (Foxx and Hake, 1977). Token reinforcement for reductions in automobile use has been backed up by special privileges such as free servicing of one's car or parking privileges. One procedure for curbing automobile use has been to encourage use of mass transit. In one programme, persons who travelled by bus received tokens (coupons) redeemable for items at local stores (Everett, Hayward and Meyers, 1974). In general, token reinforcement has been very effective in curbing the use of various forms of energy. However, large-scale applications await to be completed to determine whether significant reductions in energy consumption can be achieved.

Employment and job-related skills

Procuring and sustaining employment are issues of obvious social import. Aside from the economic implications, unemployment is associated with a number of other social problems including crime, mental illness and alcoholism. Token reinforcement procedures have been used to identify and fill available positions and to improve work performance of individuals who already have jobs.

For example, Jones and Azrin (1973) provided monetary incentives (i.e. token reinforcement), advertised in the newspapers, for persons who identified job vacancies that led to employment of prospective clients who did not have jobs. The number of job vacancies that were made available and that resulted in job placements markedly increased under this contingency. In job training studies, unemployed persons have been trained to engage in several behaviours that will help them obtain jobs, including engaging in job interviews, seeking employment opportunities and preparing résumés. Such programmes have had marked effects in procuring jobs (Azrin, Flores and Kaplan, 1975).

For persons who have jobs, token reinforcement has been used to improve performance. For example, token reinforcement, in the form of small monetary incentives, has decreased tardiness and absenteeism. Occasionally, reinforcement systems in industry have been reported to save large amounts of money by improving efficiency among employees.

Applications of reinforcement in business and industry are hardly

The token economy 75

new. The contingent delivery of wages and commissions have always provided strong incentives for performance. Contemporary research seems to have expanded the range of areas within employment that are focused upon and evaluated empirically.

Littering and recycling of waste In the United States the improper disposal of trash on the roads, in parks and other public places (i.e. littering) constitutes a major problem, not merely because of the unsightly products but also because of the expense in removing them. Reinforcement procedures have been used to increase the proper disposal of litter and to remove existing litter. Small monetary incentives or tickets with potential value (as in raffles or lotteries) constitute variations of token programmes that have controlled litter (Chapman and Risley, 1974; Powers, Osborne and Anderson, 1973). Programmes in national parks, athletic stadiums, cinemas, zoos, urban living areas and schools have helped reduce littering.

Some waste products need not be destroyed or littered, but rather can be collected and reused. Waste products such as metal cans, paper and returnable soft drink bottles can be collected and recycled. Reinforcement programmes have been successful in encouraging recycling of wastes (Geller, Chaffee and Ingram, 1975). Reinforcement programmes usually rely upon small monetary incentives or the opportunity to earn prizes based upon the collection of recyclable wastes. As with other social problems to which reinforcement techniques have been directed, several effective demonstrations exist but large-scale applications have yet to be reported.

Medical applications

Behavioural techniques increasingly have been applied to problems that relate to physical health and illness. Applications of behavioural procedures to the prevention, diagnosis, treatment and rehabilitation of problems of physical health have emerged as an area referred to as *behavioural medicine* (Schwartz and Weiss, 1978). Several problems have been studied, including adherence to medical regimens such as exercise, following a special diet and taking medicine, and the treatment of such disorders as cardiac arrhythmias, hypertension, seizures, headaches, pain and many others (McNamara, 1979; Williams and Gentry, 1977).

76 Applications of conditioning theory

Behavioural medicine actually encompasses the full range of behavioural techniques beyond those derived from operant conditioning. However, token reinforcement has been used in selected applications of behavioural techniques to medical problems. For example, a token programme was used to help an eighty-two-year-old man who suffered a heart attack (Dapcich-Miura and Hovell, 1979). After leaving the hospital the patient was instructed to increase his physical activity, to eat foods high in potassium (e.g. orange juice, bananas), and to take his medication. However, he failed to execute these behaviours. A token reinforcement programme was devised in which he earned poker chips for walking, drinking orange juice and taking medication. The poker chips could be saved for selecting the dinner menu at home or going out to dinner at a restaurant of his choice. The programme, which was monitored by his grand-daughter with whom he lived, markedly increased adherence to the medical regimen.

Reinforcement systems have been used in several applications to maintain exercise and diet regimens for such populations as diabetics, to increase activity and decrease complaints, moaning and grimacing among pain patients to increase food consumption of anorexia nervosa patients, and several other problems. In passing, it is important to note the use of punishment procedures such as time out from reinforcement for hypochondriacal complaints and shouting 'no' to interrupt and reduce the frequency of epileptic seizures (see Kazdin, 1980).

General comments

Extensions of token economies to social and medical problems only illustrate rather than exhaust recent areas of application. And in each of these areas it is not just token economies that have been extended but behavioural programmes in general. For example, the full range of behaviour therapy techniques has been extended to medical problems. Token economies represent only one of the procedures. In contrast, for social and environmental problems token economies have been relied upon more heavily. The reason for this is that social programmes often depend upon tokens already available in society, namely, money. Small monetary incentives fit in with the existing back-up events already quite familiar and valuable to most of us.

Conclusion

The accomplishments of the token economy have been remarkable in many ways. Few treatment techniques have been extended to the full range of target behaviours and clinical populations highlighted in the present paper. Yet, it is not merely the extension of the techniques to various populations that is important but also the careful empirical evaluation of token economies and their effects. Few, if any, methods of treatment, rehabilitation or education begin to approach the demonstrated efficacy of the token economy.

Although the token economy has made significant accomplishments, major issues still remain to be resolved. A salient area where research is needed is developing strategies to ensure that changes achieved during token reinforcement programmes are maintained and transfer to extra-treatment settings. To this point, programmes have emphasized demonstrations that various behaviours can be changed and that the changes are marked. This initial focus is important because of the relative paucity of research demonstrating that behaviour change can be achieved and empirically demonstrated. Now that some of the basic questions have been addressed, research needs to turn to the larger issues. Work has begun to examine techniques to maintain behaviour and to ensure its transfer. However, as noted earlier, the technology of maintenance and transfer has not reached the same level of development as the technology of behavioural change.

References

Ayllon, T. and Azrin, N.H. (1968) *The Token Economy: A Motivational System for Therapy and Rehabilitation.* New York: Appleton-Century-Crofts.

Ayllon, T. and Kelly, K. (1974) Reinstating verbal behavior in a functionally mute retardate. *Professional Psychology* 5: 385–93.

Ayllon, T., Milan, M.A., Roberts, M.D. and McKee, J.M. (1979) *Correctional Rehabilitation and Management: A Psychological Approach.* New York: Wiley.

Ayllon, T. and Rosenbaum, M.S. (1977) The behavioural treatment of disruption and hyperactivity in school settings. In B.B. Lahey and A.E. Kazdin (eds) *Advances in Clinical Child Psychology*, vol. 1. New York: Plenum.

Azrin, N.H., Flores, T. and Kaplan, S.J. (1975) Job-finding club: a group-assisted program for obtaining employment. *Behaviour Research and Therapy* 13: 17–27.

78 Applications of conditioning theory

Becker, W.C. and Carnine, D.W. (1980) Direct instruction – an effective approach to education intervention with the disadvantaged and low performers. In B.B. Lahey and A.E. Kazdin (eds) *Advances in Clinical Child Psychology*, vol. 3. New York: Plenum.

Bushell, D. Jr (1978) An engineering approach to the elementary classroom: The Behaviour Analysis Follow Through project. In A.C. Catania and T.A. Brigham (eds) *Handbook of Applied Behavior Analysis: Social and Instructional Processes*. New York: Irvington.

Chadwick, B.A. and Day, R.C. (1971) Systematic reinforcement: academic performance of underachieving students. *Journal of Applied Behavior Analysis* 4: 311–19.

Chapman, C. and Risley, T.R. (1974) Anti-litter procedures in an urban high-density area. *Journal of Applied Behavior Analysis* 7: 377–84.

Dapcich-Miura, E. and Hovell, M.R. (1979) Contingency management of adherence of a complex medical regimen in an elderly heart patient. *Behavior Therapy* 10: 193–201.

Drabman, R.S. (1973) Child versus teacher administered token programs in a psychiatric hospital school. *Journal of Abnormal Child Psychology* 1: 68–87.

Everett, P.B., Hayward, S.C. and Meyers, A.W. (1974) The effects of a token reinforcement procedure on bus ridership. *Journal of Applied Behavior Analysis* 7:1–9.

Foxx, R.M. and Hake, D.F. (1977) Gasoline conservation: a procedure for measuring and reducing the driving of college students. *Journal of Applied Behavior Analysis* 10: 61–74.

Geller, E.S., Chaffee, J.L. and Ingram, R.E. (1975) Promoting paper recycling on a university campus. *Journal of Environmental Systems* 5: 39–57.

Glynn, E.L. and Thomas, J.D. (1974) Effect of cueing on self-control of classroom behavior. *Journal of Applied Behavior Analysis* 7:299–306.

Greenberg, D.J., Scott, S.B., Pisa, A. and Friesen, D.D. (1975) Beyond the token economy: a comparison of two contingency programs. *Journal of Consulting and Clinical Psychology* 45: 498–503.

Gripp, R.F. and Magaro, P.A. (1971) A token economy program evaluation with untreated control ward comparisons. *Behaviour Research and Therapy* 9: 137–49.

Hartlage, L.C. (1970) Subprofessional therapists' use of reinforcement versus traditional psychotherapeutic techniques with schizophrenics. *Journal of Consulting and Clinical Psychology* 34: 181–3.

Jones, R.T. and Azrin, N.H. (1973) An experimental application of a social reinforcement approach to the problem of job-finding. *Journal of Applied Behavior Analysis* 6: 345–53.

Kazdin, A.E. (1973) Role of instructions and reinforcement in behavior changes in token reinforcement programs. *Journal of Educational Psychology* 64: 63–71.

Kazdin, A.E. (1977) *The Token Economy: A Review and Evaluation*. New York: Plenum.

Kazdin, A.E. (1978) *History of Behavior Modification: Experimental Founda-*

tions of Contemporary Research. Baltimore: University Park Press.
Kazdin, A.E. (1980) *Behavior Modification in Applied Settings* (second edition). Homewood, Ill.: Dorsey.
Kazdin, A.E. (in press) Behavior modification in education: contributions and limitations. *Quarterly Review of Development*.
Kazdin, A.E. and Geesey, S. (1977) Simultaneous-treatment design comparisons of the effects of earning reinforcers for one's peers versus for oneself. *Behavior Therapy 8*: 682–93.
Kazdin, A.E. and Pulaski, J.L. (1977) Joseph Lancaster and behavior modification in education. *Journal of the History of the Behavioral Sciences 13*: 261–6.
Kirigin, K.A., Wolf, M.M., Braukmann, C.J., Fixsen, D.L. and Phillips, E.L. (1979) Achievement Place: a preliminary outcome evaluation. In J.S. Stumphauzer (ed.) *Progress in Behavior Therapy with Delinquents*. Springfield, Ill.: Charles C. Thomas.
Knapczyk, D.R. and Yoppi, J.O. (1975) Development of cooperative and competitive play responses in developmentally disabled children. *American Journal of Mental Deficiency 80*: 245–55.
Koegel, R.L., Russo, D.C. and Rincover, A. (1977) Assessing and training teachers in the generalized use of behavior modification with autistic children. *Journal of Applied Behavior Analysis 10*: 197–205.
Marholin, D., II, Siegel, L.J. and Phillips, D. (1976) Treatment and transfer: a search for empirical procedures. In M. Hersen, R.M. Eisler and P.M. Miller (eds), *Progress in Behavior Modification*, vol. 3. New York: Academic Press.
McNamara, J.R. (1979) *Behavioral Approaches to Medicine: Application and Analysis*. New York: Plenum.
Nelson, G.L. and Cone, J.D. (1979) Multiple-baseline analysis of a token economy for psychiatric inpatients. *Journal of Applied Behavior Analysis 12*: 255–71.
Patterson, G.R. (1974) Interventions for boys with conduct problems: multiple settings, treatments, and criteria. *Journal of Consulting and Clinical Psychology 42*: 471–81.
Paul, G.L. and Lentz, R.J. (1977) *Psychosocial Treatment of Chronic Mental Patients: Milieu versus Social-learning Programs*. Cambridge, Mass.: Harvard University Press.
Phillips, E.L. (1968) Achievement Place: token reinforcement procedures in a home-style rehabilitation setting for 'pre-delinquent' boys. *Journal of Applied Behavior Analysis 1*: 213–23.
Phillips, E.L., Phillips, E.A., Fixsen, D.L. and Wolf, M.M. (1971) Achievement Place: modification of the behaviors of pre-delinquent boys within a token economy. *Journal of Applied Behavior Analysis 4*: 45–59.
Powers, R.B., Osborne, J.G. and Anderson, E.G. (1973) Positive reinforcement of litter removal in the natural environment. *Journal of Applied Behavior Analysis 6*: 579–86.
Schwartz, G.E. and Weiss, S.M. (1978) Yale conference on behavioral medicine: a proposed definition and statement of goals. *Journal of*

Behavioral Medicine 1: 3–12.
Seaver, W.B. and Patterson, A.H. (1976) Decreasing fuel oil consumption through feedback and social commendation. *Journal of Applied Behavior Analysis 9*: 147–52.
Shean, J.D. and Zeidberg, Z. (1971) Token reinforcement therapy: a comparison of matched groups. *Journal of Behavior Therapy and Experimental Psychiatry 2*: 95–105.
Skinner, B.F. (1953) *Science and Human Behavior*. New York: Free Press.
Stallings, J. (1975) Implementation and child effects of teaching practices in Follow Through classrooms. *Monographs of the Society for Research in Child Development 40* (7–8, Serial No.163).
Stokes, T.F. and Baer, D.M. (1977) An implicit technology of generalization. *Journal of Applied Behavior Analysis 10*: 349–67.
Stuart, R.B. (1969) Token reinforcement in marital treatment. In R.D. Rubin and C.M. Franks (eds) *Advances in Behavior Therapy, 1968*. New York: Academic Press.
Williams, R.B., Jr and Gentry, W.D. (eds) (1977) *Behavioral Approaches to Medical Treatment*. Cambridge, Mass.: Ballinger.

4 Application of behaviour modification in the rehabilitation of traumatically brain-injured patients

Rodger Ll. Wood and Peter Eames

Introduction

This chapter is based upon recent experience in attempting to apply behavioural methods of treatment to a group of severely traumatically brain-injured adults with behaviour disorders, and upon resulting theoretical and experimental considerations.

Behaviour disorders are common in the brain-injured, and can severely impede or prevent physical and psychological rehabilitation. Although behaviour modification techniques are now generally in wide clinical use, there appear to be very few publications describing their use in this type of individual (Wall, 1969; Legewie-Bertzborn et al., 1977; Dolan and Norton, 1977; Hollon, 1973), and none of these covers the possible use of group techniques like token economy (see Chapter 3).

It is natural to suppose that there might be a particular problem in applying behaviour modification techniques to this group. The techniques are thought, after all, to depend upon associational learning (particularly classical conditioning and operant learning), and learning obviously depends on the brain. Thus it would not be surprising if the ability to learn in this way were disordered by brain-injury. Nevertheless, it is known that individuals who suffer from mental subnormality because of brain-damage very early in life can and do respond to this sort of treatment; and some maladaptive behaviours seen after head-injury certainly appear to have been acquired by a process of learning.

82   Applications of conditioning theory

Radical behaviourist approaches (Skinner, 1953; Bandura, 1969) tend to ignore the very existence of the brain, considering the organism as a sort of behavioural 'black box'. But there are many theoretical reasons for taking the state of the learning-apparatus into consideration, and our experience provides considerable support for this.

The brain is alive (though not necessarily well) and living at the bottom of all behaviour

Even at the level of current understanding, neural mechanisms are exceedingly complex. Various models of brain function have been advanced, of which perhaps the most useful is the highly interactive model of Luria (1973). What all current models have in common, however, is the concept of interaction between cortical localization of specific analytical and synthetic functions (e.g. perceptual processing, polymodal integration and initiation of voluntary movement), and subcortical modulating systems (e.g. arousal, attentic and memory). Although the neural mechanisms involved in associational learning are far from known, there are reasons for thinking that it is subserved by subcortical systems. (Discussion of this area is beyond the scope of this chapter, but see Eames and Wood (in preparation)).

At a rather more accessible level, brain function may be looked at in terms of neuropsychological phenomena, and certainly more is known about these in relation to learning. In particular, orientation towards cue stimuli (Bandura, 1969), selective attention to relevant stimulus dimensions (Cullen, 1976; Jones and Cullen, personal communication; Zeaman and House, 1963), and short-term information storage (Sperling, 1960; Barber and Legge, 1976) are all of central importance in associational learning.

At the developmental level, it is clear that innate behaviours, and those learned at earlier stages, are not eliminated by the later learning of incompatible alternative behaviours. Rather they are inhibited, and thus they remain available for expression, should the later behaviours be somehow deleted, or the inhibition reduced. (Evidence for this appears not only in the release of 'primitive behaviours' by damage to the brain, but also in the 'regressions' of hypnotic trances, and the 'abreactions' produced

Behavioural modification and brain injury

by conditions which reduce arousal.) The inhibition responsible for such developmental control must be mediated by neural (or neurohumoral) mechanisms.

Brain damage produced by trauma to the head is particularly complex, because it results from a variety of forces. The direct force of a blow (and possible direct damage from skull fragments, if there is fracture) damages the subjacent cortex. Rapid oscillations of the brain within the skull produce bruising of the cortex at the poles of the hemispheres, and also diffuse shearing of fibres in the white matter and brain stem. Rises in intracranial pressure cause compression damage of the diencephalon (including hypothalamus) and the brainstem. The actual damage produced in a particular case will depend on the actual conditions: for example, the occurrence of a fracture may dissipate much of the energy of the blow, thus diminishing diffuse damage. Depending on the sites of damage, there may be disruptions of any of the 'specific' cortical areas, of any of the deeper (subcortical) modulating mechanisms, or, more importantly, of a large number of connecting fibres.

The ways in which such damage may be related to abnormalities of behaviour are well demonstrated by Lishman (1978) (see also Eames and Wood (in preparation)). It is useful to consider such disruptions in two groups: the main group consists of behaviours resulting from loss of specific functions and modulatory controls; the second consists of behaviours positively produced by sudden spontaneous electrical disturbances (i.e. epilepsy). With the former, the objective of behavioural treatment will be to achieve learning of new modulatory controls, new strategies for the recognition of cues in the environment, and new processes for the production of behaviour. With the second group, however, it will be necessary to find other means (mainly pharmacological) of controlling the epileptic disturbances; behavioural management will contribute mainly by manipulating responses to the produced behaviours such that they are never positively reinforced.

More important than behavioural deficits in the present context is the fact that brain mechanisms involved in associational learning may also be disrupted by brain damage.

Problems in the application of behaviour modification to the brain-injured

'Constraints'

As was mentioned in the introduction, we have found it of great importance to take into account the state of the 'learning-apparatus' when planning behavioural management.

Introduction In general, current models of 'behaviour modification technology' see the essential components for analysis of behaviour as the interaction and association between environmental and behavioural events. This 'radical behaviourism' is discussed by Thomas and Blackman (1976) as a method of explaining behaviour without any reference to 'inner causes'. Interestingly enough, earlier models (see e.g. Woodworth, 1929; Lindsley, 1964; Keehn, 1969) took the form 'S-O-R' where O represented the condition of the behaving organism considered in mentalistic terms involving intentions, purposes or wishes. Our group, in whom disruption of neural mechanisms is a known and central feature, appear to demonstrate that this latter model is the more useful if 'O' is considered in mechanistic (neural) terms. Indeed, our experience has led us inexorably to the point where much of our initial assessment is concerned with the search for 'constraints'. Constraints may perhaps best be defined in the present context as neurological and neuropsychological abnormalities affecting 'O'. One problem with this definition is that *all* of the mechanisms involved are, of course, ultimately neural. The distinction between the neurological and the neuropsychological seems necessary largely because of our ignorance of the exact nature of the neural basis of many functional mechanisms. However, there may exist a more fundamental distinction, which is hinted at by a practical, clinical difference: it is helpful, indeed necessary, to distinguish between constraints on behaviours (which happen to be those currently perceivable as 'neurological') and constraints on learning (which happen to be largely the 'neuropsychological'). (The exceptions to this are neurological conditions directly affecting stimulus–reception – i.e. primary sensation – like defects of vision or hearing.) Some examples may help to make this clear.

Constraints on behaviour In a particular individual, if explosive or impulsive behaviours arise from intermittent ('paroxysmal') electrical disturbances of an epileptic nature, then such behaviours are unwilled (and unexpected) and will not be controllable by the individual (Ervin and Mark, 1970). Thus, a behaviour modification programme is likely to effect reduction of such behaviours only to the extent to which similar behaviours have been learned (as a result, say, of the reinforcing properties of the responses of other people to the 'true' explosive or impulsive behaviours). The primarily epileptic behaviours are inaccessible to learned control.

Again, if diffuse diencephalic damage occurs, it may disturb the functioning of any of the many hormonal and neurohumoral systems controlled by the hypothalamus. Marked changes can appear in, for example, the behaviours and drive-level related to eating, which are unlikely to be subject to voluntary or learned control. Similar considerations apply to sexual drive and behaviours.

Certain types of brain damage may cause, or more often allow the emergence of, states resembling mental illness (schizophrenia-like syndromes or manic-depressive illness). As has been well established, behaviour modification techniques can sometimes alter outward behaviours produced by such states (Ayllon and Michael, 1959), but arguably do not alter their unexpressed mental states.

Serious problems arise in the assessment and management of behaviour disorders in the brain-injured because abnormal behaviours are responded to by other people, very often in ways which are positively reinforcing. (This is especially true because most people have an inherent sympathy for the victims of head-injury.) There are two important effects of this interaction. Firstly, there is often a relative failure of positive organic 'symptom' behaviours to respond to appropriate medical treatment alone in the absence of concurrent behavioural management. Secondly, the superimposed 'learned versions' of the behaviours, being often more pleomorphic (or less stereotyped), may obscure the organic nature of the primary disorder. One particularly interesting patient who displays this problem well is discussed later on p. 93.

Constraints on learning Functional systems necessary to learning include the various modalities of primary sensation, perception, arousal and selective attention, short-term information storage, and possibly learning and associative mechanisms themselves. Disruption of such functions causes the defects known as 'neuropsychological', and two major problems in behaviour modification are to understand the nature of their impacts on the learning process, and to devise means of circumventing the constraints they produce. These problems form the subject matter of the next three sections.

The slowness of the learning process

Two significant and related problems in the application of behaviour modification in this group are the time necessary for conditioning to occur, and the kind of reinforcement schedule necessary to achieve it. Our findings are that brain-injured patients characteristically take much longer to condition than 'normals', and need a continuous reinforcement schedule for a much longer period than is usual.

It is well established that intermittent schedules produce greater resistance to extinction, and are more efficient in terms of the cost of the reinforcement per response and reduce the likelihood of satiation. However, neuropsychological constraints appear to reduce the effectiveness of the conditioning procedure if it is not maintained on a near-continuous schedule. This may well be related particularly to the disturbance of short-term information storage (memory) which is so typical of brain-injured individuals. We have to accept that, in a real life token economy, some instances of behaviours requiring reinforcement do go unobserved, and that therefore, to some extent, an intermittent reinforcement schedule is practised. This is probably easier to avoid in a setting in which the same programme is applied to all the subjects (e.g. Staats et al., 1967). However, in a clinical setting, practical difficulties of limited staff/patient ratios, and a wide variety of target behaviours requiring numbers of continuous behavioural programmes (often several different ones for any one patient), mean that schedules are bound to be less than perfectly continuous.

The difficulties demonstrated by our patients in the acquisition of conditioned responses resemble those of Oakley's (1978) decorticate rats (rats which had all neocortex surgically removed). These animals acquired instrumental responses more slowly and less efficiently than normal rats. Although, of course, our patients are not strictly decorticate, the combination of cortical damage and the effective cortical disconnections caused by the diffuse shearing of fibres subcortically, does amount at least to a diffuse partial decortication. Later examples (see p. 90) show that similarities exist between the patients and decorticate rats in the slowness and fragility of acquired conditioned responses, how long they take to consolidate, and their tendency to break down when changes are introduced into the reinforcement schedules.

Another similarity with Oakley's findings is that although our patients do demonstrate the ability to acquire or lose responses within a given learning paradigm, they have so far shown little tendency to develop learning sets or strategies – i.e. to develop rules which lead to the solution of problems generally.

Selective attention

Oakley's work points to yet another way in which brain-injury can interfere with behaviour modification by reducing the efficiency of associational learning. He considers that the neodecorticate's difficulties in the instrumental situation lie in defining the salient features of cues in the environment, rather than in learning the relationship between responses and reinforcements. This seems to imply that deficits in attentional mechanisms are crucial to the problem – and such deficits are virtually the rule following severe head-injury. Many of our patients have severe attentional deficits which profoundly interfere with their ability on formal tests of discriminative learning (Wood, in preparation). (The view that this interference stems from attentional deficits is strongly supported by the similarity of the patients' performances on such tests to those of severely subnormal individuals in the study by Zeaman and House (1963)). Our experience has been that the more severe the attentional deficit, the slower and less efficient is the acquisition of conditioned behavioural change, and the more easily it may be lost.

Motivation

Finally, a major stumbling-block in the application of behaviour modification to the brain-injured is that many of these individuals suffer from disorders of motivation, such that they produce less behaviour in general – and often, therefore, behaviours appear

88 Applications of conditioning theory

too infrequently to allow conditioning to occur. Such patients may appear intact on casual observation, but they have a marked degree of apathy which severely undermines the value of reinforcers.

This is an area in which it is important to clarify terms, since they are often confused, or used very loosely. *Drive* is a property of the organism, a measure of the initiation of production of behaviour, or of the size of responses to stimuli. *Incentive* refers to the amount of desirability attached to a particular goal, and depends on the balance between inherent properties of the goal (or reinforcer) and the particular appetites of the organism. (For example, Smarties may hold little incentive for someone who dislikes chocolate!) This also means that the ability to experience pleasure (or pain) is a necessary ingredient, one which might be referred to as *hedonic responsiveness*. The task required to reach a goal may require any level of *effort*. *Motivation*, then, can be seen as the amount of effort the individual of given drive is prepared and able to exert in order to achieve a given goal.

Motivation is central to rehabilitation following any form of disablement, but in head-injury it is a major problem, because various aspects of motivation can be disturbed (Field, 1976). For example, an apparently desirable and achieveable goal may hold no attraction for the head-injured patient, who may be strongly motivated towards other, unrealistic, goals. On the other hand, the cost in terms of effort may appear to the patient to be excessive in relation to the nature of the reward. The situation may be aggravated by the almost universal apathy which determines that there is insufficient incentive in any reward, whether material or social. Furthermore, the use of positive or negative punishment may create problems by exacerbating apathy, or provoking withdrawal or depression. (Such factors presumably underlie the findings of Belmont et al. (1969) who found during a controlled trial that brain-injured patients showed motivated and directed behaviour only whilst the therapist was actually present. They point out the implications of this for staff/patient ratios, and the need for 'programmed-therapy techniques'.

We see evidence in our patients of disorders in three relevant areas. Reduction of drive (possibly from hypothalamic damage) shows in general lethargy, as well as in problems of motivation. In some (notably in those who show dissociative or hysterical features) there is a lack of hedonic responsiveness, which also radically reduces motivation. This problem is likely to be the result of damage to the frontal or septal regions or their connections. Lastly, there are the traditionally recognized frontal lobe problems of indifference to social approval and inability to consider the future consequences of actions. The effect of such deficits on the value of social and other reinforcements is clear.

Traditional approaches to behaviour modification presuppose that the practice of operant conditioning has little need of the concept of motivation, and need consider only incentive. Apart from objections to this based on the considerations above, there are two problems met with in clinical practice. In the first place, we have to work within acceptable ethical limits in the manipulation of incentives, particularly where any deprivation is involved. In the second place, the intrinsic lack of drive and hedonic responsiveness of some patients limits the apparent incentive value of many reinforcers. In such circumstances, any degree of co-operation or positive response from the individual is an improvement, and in order to capitalize on this it is usually necessary to find a means of checking, in each patient, the effects of reinforcement of various types, particularly of social reinforcement. We have also found it of the greatest importance to reinforce any and every spontaneous behaviour (whether a target behaviour or not) that is adaptive.

Thus our experience is in agreement with certain studies (O'Brian and Azrin, 1972; Herson et al., 1972) showing that reinforcing any 'functional behaviours' (e.g. social skills, personal hygiene, social interaction) leads to improvement in generally desirable behaviours, and to reduction in symptomatic behaviours.

Some examples of behaviour modification with the brain-injured

There are three main ways in which behaviour modification is applied to the sorts of behaviour disorders seen in brain-injured individuals:

(a) to control or eliminate undesirable behaviours (e.g. temper outbursts, and antisocial or disinhibited behaviours);
(b) to shape existing behaviours into more appropriate or constructive forms (e.g. social skills);

(c) to evince behaviours where drive and motivation deficits are prominent.

Control of inappropriate behaviours

One effective way of dealing with undesirable behaviours is to introduce the traditional period of 'time-out from positive reinforcement'. This is a deliberate attempt to eliminate any reinforcement from any source for a short period of time. Usually this involves some form of social isolation for the duration of the time-out period, and this can be achieved in either of two ways: by the use of the 'time-out room', or by contriving brief isolation 'on the spot'. A 'time-out room' is usually a small and completely bare and empty room into which the patient is put for a brief period of time (of the order of five to ten minutes). We have found the time-out room to be the most appropriate method for dealing with outbursts of aggression. Although these frequently have an epileptic basis, related to damage to the temporal lobes, and thus are amenable to medical control, by the time we see the patients there is almost inevitably a corresponding pattern of learned behaviour overlying the epileptically induced behaviours, and often occurring quite independently of any actual temporal lobe electrical disturbance. Such patients tend to learn to respond to aversive stimuli in a disproportionate and usually aggressive way. Thus, although medication may control the truly epileptic aspects of explosive behaviour, it does little for the ways in which a patient has learned to respond to aversive situations generally. We have frequently found with our patients the same situation which we have found with those in other behavioural settings who have explosive and impulsive behaviour disorders related to a primary problem of temporal lobe epilepsy: either anticonvulsant (drug) treatment or extinction programmes using time-out, used alone, result in only relative reductions in frequency of explosive or impulsive behaviours, whereas the combination of both approaches almost always leads to near-elimination of these behaviours, with learning curves typical of extinction. Figure 4.1 shows examples of this.

Sometimes the use of a time-out room is inappropriate. This may be because explosive behaviours fall short of actual physical aggression. More usually, it is because the individual learns to use

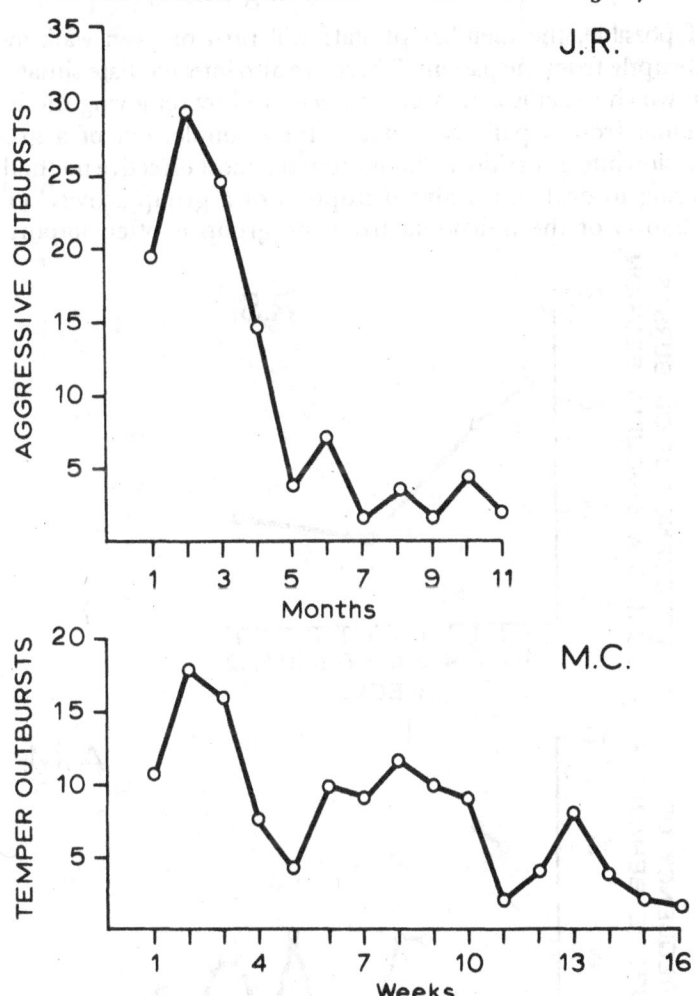

Fig. 4.1 The effects of time-out programmes on the frequency of aggressive outbursts (top panel) and temper outbursts (bottom panel). See text for further details.

aggression to achieve being put in the time-out room, as a means of avoiding some other situation (usually a work or therapy situation). If this happens, 'time-out on the spot' needs to be used. In this case, the patient is completely ignored – not looked at, talked to or touched – again for a brief, usually specified, period of time.

92   Applications of conditioning theory

If possible, the member of staff will turn or even walk away abruptly from the patient. There are also intermediate situations in which social isolation may be achieved by removing the individual from a particular area – for example, out of a group session into a corridor. This is often the most effective method of trying to deal with active disruption of a group activity. (The removal of the individual from the group is often important

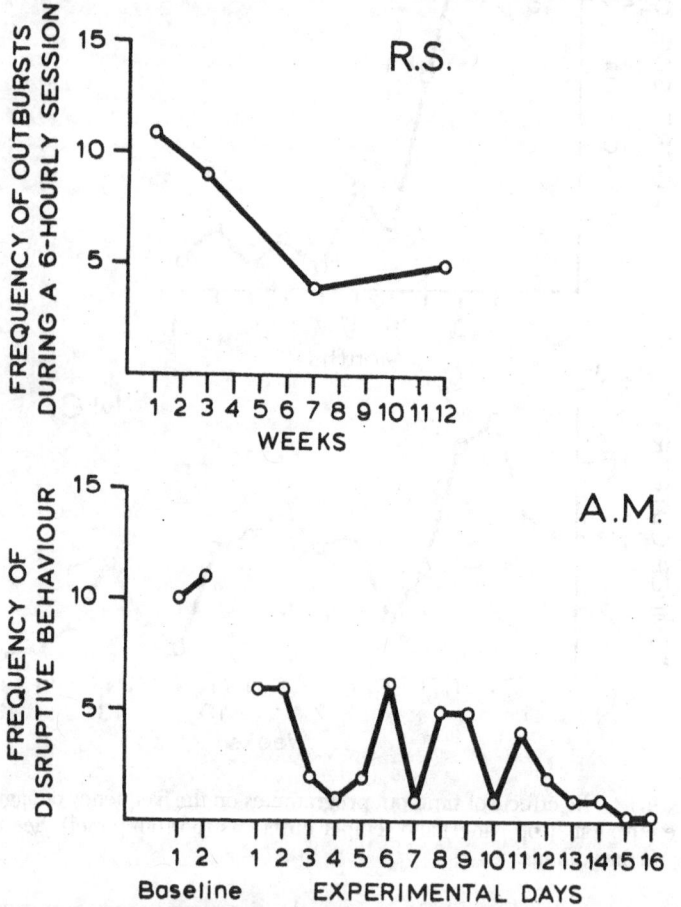

Fig. 4.2   Effect of time-out programmes on the frequency of aggressive outbursts (top panel) and disruptive behaviour (bottom panel). The former programme used 'time-out-on-the-spot' (removal of attention) as the consequence of inappropriate behaviour, the latter used removal from the group room to the corridor.

because, although staff members may very well have sufficient understanding and control to apply 'time-out on the spot' in such circumstances, other patients usually do not.) Some results from the use of these methods are shown in Figure 4.2

There are occasions, however, when a positively punishing event is more effective than the negative punishment of 'time-out', and sometimes this may be the only technique adequate to eliminate unwanted behaviours. Positive punishment has been used in a variety of ways, usually involving the delivery of an electric shock or unpleasant noise. Because there are practical difficulties in administering these forms of reinforcement in a clinical environment, we have used a very simple form, namely an unpleasant smell (in particular, aromatic ammonia vapour, kept in easily carried small wick-bottles), held for a second or so under the patient's nose immediately after the observation of a specific undesirable behaviour. This particular punishing stimulus was chosen because it has had extensive use in other settings, especially in the elimination of undesirable behaviours with retarded individuals. We have applied this method to reduce the frequency of spitting, after it had been found that the general token system failed completely to reduce the frequency of this behaviour. This is illustrated in Figure 4.3 (and this figure particularly well demonstrates the problem of slowness of responses, discussed earlier).

Positive or negative punishment procedures sometimes fail to produce the necessary changes, even though linked to positive reinforcement for appropriate behaviour, and this can be due to neurological constraints. Although the individual may be able to recognize and react to various reinforcement contingencies appropriately, he/she may need an intensive period of conditioning, usually on a sessional basis, to be able to consolidate a modified form of behaviour which can then be maintained by the pressures of the token economy. A particularly good example of this is one patient who had made a relatively good (though not full) recovery physically and intellectually, but whose reintegration into the outside world was prevented by the fact that she produced almost continuous, very irritating, repetitive conservational themes, which were nearly all socially inappropriate and irrelevant. In addition her speech delivery was very rapid and somewhat explosive. Superficially, this problem resembled that of Ayllon and Michael's 1959 case, particularly as she had had much positive reinforcement from people paying attention to her nonsense output. But many months of applying their classical behaviour modification method produced no significant change.

Her transfer from a traditional behaviour modification area into our behavioural head-injury rehabilitation unit fortunately led to a full speech and language assessment, as a result of which a clearer analysis of her speech production was available. Shortly afterwards, our speech therapist was referred a patient with a well-known but uncommon organic syndrome known as 'Cluttering' (Weiss, 1964). The marked similarities in the speech production of the two individuals made it apparent that there was, in our patient, an organic basis for her most significantly unacceptable

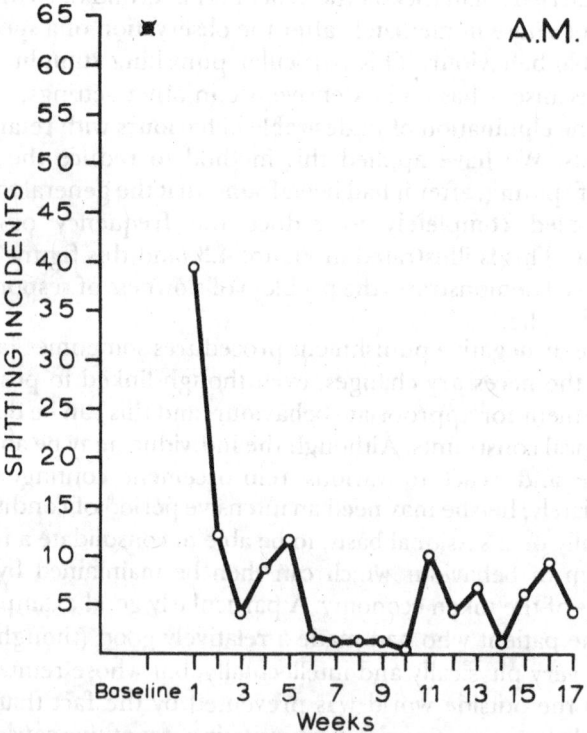

Fig. 4.3 The reduction of spitting behaviour following a programme of contingent positive punishment using an unpleasant smell (aromatic ammonia vapour) as the punishment stimulus.

Behavioural modification and brain injury   95

behaviour. The application of specific speech therapy techniques finally made some chinks appear in the constancy of the problem. With this beginning, and the knowledge that cognitive control over the organically determined outpouring of 'empty' repetitive speech, though difficult, could be achieved, a new programme was introduced. This involved three elements: specific speech therapy to establish the means of control over speech production; a sessional programme of cognitive over-learning of the need to

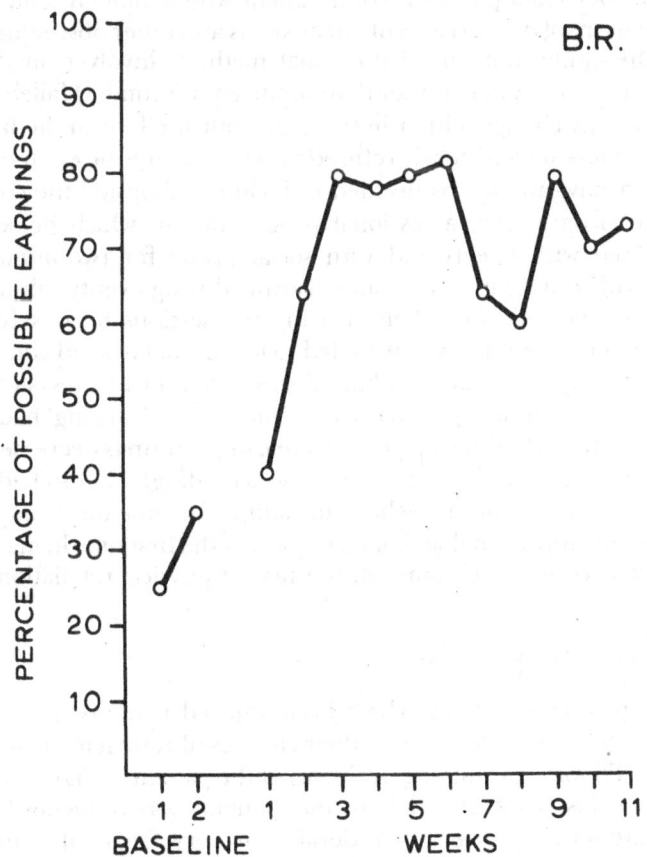

Fig. 4.4   During a twenty-minute daily session, swearing behaviour was reduced by reinforcing two-minute periods of conversation without swearing. This figure shows the concomitant increase in earnings on a token economy programme following the introduction of these parallel sessions.

control, and of the form of what was unacceptable (to try to overcome the neuropsychological constraints imposed by her intellectual blunting); and re-establishment of the previous classical method of Ayllon and Michael, consisting of 'time-out on the spot' for the unwanted behaviour plus positive reinforcement for all acceptable behaviours. The result of this new initiative was an impressive and progressive reduction of the unacceptable proportion of her speech output.

A further example is that of a patient who exhibited temper outbursts involving streams of swearwords and other obscenities. Lengthy application of all the usual methods involved in the token economy system (other than positive punishment) failed to produce any change, either in the behaviour itself, or in the fact that the patient consistently refused to acknowledge the existence of the behaviour. It was decided to include, alongside the continuous programme, a sessional programme in which he was reinforced with sweets and with social praise for two-minute periods of conversation without swearing, during twenty-minute sessions repeated twice daily. During the sessions he was frequently reminded that swearing led to loss of tokens, and consequently to loss of rewards and privileges under the token system. As Figure 4.4 shows, this form of 'cognitive over-learning' had a markedly beneficial result, and his swearing outbursts decreased, allowing his token earnings to increase accordingly. It also had a generalized effect on his behaviour, and he became much more affable and approachable. For example, for the first time in many years staff could touch him without fear of physical retaliation.

Shaping of existing behaviours

There are many ways in which brain-injured patients need to develop behaviours to increase their chances of return to normal society. To some extent, the problems of the patient in Figure 4.4 illustrate this point. Another of our patients was reducing his social attractiveness very considerably by very frequent manipulative and ingratiating behaviours. He admitted to little insight into these behaviours, and no useful response was achieved by attempts to explain their unacceptability. A programme was set up which was limited to the earning of week-ends at home, a powerful reinforcer for this young man. First, a baseline record-

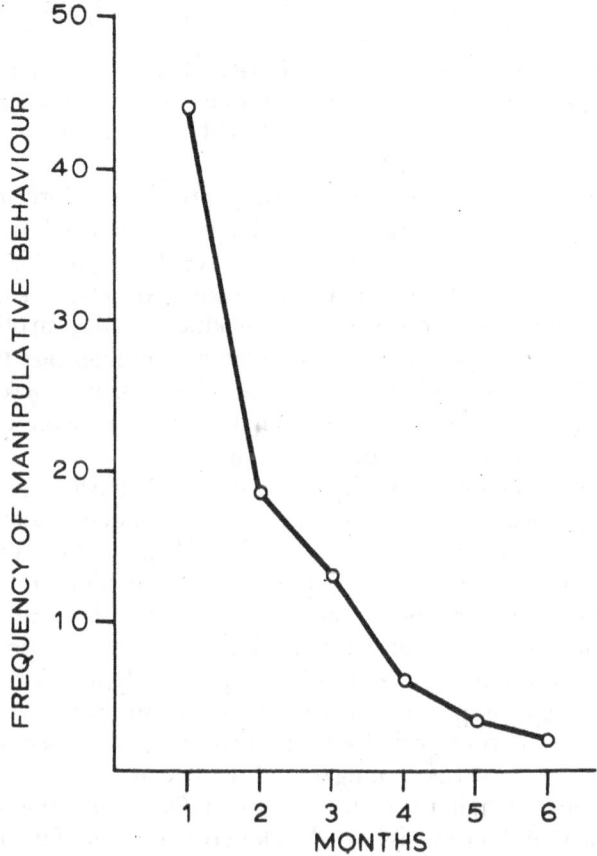

Fig. 4.5 Frequency of manipulative behaviour during a punishment programme. See text for explanation.

ing was made of the number of manipulative behaviours, witnessed by at least two staff members, occurring in the course of a week. As a result, an appropriate 'allowance' was decided, somewhat less than the baseline number. From then on, a 'black mark' was awarded for any example of such behaviour, and if the 'allowance' was exceeded, weekend leave was forfeited. As the weekly number of 'black marks' reduced, so the 'allowance' was reduced. Figure 4.5 demonstrates the reduction in the frequency of the behaviours as a consequence.

Applications of conditioning theory

Evincing behaviours

It is in attempts to promote productive and versatile behaviours that the problem of motivation assumes its greatest importance. We have used two particular methods with gratifying degrees of success.

The first involves promoting, through positive reinforcement, any spontaneous and desirable behaviour produced by the patient, and this leads to a sort of 'backwash' of positive reinforcement within the unit. This often results in a chain reaction such that alteration of one behaviour produces changes in others, and may thus allow new reinforcement contingencies to be selected for further adaptive behaviour changes, and increased motivation. (In addition to this, such a 'backwash' increases the contrast involved in 'time-out on the spot'.)

The other technique has been to look at a behaviour pattern resulting in a short-term goal (for example, a patient's 'morning programme', in which he has to be out of bed, washed, shaved and dressed appropriately, before presenting himself at the apropriate time in the breakfast room). By dividing such behavioural sets into small units of behaviour, it becomes possible to control these in a more detailed way. Initially, the patient is allowed one prompt for each item of behaviour, and if he then performs it, he is rewarded with a token. If he fails, then that is one token less towards earning breakfast. The process is repeated with the next item in the series, and so on. Once some fluency in the behavioural series has been developed, a number of items can be grouped together to form a larger and more meaningful unit, requiring the patient to produce more behaviour before reinforcement is given. Once these larger units have been successfully developed, prompting is gradually reduced, and ultimately the position is reached where the whole behavioural set is performed without prompting, and with reinforcement only at the end. The last stage, of course, once the behavioural set is firmly established, is to discontinue specific reinforcement attached to it.

In cases where patients show no interest in the token system, or fail to attend for meals (as, for example, in the case of patients who have some relative difficulty with walking), the time taken for the inherent pressures of the token system to produce helpful results can be very protracted, and great care must be taken to make sure that their physical condition does not suffer from any loss of nutrition. (We should perhaps stress that where meals are not earned the uninteresting but nutritious alternative of Complan is given.) Our experience so far has shown that most such patients do ultimately respond, and continue to make reasonable progress thereafter. Figure 4.6 concerns a patient who would not accept payment of tokens earned. It was difficult to know whether this was as a result of a known trait of stubbornness from long before the injury, or whether it was a feature of his organically determined psychiatric state (a Capgras syndrome, in which he held the delusion that he and his family had all been replaced by identical substitutes). In any event, it inevitably led to loss of the privileges he could have achieved, but the problem was eventually rectified by the contingent withdrawal of social reinforcements for refusal of tokens.

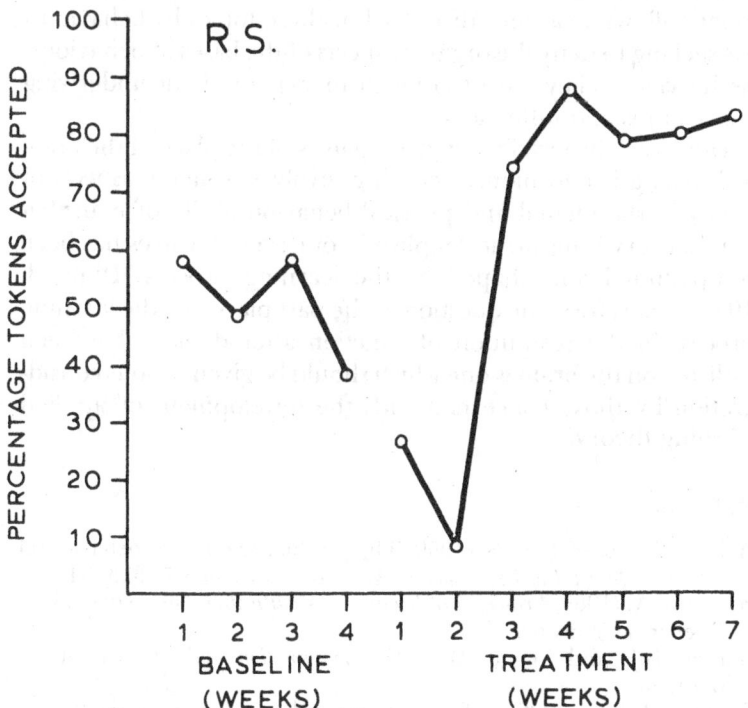

Fig. 4.6 Percentage of earned tokens which were accepted by a patient both before (baseline) and after (treatment) the introduction of a programme specifying contingent withdrawal of social reinforcement and attention by nursing staff for refusal to accept earned tokens.

Conclusions

We may conclude that the varied and complex patterns of brain damage caused by head trauma do not prevent the acquisition of behaviours through associational learning, but may nevertheless have profound effects on the efficiency of the process and the scope of what may be learned.

We believe that those aspects of our experience which have led to the concept of 'constraints' are of the greatest importance, not only for treatment, but also as an avenue for research. The effects that brain damage has upon the potential for behavioural learning in man should allow a new kind of analysis of the parts played by the brain in the control of learning.

Quite recently, Kimble (1973) stated that knowledge obtained in the studies of the reticular formation and limbic system no longer allows a cavalier disregard of these topics by behaviourists seeking to deny the organic aspects of the bases of behaviour. As he says, ' They have too much to suggest about underlying mechanisms and influences.'

However, the task facing investigators of the place of the brain in learning is enormous. Learning involves so many aspects of ability in the mental and physical behavioural life of man that almost everything we accomplish in our everyday lives has been compounded and shaped by the learning process (Dimond, 1980). Therefore, the question of the part played by the learning process in the restitution of function after damage has been inflicted on the brain is one which should be given serious consideration by those concerned with the development of applied learning theory.

References

Ayllon, T. and Michael, S. (1959) The psychiatric nurse as behavioural engineer. *Journal of Experimental Analysis of Behaviour 2:* 323–34.

Bandura, A. (1969) *Principles of Behaviour Modification* New York: Holt, Rinehart & Winston.

Barber, B.J. and Legge, D. (1976) *Information and Skill.* London: Methuen.

Belmont, I. et al. (1969) Effects of cerebral damage on motivation in rehabilitation. *Archives of Physical Medicine and Rehabilitation 50:* 507–11.

Cullen, C.N. (1968) Errorless learning with the retarded *Journal of Practical Approaches to Developmental Handicap 2 (3):* 21–4.

Dimond, S. (1980) *Neuropsychology* London: Butterworth.
Dolan, M.P. and Norton, C. (1977) A programmed training technique that uses reinforcement to facilitate acquisition and retention in brain-damaged patients. *Journal of Clinical Psychology 33(2):* 496–501.
Ervin, F.R. and Mark, V.H. (1970) *Violence and the Brain* New York: Harper & Rowe.
Field, J.H. (1976) The epidemiology of head injuries in England and Wales. London: HMSO.
Hollon, T.H. (1973) Behaviour modification in a community hospital rehabilitation unit. *Archives of Physical Medicine and Rehabilitation 54:* 65–8.
Keehn, J.D. (1969) Consciousness, discrimination and the stimulus control of behaviour. In R.M. Gilbert and N.S. Sutherland, (eds), *Animal Discrimination Learning.* London: Academic Press.
Kimble, G.A. (1973) Scientific psychology in transition. In F.J. McGuigan and B. Lumsden, New York: Wiley.
Legewie-Bertzborn, H., Legewie, H., Foit, J. and Brinkman, R. (1977 Verhaltenstherapeutische Rehabilitation Nach Schädelhirntrauma. *Psychiat. Praxis, 4:* 223–31.
Lindsley, O.R. (1964) Geriatric behavioural prosthetics. In R. Kastenbaum, (ed.), *New Thoughts on Old Age.* New York; Springer.
Lishman, W.A. (1978) *Organic Psychiatry.* Oxford: Blackwell.
Luria, A.R. (1973) *The Working Brain.* Harmondsworth: Penguin.
Oakley, D.A. (1979) Cerebral cortex and adaptive behaviour. In D.A. Oakley and H. Plotkin (eds) *Brain, Behaviour and Evolution.* London: Methuen.
O'Brian, F. and Azrin, N.H. (1972) Symptom reduction by functional displacement in the token economy: a case study, *Journal of Behaviour Therapy and Experimental Psychiatry, 3 (3):* 205–7.
Skinner, B.F. (1953) *Science and Human Behaviour.* New York: Macmillan.
Sperling, G. (1960) The information available in brief visual presentations. *Psychological Monographs: General and Applied, 74:* 1–29
Staats, A.W., Minke, K.A. Goodwin, W. and Landeen, J. (1967) Cognitive behaviour modification: 'motivated learning' reading, treatment with sub-professional therapy technicians. *Behaviour Research and Theory 5:* 283–99
Thomas, G.V. and Blackman, D.E. (1976) Operant conditioning and clinical psychology In M.P. Feldman and A. Broadhurst *Theoretical and Experimental Bases of the Behaviour Therapies'* New York: Wiley.
Wall, R.T. (1969) Behaviour modification and rehabilitation. *Rehabilitation Counseling Bulletin* (Dec. 1969): 173–83
Weiss, D.A. (1964) *Cluttering.* New Jersey: Prentice-Hall.
Woodworth, R.S. (1929) *Psychology* New York: Holt.
Zeaman, D. and House, B.J. (1963) The role of attention in retardate discrimination learning. In N.R. Ellis *Handbook of Mental Retardation,* New York: McGraw Hill.

5 Behaviour modification in organizations

Graham Davey

Most students of psychology are familiar with the use of conditioning principles in the treatment of behavioural problems, and indeed most of the chapters in this volume concern the clinical aspects of behaviour modification and behaviour therapy. However, it was not until the late 1960s and early 1970s that the broader implications of a technology of behaviour change became apparent. Throughout the 1960s articles had sporadically appeared, hinting at the possible applications of behaviour modification techniques outside the clinical sphere, but it was perhaps Skinner's book *Beyond Freedom and Dignity*, published in 1971, which aroused most interest. In this book Skinner set out to convince his audience of two things: firstly, that man was not an autonomous agent but was a product of his heredity and his environment (in effect he was a product of reinforcement contingencies), and secondly, that only a conscious technology of behaviour based on conditioning principles could overcome major social problems such as famine, poverty, overpopulation and pollution – problems that threatened the survival of our cultures. Unfortunately, all the book really succeeded in doing was to harden the resolve of those already convinced by Skinner's theories, and to create a broad spectrum of opponents ranging from those who saw it in an ideological light as a recipe for tyranny (e.g. Chomsky, 1972) to those who saw it as an unwarranted attack on man's dignity and achievements as a 'self-determining' animal.

However, almost a decade has since passed and it should now be possible to evaluate some of the attributes of Skinner's thesis in a more dispassionate light despite these quarrels. That is part of what I hope this chapter will achieve, but rather than simply reiterate the ideological, ethical and paradigmatic arguments that followed the publication of *Beyond Freedom and Dignity*, I want to view Skinner's notions in the light of more practical evidence relating to the application of conditioning principles. For instance, conditioning principles have been applied in programmes geared towards decreasing littering and pollution (Geller, Witmer and Tuso, 1977; Kohlenberg and Phillips, 1973; Powers, Osbourne and Anderson, 1973; Witmer and Geller, 1976) and the conservation of energy supplies and raw materials (Palmer, Lloyd and Lloyd, 1977; Kohlenberg, Phillips and Proctor, 1976; Deslauriers and Everett, 1977).

However, perhaps the greatest attention has been paid to that aspect of human resource management required in organizations. All societies, whether socialist or capitalist, strive for efficient work organizations, industrial and commercial, which create the wealth and economic standards of that society. In the last ten years organizational behaviour modification (OBM as it has come to be known) has been attempting to apply principles of contingency management to industry. Where it has been applied this has so far resulted in more efficient training programmes for employees, new job-enrichment and job-enlargement schemes, increased productivity, and has provided insights into the relationship between job performance and job satisfaction. However, arguably the most important outcome of OBM research has been the light it has cast on the inefficiency of organizations produced by 'sloppy' contingency management. All work organizations require of their participants that they meet certain behavioural requirements (e.g. being present during certain hours of the day and indulging in certain specified 'work' behaviours); yet apart from informing the member that this is what he *should* do, there is little attempt made to ensure that the environmental contingencies in the organization are conducive to generating or maintaining these behaviours. The following sections deal with the kinds of analyses necessary for identifying contingency management problems (e.g. identifying the causes of behaviour, identifying appropriate reinforcers, and setting up appropriate contingen-

104 Applications of conditioning theory

cies), and concludes with a discussion of some actual applied studies and some critical issues which extend beyond the mere academic application of behaviour modification principles to organizations.

Organizational behaviour modification

Organizational behaviour modification is that branch of psychology which attempts to relate operant conditioning principles to organizational behaviour. It tries to achieve this in three ways. Firstly, by attempting to operationalize traditional organizational terminology into a language which involves only measurable and observable events, whether they be environmental or behavioural. Secondly, by allocating the causes of behavior to the contingencies which exist between environment and behaviour; this involves analysing the antecedents and consequences of organizational behaviour and identifying actual and potential reinforcers and punishers. And, thirdly, by manipulating the contingencies of reinforcement avaiable in organizations in order to facilitate organizational performance and productivity. The following sections explore some of these aims and achievements in more detail.

Internal states vs. environmental control

In more traditional treatments of organizational behaviour the causes of efficient or inefficient performance on a job are often localized in the individual or in the nature of the job itself. For instance, the individual may be 'motivated' to carry out the tasks required of him, and he may perform his tasks rapidly and efficiently because he obtains a high degree of 'job satisfaction'. Alternatively a job may be 'intrinsically rewarding' or, if not, it may require a boost from a 'job enrichment' scheme. The factors which control good organizational behaviour in these examples are located either in the individual or in the job. To give further examples of the traditional view, McGregor (1960) states that 'people will exercise self-direction and self-control in the achievement of organizational objectives to the degree that they are committed to the objectives' – the locus of control is seen to rest in the individual. Herzberg (1968) has made the claim that

Behaviour modification in organizations 105

some jobs just cannot be made more motivating in themselves, but control of efficient or inefficient behaviour is seen to rest in the nature of the job.

This view of the causes of organizational behaviour is not one that is shared by those concerned with organizational behaviour modification. In an influential paper, Nord (1969) outlined the behaviourists' view that organizational behaviour was a function of environmental contingencies and not of attributes located solely in the individual or the job; in effect, it was the relationship between observable behaviour and reinforcement contingencies which controlled performance. He continued by interpreting some of the traditional organizational notions into behaviourist terms. For instance, *job motivation* is seen by many as an internal attribute, but how do we identify a worker who is 'highly motivated'? We identify a worker who is highly motivated simply as one who emits the desired response at a high rate (Nord, 1969; Mawhinney, 1975). In effect, we are simply *redescribing* what we observe and are therefore not explaining 'good performance' by alluding to 'high motivation' at all (see Skinner, 1953).

In similar fashion, Nord points out that the apparent internal causes of organizational behaviour stressed by McGregor above, can be unpacked in terms of external determinants. Indeed, McGregor himself states that the 'degree to which individuals are committed to the objectives of the organization' (the internal causes of good performance) can be materially affected by 'managerial policies and practices' (an external variable). Nord also points out that the motivational value of a task can be substantially affected by the reinforcement schedule for performing on that job. For instance, what could be more boring than the task of putting small tokens on a numbered card (the game of bingo), yet this behaviour can be generated and maintained at great length simply by appropriate scheduling of rewards. In this sense, what 'job enrichment' or 'job enlargement' schemes may be required to do to achieve their objective of increased efficiency and increased job satisfaction is: (i) to schedule rewards contingently on the required behaviour, and (ii) to increase the number of potential reinforcers. Most organizations achieve one of these objectives but rarely the other; for instance, monetary reward may be seen as the sole incentive necessary for a worker if he is on 'piece-rate' (i.e. money is contingent upon his productivity), alternatively an

106 Applications of conditioning theory

organization may provide incentives such as sick pay, recreation programmes, employee lounges, work breaks, annual salary increments, etc., all of which are potential rewards but none of which may be contingent upon the behaviour required of the worker by the organization.

Perhaps more interesting in this context is the relationship between task performance and reports of 'task satisfaction'. Again, many traditional views of organizational behaviour regard job satisfaction as an important determinant of efficient job performance — another example of an internal state supposedly controlling an external behaviour. However, the organizational behaviour modifier would regard satisfaction and performance in a completely different way. Skinner (1969) has suggested that internal feelings, such as satisfaction, are at best only *accompaniments* rather than *causes* of behaviour. Therefore, verbal reports of satisfaction and performance on a task are both considered as behaviours each of which is susceptible to control by external factors. If this is true, implementing procedures which increase verbal reports of job satisfaction would be unlikely significantly to affect productivity unless those procedures also directly affected the task behaviour itself. In a laboratory experiment designed to assess the relationship between reports of task satisfaction, productivity and contingent reward, Cherrington, Reitz and Scott (1971) found positive correlations between reports of task satisfaction and productivity only after rewards had been given contingent upon productivity; conversely they found a negative correlation between satisfaction and productivity when inappropriate reward had been given to low performers. What this suggests is that there is no necessary cause-effect relationship between productivity and satisfaction. Instead, contingent reward has both a performance reinforcing and a satisfaction increasing potential (see also Osipow, 1972; and Osipow and Scheid, 1971). It is also interesting to note that although productivity under non-contingent reward was maintained at a reasonable level, job satisfaction was *inversely* related to the degree of productivity. Such a finding might have important implications for those organizations which provide non-contingent pay rises, dependent not on productivity but on age and seniority.

In summary, the organizational behaviour modifier sees control of organizational behaviour as being determined by external

Behaviour modification in organizations

contingencies of reinforcement, and not by internal states located in the individual nor by any intrinsic attributes of the job or task itself. More precisely, (i) internal states such as 'job satisfaction' are seen as behaviours which are independent of, rather than causes of, levels of productivity, and as such can be independently manipulated by programming appropriate reinforcement contingencies, and (ii) perceived attributes of the job or task such as its tedium or its 'motivating properties' are seen not as intrinsic attributes of the job but as a function of reinforcement contingencies related to that task. As we have seen and shall see later, contingent reinforcement can increase both productivity and reports of greater task satisfaction.

Reinforcers

The first task for any organizational behaviour modifier is to identify the behavioural consequences which are important in maintaining those behaviours. The most immediately obvious potential reinforcer is, of course, money – the wage that the individual receives in return for his/her labour. But this is by no means the only reinforcer, and in many cases when it is used it is scheduled so inefficiently in organizations that it is of little value in maintaining the behaviours desired by the organization. However, although one might consider that money is the prime incentive for attending and performing on a job, in reality the contingencies are much more subtle than this. In effect most organizations maintain required behaviour by punishment or threats of punishment. As Skinner (1969) points out:

> No one works on Monday morning because he is reinforced by a pay cheque on Friday afternoon. The employee who is paid by the week works during the week to avoid losing the standard of living which depends on a weekly system.

That is, the system may look like one of positive reinforcement, but the employee's behaviour is actually aversively controlled. More explicit forms of aversive control are found in disciplinary regulations such as wage 'docking' for tardiness or suspension for absenteeism, and more informal punishment such as verbal haranging by organizational superiors when failing to meet the necessary performance requirements. Control by punishment is pervasive in organizations for many reasons. For instance: (1) many organizations feel they have a right to expect an employee to perform up to a particular standard in return for a pay cheque, failure to meet this standard is then seen as a breach of faith for which the organization feels that it has a legitimate and moral right to exact retribution. (2) Punishment can often be seen to have an immediate effect. Even though the effect of punishing undesirable behaviours may be relatively transient in comparison with reinforcing desired behaviours, the perceived immediacy of the effect of punishment actually reinforces the punisher for using it. (3) People who punish are usually emitting an escape response themselves; for instance, the shop floor manager who disciplines a production line worker for failing to meet a production requirement is probably doing so in order to avoid a bad report from his organizational superiors. Nevertheless, despite these reasons for the continued use of punishment contingencies in organizations, punishment is an inefficient method of control in comparison to positive reinforcement. For instance, punishment rarely eliminates a behaviour but merely suppresses it temporarily (cf. Azrin and Holz, 1966; Davey 1981a, pp. 121–30). Perhaps more importantly, the implementation of punishment contingencies does not necessary imply that desired behaviours will increase. The punished individual is subsequently likely to indulge merely in behaviour which helps him to *avoid* the punishment – whether these behaviours are desired or not. For example, if an employee is punished for his perpetual tardiness by receiving a disciplinary interview, rather than avoid these punishers by becoming punctual, he/she is often just as likely to try and avoid them by complete absenteeism (Hermann, de Montes, Dominques, Montes and Hopkins, 1973; Schneier, 1974).

The alternative means of controlling behaviour, and that which is recommended by organizational behaviour modifiers, is to positively reinforce desired behaviours. There are two important steps here. Firstly, identify potential reinforcers in the organizational setting – which we will discuss here – and secondly, ensuring that these reinforcers are contingent upon the appropriate behaviours – which we will discuss in the next section.

In its simplest form, Nord (1969) portrayed organizational behaviour as an exchange, with the participant being reinforced

Behaviour modification in organizations

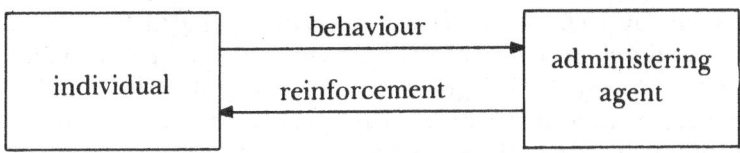

Fig. 5.1

by an organizational superior (see Figure 5.1). The most obvious reinforcer at the disposal of the organization is money, a generalized conditioned reinforcer which is likely to act as a reinforcer for most, if not all, members of the organization (cf. Vroom, 1964). However, other reinforcers may be acting to reduce the potency of a monetary reinforcer. For instance, Jablonsky and De Vries (1972) proposed a multi-person exchange model of operant interactions in organizations, in which there were at least two important sources of reinforcement: organizational superiors who in general dispensed programmed reinforcers such as managerial approval and wages, and the individual's peer-group who provided general social consequences to attending and performing on the job. As they rightly point out, the second source of reinforcers can often diminish the potency of monetary rewards. For instance, a company's policy of rewarding good work with promotion may not result in individual striving to achieve 'good work', simply because promotion might mean loss of contact with peers whose reinforcing value might be higher.

However, money and promotion are by no means the only ways that organizational superiors can reinforce good work. Perhaps one of the most potent reinforcers in any organizational setting is a combination of detailed praise accompanied by feedback given in quantitative terms. For instance, it is extremely difficult for individuals to enhance their work performance if they are unable to *discriminate* the levels at which they are already performing. If a typist is not keeping a record of how many memos she is typing per day it may be very difficult for her to respond to a request to increase her daily output. In effect it is analogous to asking someone to increase the rate of peristaltic movements in their duodenum: because they are unaware of the moment-to-moment changes in the rate of this behaviour it is thus difficult to bring it under voluntary control. Similarly, if the typist is unaware of her

110 Applications of conditioning theory

day-to-day performance it will be difficult to bring this behaviour under the control of reinforcement contingencies. In an applied study at Emery Air Freight Company (that we shall discuss later) managers were given detailed training in the need to proffer continuous feedback to employees and praise appropriate behaviour. For example, it is not enough simply to acknowledge good or improved work with the phrase 'well done, keep it up', but a phrase such as 'I liked the method you used to reduce the number of sheets of carbon paper we use, and by the way you typed seventy-eight memos yesterday which is 15 per cent up on your average for last week', imparts both praise and feedback simply and quickly. Eventually, continuous feedback can be achieved by giving the worker a daily sheet on which he/she can mark his/her performance and compare this with the required standards. Furthermore, acknowledgement of good work does not simply have to involve a phrase such as 'well done, keep it up'. In the Emery Air Freight study (pp. 118–19) managers were given a booklet suggesting up to 150 ways of recognizing and rewarding appropriate behaviour. These ranged from the simple 'good work, you're running pretty consistently at 98 per cent of standard' to 'let me buy you a cup of coffee'.

Apart from the importance of performance feedback as a reinforcer in organizations, other techniques are available for identifying reinforcers. Luthans and Kreitner (1975) mention three useful techniques.

(1) *Ipsative tests* (Blood, 1973). This test contains 45 pairs of statements, and the individual selects his/her preference in each pair. Eventually, this gives a hierarchy of preferences in ten reward categories.

These reward categories are:

(1) Achievement or sense of accomplishment.
(2) Responsibility or control.
(3) Opportunity for personal growth.
(4) Recognition from the community and from friends.
(5) Job or company status.
(6) Interpersonal relationships or friendships.
(7) Pay or monetary reward.
(8) Job security.
(9) Provision for family.

(10) Support for hobbies or avocational activities.
(From Luthans and Kreitner, 1975, p. 95.)

(2) *Contingency questionnaires* (Reitz, 1971). Employees select one of six responses ranging from 100 per cent certain to very improbable to each of twenty items. These answers can give the manager a pretty good idea of what kinds of consequences are important to individuals. The statements include the following:

(1) Your supervisor would personally pay you a compliment if you did outstanding work.
(2) You would be promoted if your work was better than others who were otherwise equally qualified.
(3) Your next pay increase will be consistent with the amount recommended by your supervisor, etc.

Although the details of potential reinforcers may not be as precise as other methods, this approach does help to indicate behaviour which might be in need of reinforcement, as well as potential reinforcers.

(3) *Self-selection techniques* (Cathey, 1970; Oates, 1973). In this method for identifying potential reinforcers, individuals are allowed to choose their reward from an assortment of options. For example, on having completed a job up to the required standards, an employee may be given the choice of more time off as opposed to cash benefits, a deferred income plan as against immediate cash, etc. In effect, having a *menu* of reinforcers from which employees can choose increases the likelihood that the organization will be using effective reinforcers across most of its employees.

Finally, in this section, it is perhaps important to discuss the relationship between external and intrinsic reinforcement for organizational behaviour. Certain theorists (e.g. De Charms, 1968; Deci, 1971; 1972) have claimed that extrinsically reinforcing an intrinsically motivated behaviour will decrease intrinsic motivation and therefore decrease the level of behaviour determined by it. Scott (1976) has addressed a paper to this problem, and draws a number of conclusions from a review of the animal and human literature: (1) In the animal literature, puzzle-solving behaviours in monkeys can be acquired and maintained in the absence of extrinsic rewards (e.g. Davis, Settlage and Harlow, 1950), but this behaviour often declines rapidly unless new response contingent reinforcers are introduced. The conclusion is that in the animal literature there are numerous examples of intrinsically motivated behaviour which can be facilitated by subsequent external reinforcement. (2) De Charms (1968) claims that 'intrinsic motivation refers to an internal state resulting from knowledge of having accomplished something by individual effort.' However, as Scott suggests, this kind of analysis is not particularly helpful in the applied situation because we are not told how the motivational state produces behaviour, nor are we told how to produce changes in this state. (3) As Nord (1969) points out, it seems quite reasonable to assume that certain tasks are intrinsically rewarding, but this can be unpacked in a much more practically meaningful way. For instance, an individual's rate of performance may increase because he completes a job which perhaps had a high probability of failure. In this case the reinforcer is the completion of the job itself, not any characteristic of the task behaviour. McGregor (1966) has suggested that intrinsic rewards such as this are more powerful than extrinsic rewards but this may be so simply because intrinsic rewards are scheduled more contingently than extrinsic rewards. That is, if the reinforcer is the completion of the task it is impossible to get more contingent than that, and contingent reward, as we shall see, is the most potent method for generating desired behaviour. For a fuller exposition of the behaviourist views on extrinsically and intrinsically motivated behaviour, the reader is referred to reviews by Dunham (1977) and Mawhinney (1979).

Contingencies

Having identified actual and potential reinforcers the next step is to identify the contingencies which relate these reinforcers to behaviours in the organization, and, if necessary, subsequently to design contingencies which will more effectively generate desired organizational behaviour. Whether they are intentionally designed or not, all organizations contain contingencies of reinforcement and either one manages the contingencies or they will get managed by accident. Either way there will be contingencies and they will have their effect. A prime instance of 'sloppy' contingency management can be seen in the weekly wage system of payment. Here the monetary reinforcer is contingent neither upon the work behaviour of the employee nor his level of performance, but simply

Behaviour modification in organizations 113

on his attending the place of work. Other consequences, usually punitive, are programmed to control his rate of performance on the job. Similarly, organizations regularly provide reinforcers which are not contingent upon desired behaviours; we have already mentioned sick pay, recreation programmes, employee lounges, work breaks and so on, most of which are provided without regard to the employee's performance on the job. However, we must point out that these factors may have other benefits even if they do not directly affect job performance; for instance, they may reduce turnover of staff when high turnover would be costly for the organization. Furthermore, this general disregard for the importance of contingencies can be seen on a much wider level. Governments may introduce reductions in income tax in order to stimulate industrial growth and increase productivity, yet such 'incentives' are not contingent in any way upon the behavioural goals desired of the population by the government (i.e. increased productivity) and therefore, according to conditioning theory their effectiveness should be minimal.

The next question concerns the implementation of appropriate contingencies in organizations. Conditioning theory provides us with two specific rules for generating stable behaviour which are resistant to extinction. Firstly, reward should be administered as soon as possible after the completion of the required response (contiguity of reward). This is perhaps why intrinsic reinforcement *appears* to be more powerful than extrinsic reinforcement in determining performance on a task. As suggested above, the completion of a task which has perhaps proved arduous is reinforcing, and the reinforcer is by necessity gained immediately on completion of the task. When extrinsic rewards are used they are often difficult to schedule immediately following the required behaviour. Even piece-rate systems of payment, where the employee receives payment in relation to his productivity, may not provide the employee with the actual reinforcer until the end of the working week, this entailing at least some delay of reinforcement. The second rule concerns the frequency of reward. It is well known from the animal and human literatures that intermittent reinforcement is superior to continuous reinforcement in two respects: one, it produces a higher *rate* of responding, and two, it increases resistance to extinction. Furthermore, the scheduling of intermittent reinforcement produces distinctive fluctuations in the patterning of behaviour which

114　Applications of conditioning theory

may have important relevance for organizational behaviour modifiers. There are four basic schedules of intermittent reinforcement, fixed-interval, fixed-ratio, variable-interval and variable-ratio. A fixed-interval schedule reinforces the first instance of the desired response that occurs after a specified period of time, and in a wide variety of animals (including man) this schedule usually generates a positively accelerated gradient of responding (known as the 'fixed-interval scallop'). This gradient consists of a pause after each reinforcement with responding gradually increasing up to the time for the next reinforcer's availability. In effect, a fixed-interval schedule is loosely analogous to the schedule under which an employee earning a weekly or monthly salary is performing (although it is only loosely analogous because in most cases the behaviour which is necessary to obtain the reinforcer at the end of the fixed-interval is merely attending the place of work and not indulging in the required job). In such cases, the organizational behaviour modifier might reasonably expect that this schedule would produce fluctuations in the rate of organizational behaviour concomitant with a fixed-interval basis (e.g. fixed-interval one week) then one might reasonably expect this behaviour to be extremely low in frequency early in the week. That is, all other things being equal, tardiness or absenteeism can be expected to be highest on Monday, slightly less on Tuesday, and so on, until reward is available on Friday.

A fixed-ratio schedule differs from a fixed-interval schedule in that reward is scheduled according to number of responses rather than the passage of time. For instance, on a fixed-ratio twenty schedule, every twentieth response produces the reinforcer. However, even though this schedule requires that a number of responses be emitted before the reinforcer is delivered, it still produces a pattern of behaviour consisting of a pause after reinforcement followed by an abrupt transition to a relatively high rate of responding which is maintained until reward is achieved. This schedule is loosely analogous to the reward conditions experienced by a worker on piece-rate (i.e. one who is rewarded for his productivity). The amount of money he receives at the end of the week (i.e. the number of reinforcers) will be proportional to the number of 'ratios' he has completed (i.e. how many job units he has completed). Nevertheless, even a fixed-ratio schedule produces a post-reinforcement pause, and one might legitimately expect performance to be poor and productivity low on days immediately following the receipt of the wage packet.

The remaining two schedules, variable-interval and variable-ratio, are counterparts of the two schedules we have already discussed, except that reinforcers are scheduled on a variable time and variable number of responses basis respectively. In animals these schedules generate stable high rates of responding with little or no post-reinforcement pause. Because of this characteristic of variable schedules they appear to be the most appropriate for use in organizational settings where stable high levels of performance are required.

However, in practical terms this does not mean that the employee should simply be given his/her wage packet on different days each week, or irregularly following the production of a specified number of job units. For instance, Aldis (1966) has suggested one way in which variable-ratio (VR) schedules can be adopted in organizations. Instead of giving an expected Christmas box to workers, the names of workers who have achieved production above a specific level can be put into a hat and the winners paid according to the number of units they have produced above this specified level. Lotteries have been successfully adopted in other studies as a means of implementing a variable-ratio schedule of reinforcement. Pedalino and Gamboa (1974) successfully decreased the level of absenteeism in a manufacturing/distribution centre by presenting each worker with a lottery ticket when he attended work; this also had the side effect of decreasing tardiness because the employee had to be on time to become eligible. Stephens and Burroughs (1978), in a similar study designed to decrease absenteeism, instigated a system whereby hospital employees became eligible for a lottery ticket for a $20 cash prize if they were *not* absent on eight days randomly selected from a three-week period. This system also resulted in significant decreases in absenteeism. However, it must be pointed out that these studies were concerned with the application of variable schedules of reinforcement to behaviours only peripheral to that of production. They did not alter the fundamental contingencies relating productivity and job performance to earnings. One study has attempted to compare continuous and variable schedules of monetary reinforcement and their effect on production, but this produced results which were not in agreement with the expectations of conditioning theory. Yukl and Latham (1975) set up continuous and variable reinforcement contingencies for fores-

116   Applications of conditioning theory

try work crews who were planting trees. One group was given a $2 bonus for each bag of trees planted (continuous reinforcement), a second group received a $4 bonus when they had planted a bag of trees *and* then correctly guessed the outcome of a coin toss (variable-ratio 2), and a third group received a $8 bonus when they had planted a bag of trees and correctly guessed the outcome of two coin tosses (variable-ratio 4). At the end of the day each worker had received approximately the same amount of money in bonuses, but they differed only in the scheduling of this money. Contrary to Yukl and Latham's expectations the continuous reinforcement group had the highest productivity. They interpret this discrepancy between theory and practice in a number of ways. Firstly, many of the women participating in the study felt that coin tossing was a form of gambling, and thus frowned upon this new method of payment; a method of arranging the VR schedule which was less directly related to gambling might have proved more successful. Secondly, they point out that none of the schedules in their study were in fact 'pure' because the workers also received an hourly wage. Whether these interpretations account for this discrepancy or whether variable schedules have only limited applicability to organizational performance is a matter for further investigation. What this study does suggest though, is that one should perhaps be wary about implementing variable-ratio schedules when the contingency relates the employee's task behaviour to monetary reinforcers, and the system is conceived of in a 'gambling-like' framework (e.g. as in a lottery or coin tossing method of generating the variable contingency). Individuals may quite reasonably object if they feel that their earnings, and hence their livelihood, are dependent on 'a gamble' – even if in reality they are not.

What might be required to make variable schedules successful in the kinds of situations used by Yukl and Latham is merely a method of generating the variable schedule which appears to have no more 'risk' attached to it than does a continuous reinforcement schedule. Perhaps this might be achieved simply by making employees clearly aware that although payment may occur irregularly their earnings will be directly related to their productivity.

Some applied studies

In a questionnaire given to workers some years ago, over 50 per cent of wage earners admitted they could accomplish more each day if they tried (Luthans and Kreitner, 1975, p. 90), so it is perhaps not surprising that organizational psychologists have been striving for some years to find techniques which might unlock this potential. We have talked so far in this chapter about how the organizational behaviour modifier would conceptualize organizational behaviour, and also about some of the possible ways in which conditioning theory might be applied to organizations. Now it is necessary to look at some applied studies and assess their accomplishments.

Before commencing the implementation of any organizational programme it is necessary to analyse fully the existing regime. Organizational behaviour modifiers approach this in a particular way, which enables them to translate the practicalities of the existing system into a vocabulary consistent with their own conceptual framework. Luthans and Kreitner (1975) call this the OBM problem-solving model, and it contains five specific steps which define the OBM procedure.

(1) *Identify* This involves identifying the specific behaviours that either exist in the organization already or are required by the organization. This identification process requires that behaviours be defined in terms which allow them to be observed and measured. For instance, if it is an advertising executive's job to think of new advertising campaigns for his company's clients, we cannot observe or readily measure the amount of time he spends 'thinking' about a particular job. However, we might be able to rather loosely operationally define this behaviour in terms of the amount of time he spends attending to papers concerned with this work and the amount of time he spends writing about this job, as opposed, say, to looking out of the window, talking informally with colleagues, etc.

(2) *Measure* Having identified the important behaviours, their baseline frequency prior to any intervention must be measured (see Luthans and Kreitner, 1975, p. 73 for further details of the practicalities involved in this stage).

(3) *Analyse* Following measurement of the relevant behaviours it is then necessary to analyse the behaviour-environment relationships that might be acting to maintain or suppress these behaviours. In effect, this requires us to identify the events preceding these

behaviours (and hence that might act as environmental stimuli setting the occasion for the emission of the behaviour), and also that we identify any consequences of behaviour (the events that might reinforce or punish the behaviour). This stage might also require us to identify possible new reinforcers that can be used in the intervention phase.

(4) *Intervention* This is the stage where the organizational behaviour modifier intervenes to set up the contingencies which will generate the behaviours required by the organization. These contingencies should be consistent with principles derived from operant conditioning and adapted, if necessary, to fit the practicalities of the organizational situation.

(5) *Evaluation* An objective evaluation of the effectiveness of the OBM programme must be made by comparing baseline levels of performance recorded in stage two with the levels of behaviour recorded following a period of intervention with the redesigned contingencies. Although it is often the case that evaluation consists of recording the level of change in target behaviours (i.e. behaviours to which the OBM programme is directly addressed) it is often also important to monitor behaviours peripheral to this, since a change in the contingencies related to one behaviour can have profound influences on other, related, behaviours. For instance, by setting up programmes designed to alleviate tardiness in employees we may also affect the way in which the employee's family react to him. Because he leaves home earlier to arrive at work on time his wife may feel he is beginning to neglect her, and since his wife is probably a source of reinforcement for other behaviours these, too, may be affected. Although it is not always easy to know in advance what behaviours to monitor it is wise to at least be aware that a programme may affect more than just the target behaviour (Willems, 1974).

The Emery Air Freight experience Perhaps the most widely known example of the application of OBM in large organizations is known as the Emery Air Freight experience (At Emery Air Freight, 1973). During the first stage of this study the company carried out a performance audit designed to identify the job behaviours with the greatest impact on profits. Since Emery requires the extensive use

Behaviour modification in organizations 119

of large freight containers they deduced that most money could be saved if maximum use was made of all container space. Although managers and warehousemen who loaded the containers had been trained and encouraged to increase the use of empty container space, an audit team found container utilization to be only around 45 per cent, whereas the managers and warehousemen actually believed they were using around 90 per cent. What was obviously required in this situation was a constant feedback programme whereby warehousemen were kept informed of their level of performance in filling containers. Once this feedback provided them with the ability to discriminate their own performance levels, new performance standards could be introduced and their attainment suitably reinforced. The warehousemen were in fact given the opportunity to provide themselves with feedback of their performance as they kept a checklist when their container utilization rate fell between 45 per cent and 95 per cent a day. Subsequently, when they were each given daily performance targets, warehouse managers would provide positive reinforcement for their attainment. In effect, although the warehouseman was keeping a check on his own daily performance level, the manager would provide further feedback and reinforce desired performance levels. In order that managers were able to act as 'contingency managers' and 'reinforcer dispensers', they, too, were given detailed training in feedback and recognition and reward. Workbooks given to the managers outlined over 150 ways of rewarding employees, 'ranging from a smile and a nod of encouragement, to "let me buy you a coffee" to detailed praise for a job well done'.

As a consequence of this programme, Emery Air Freight made a saving of $520,000 in the first year and a reported $2 million over a three-year period. Apart from its obvious benefit to the company, this study has a number of interesting aspects. (1) It outlines neatly the important stages that an OBM programme should follow. Firstly, it identifies those behaviours which are most importantly related to overall performance, secondly, it provides the employees with feedback, informing them of their own performance levels, and thirdly, it provides positive reinforcement for performance standards required by the organization. (2) It suggests how performance standards can be increased without the complexity and conflict of incentive systems where standards, performance and earnings are inextricably linked. Although the employees are not given monetary remuneration for their increased efficiency, the savings that Emery made through the programme did allow them to offer peripheral benefits which were bigger and better than rival companies – a fact which employees recognized.

Improving performance in small businesses The Emery Air Freight experience gives one example of the use of OBM in relatively large companies, but these same principles are equally applicable to improving performance in small businesses. Two studies by Komaki, Waddell and Pearce (1977) give the reader some idea of the kinds of contingencies that can be manipulated in smaller organizational settings.

The first study of Komaki et al. involved the behaviour of two clerks in a neighbourhood grocery store. Three behavioural goals were specified: (1) At least one of the workers should be in the store and within three feet of a display shelf when the store was open. (2) Whenever a customer was in the store one of the workers should approach within three feet and, with a smile, ask the customer 'may I help you?' Whenever a customer requested assistance, this should be given within five seconds of the request. (3) The merchandise display shelves, the produce counter, and the package meat counter should be filled to at least 50 per cent of their capacity at times when the store was open. Whenever the clerks achieved at least 90 per cent on the desired behaviours they were given time off with pay each week. Similarly, they were given feedback daily on their performance levels on each behaviour. On the basis of daily observation audits, mean performance levels of the three behaviours improved from 53, 35 and 57 per cent to 86, 87 and 86 per cent respectively over a five-week period.

The second study took place in a game room located in the downtown area of a metropolitan city, and the subject was a male game room attendant who was in imminent danger of being dismissed because of inefficient performance on the job. Three desired behaviours were defined on consultation with the manager: (1) being within ten feet of the change counter whenever a customer was within ten feet of the change counter, (2) either 'making good' a machine malfunction or refunding a customer's money when a customer indicated a problem with one of the machines, (3) cleaning the premises or the machines whenever less than five people

Behaviour modification in organizations

were in the room. The attendant was informed that his take home pay would correspond to the number of cleaning duties he performed in (3) and he was given feedback on his performance levels. Over a seven-week period all aspects of the employee's performance improved, customers were receiving change promptly, machine malfunctions were being taken care of swiftly, and the premises were being cleaned daily.

These two studies also provide a number of interesting points. (1) The importance of goal clarification cannot be overstated. In each of these studies each behaviour was explicitly defined so that both the employee and the manager would be in no doubt as to what they were. This is important for the employee because he/she cannot easily increase his/her level of performance if the definition of the behaviour required is 'loose' or 'woolly'. It is also important for the manager, because if he/she is to be the dispenser of reinforcers he/she, too, must be able to identify clearly when performance levels have been met – especially if the reinforcer is praise or recognition of achievements. The control exercised by many managers and supervisors is by necessity aversive simply because they are unable to clearly identify good or improved performance and hence reinforce it. (2) In the second study, mere feedback on performance levels enabled the employee who was in danger of being dismissed to improve the levels of performance required on the job. Similarly, a potentially reinforcing – but typically noncontingent item – pay – was made contingent on a certain level of performance, with a resultant increase in those levels.

Some critical issues

No discussion of OBM would be complete without discussion of some of the wider ranging issues that surround the moral and practical acceptability of behaviour modification techniques in general. Criticisms of a conditioning approach to behaviour management range from theoretical and practical criticisms, for example, 'conditioning principles just do not work consistently when it comes to human subjects', to the moral and ethical criticisms of the kind 'behaviour management techniques based on environmental manipulation invite tyrannical control of individuals and societies' and 'the conception of man as controlled by his environment is an affront to human dignity and achievement'. Most of these issues have been discussed at length elsewhere, especially in the wake of the publication of Skinner's *Beyond Freedom and Dignity*. Rather than simply summarize these general discussions here, the interested reader is referred to Carpenter (1974), Davey (1981a, pp. 401–10), Luthans and Kreitner (1975, pp. 174–85, Wheeler (1973), and Chomsky (1972) for a spectrum of views related to this topic. However, what does concern us here is how general theoretical and moral issues relate to the use of behaviour modification in organizations. Even if one were to admit that behaviour modification techniques were manipulative, at least those who use such techniques in clinical psychology could argue that they were at least using these methods to alleviate suffering and that might be justification enough; the organizational behaviour modifier does not even have this argument to fall back on. Let us look at some of the practical issues first and ethical issues later.

(1) Although one might admit that conditioning principles do apply to man, it might be argued that the complexities of life in large organizations make their application to organizations impossible (cf. Whyte, 1972). Whyte points out that (i) dispensing reinforcers in work organizations would prove difficult due to the practical problems faced in defining and measuring complex behaviour, (ii) a worker may be simultaneously rewarded from one group and punished from another (e.g. promotion is a reward supplied by the management, but this may result in punishing anti-social reactions from workmates), (iii) environmental contingencies may be difficult to manage because of time lags between performance and reward resulting from unpredictable behaviour from those dispensing the rewards, (iv) little attention is paid to the behavioural control of those who are reinforcing other employees (i.e. managers and supervisors). In reply, it must be stated that these are not theoretical criticisms which undermine the application of conditioning theory to organizations, they are practical problems which a conditioning model could come to terms with. We have already noted that some studies have come to terms with Whyte's first criticism and the third and fourth criticisms are ones which could be corrected with appropriate managerial training schemes. The second criticism is one which can be ameliorated with the use of more detailed analysis of existing contingencies prior to any OBM intervention; certainly an event can act as both a punisher for some behaviours and a reinforcer for others; it is up to the management to

have recognized this fact before they utilize that event in a new programme.

(2) Who benefits from the implementation of an OBM programme? In most cases the organization itself has called for the implementation of the programme and it is thus the organization that gains either in terms of increases in profits or performance efficiency. Putting aside economic and commercial considerations for a moment, this is perhaps a vital issue when one considers the broader criticisms ranged at OBM from those who see it as manipulative, control oriented and ignoring the individuality of the participants. In any behaviour modification scheme benefits can come in three packages. The recipient or target of the programme may benefit – this is especially so in behaviour therapy; the modifier or individual arranging the contingencies may benefit – this is usually the case when behaviour modification techniques are used to control irritating social problems or keep groups of individuals (e.g. army recruits) in order (Holland, 1973); or both target and modifier may benefit. It is arguably this last category into which OBM should fall. Of the applied studies we have discussed, the management or organization has gained in terms of increased profits and efficiency of performance. But has the employee benefited from the programme, and in what ways could he benefit?

There are at least two ways in which an employee might be able to benefit from an OBM scheme – these are financially and psychologically. He may benefit financially by receiving a percentage of the increased profit he has helped to create, or by receiving direct monetary reward contingent upon his increased performance levels. He may benefit 'psychologically' through the OBM programme resulting in his reporting greater satisfaction with his job – as we have already noted, contingent reward has been found to be highly correlated with reports of job satisfaction (Cherrington, Reitz and Scott, 1971). Whether such reciprocity of benefits would satisfy those who point to the possible manipulative aspects of OBM is arguable. However, as Luthans and Kreitner (1975) point out, one thing is clear – most work organizations involve one group of individuals directing another group of individuals on where to go and what to do, and OBM in its strict amoral sense is merely a more efficient way of doing this (Where Skinner's theories work, 1972).

(3) Although we might reasonably claim that OBM is a more efficient means of 'telling people what to do and where to go' it

124   Applications of conditioning theory

might be argued that it is the least desirable way of doing it in that it fails to appreciate the feelings, ambitions or individuality of its participants. Certainly these are aspects of the individual's psychological make-up that the organizational behaviour modifier does not consider directly when changing behaviour. Yet OBM need not ignore such factors. It denies individuality only in the sense that it believes organizational behaviour is determined by the same processes (e.g. the operant reinforcement process) in all individuals. This does not mean that all individuals should be, or can be, treated identically. For instance, different reinforcers may be required for different individuals in a particular OBM programme (a situation in which a 'menu' of reinforcers can be used to cater for all participants, see p. 111); similarly, behavioural goals may have to be geared differently for individuals of differing ability and different levels of training. Indeed, these behavioural goals are usually best determined and have most likelihood of being achieved if they are set in joint consultation with the participants of the programme (e.g. Latham and Kinne, 1974). Finally, and perhaps most importantly as far as future development is concerned, OBM need not involve the modifier-modified relationship that for many people gives it the flavour of 'control'. Self-control of behaviour is just as much a matter of appropriate reinforcement contingencies as is external control. As long ago as 1953 Skinner wrote:

> When a man controls himself, chooses a course of action, thinks out the situation to a problem, or strives toward an increase in self-knowledge, he is *behaving*. He controls himself precisely as he would control the behaviour of anyone else – through the manipulation of variables of which behaviour is a function.

Without going into the details of this branch of behaviour modification (see Thoresen and Mahoney, 1974, for an introductory account), an individual can exercise some degree of control over his own behaviour by reinforcing himself for those behaviours he wishes to increase and punishing himself for those behaviours he wishes to eradicate. For example, the accounts clerk may allow himself the cup of coffee he so desires during midmorning only when he has finished a specified amount of work. In this situation the individual sets his/her own behavioural targets, sets up the reinforcement contingency himself and provides his/her own reinforcer. To make use of such a technique in organizations, manage-

Behaviour modification in organizations 125

ment and employees would have to agree, first on performance targets required of the employees by the management, and second, on the willingness of the management to provide the reinforcers that the employees require to carry out their self-control programmes. The employees would formulate their own work contingencies and the job of management would be to ensure that reinforcers were forthcoming at the appropriate times. The responsibility for designing, instigating and fulfilling the self-control programme rests squarely with the employee.

Conclusions

Skinner's book *Beyond Freedom and Dignity* implored us to look closely at the contingencies which govern our everyday lives. Problems such as overpopulation, pollution and poverty – which plague many societies – can often be conceived of as behavioural problems where inappropriate contingencies of reinforcement maintain behaviours which are contrary to the best long-term interests of the individual and his society. It was mentioned at the beginning of this chapter that some attempts have already been made to apply contingency analyses and contingency management programmes to some of these problems – if only on a small scale (Davey, 1981b). However, the recent growth in the use of organizational behaviour modification programmes has provided a more detailed indication of the potency and utility of Skinner's principles to everyday living and working. The wealth of most societies is created not by individuals working alone but by individuals behaving in organizations, and those organizations require that their participants fulfil specified behavioural functions. In order to ensure that organizations function efficiently, and thus profitably for the society, we need a positive and practical technology of human resource management. Conditioning principles have provided a viable framework for analysing the variables controlling organizational behaviour, they also suggest techniques for changing this behaviour where necessary. When they have been applied, they have usually achieved their aims of improved organizational performance. Once the value of these techniques of analysis has been generally recognized it is necessary for the future that:

(1) we instigate training programmes designed to educate both managers and employees in the principles of contingency analysis and management,
(2) we develop programmes more suited to the practicalities of the organizational settings but which are soundly based on principles of behaviour analysis and conditioning, and
(3) we should understand more fully the relationships between OBM programmes and the participants' evaluations of them, measured in terms of such traditional organizational concepts as job satisfaction, perceived autonomy, degree of commitment to the objectives of the programme and the organization, etc.

If scores on these variables reflect favourably upon the implementation of OBM principles, it will go some way to removing the stigma of control and manipulation that has tended to be associated with OBM because of its animal conditioning heritage.

References

Aldis, O. (1966) Of pigeons and men. In R. Ulrich, T. Stachnik and J. Mabry (eds) *Control of Human Behaviour*. Glenview, Ill.: Scott, Foresman.
At Emery Air Freight: positive reinforcement boosts performance. (173) *Organizational Dynamics*: 41–50.
Azrin, N.H. and Holz, W.C. (1966) Punishment. In W.K. Honig (ed.) *Operant Behaviour: Areas of Research and Application*. New York: Appleton-Century-Crofts.
Blood, M.R. (1973) Intergroup comparisons of intraperson differences: rewards from the job. *Personnel Psychology 26*: 1–9.
Carpenter, F. (1974) *The Skinner Primer*. London: The Free Press.
Cathey, P.J. (1970) Wage plans: Smorgasbord, anyone? *Iron Age 205*: 56–7.
Cherrington, D.J., Reitz, H.J. and Scott, W.E. (1971) Effects of contingent and noncontingent reward on the relationship between satisfaction and task performance. *Journal of Applied Psychology 55*: 531–6.
Chomsky, N. (1972) Psychology and ideology. *Cognition 1*: 11–46.
Davey, G.C.L. (1981) *Animal Learning and Conditioning*. London: Macmillan Press.
Davey, G.C.L. (1981b) How Skinner's theories work: behaviour analysis and environmental problems. *Bulletin of the British Psychological Society 34*: 57–60.
Davis, R.T., Settlage, P.H. and Harlow, H.F. (1950) Performance of normal and brain-operated monkeys on mechanical puzzles with and without food incentive. *Journal of Genetic Psychology 77*: 305–11.
De Charms, R. (1968) *Personal causation: the internal affective determinants of behaviour*. New York: Academic Press.

Deci, E.L. (1971) Effects of externally mediated rewards on intrinsic motivation. *Journal of Personality and Social Psychology 18*: 105–15.
Deci, E.L. (1972) Intrinsic motivation, extrinsic motivation, and inequity. *Journal of Personality and Social Psychology 22*: 113–20.
Deslauriers, B.C. and Everett, P.B. (1977) Effects of intermittent and continuous token reinforcement on bus ridership. *Journal of Applied Psychology 62*: 369–75.
Dunham, P. (1977) The nature of reinforcing stimuli. In W.K. Honig and J.E.R. Staddon (eds) *Handbook of Operant Behavior*. Englewood Cliffs, N.J.: Prentice-Hall.
Geller, E.S., Witmer, J.F. and Tuso, M.A. (1977) Environmental interventions for litter control. *Journal of Applied Psychology 63*: 344–51.
Hermann, J.A., de Montes, A.I.,Dominques, B., Montes, F. and Hopkins, B.L. (1973) Effects of bonuses for punctuality on the tardiness of industrial workers. *Journal of Applied Behavioural Analysis 6*: 563–70.
Herzberg, F. (1968) *Work and the Nature of Man*. Cleveland: World.
Holland, J.G. (1973) Political implications of applying behavioural psychology. In R. Ulrich, T. Stachnik and J. Mabry (eds) *Control of Human Behavior*. New York: Scott, Foresman.
Jablonsky, S.F. and Devries, D.L. (1972) Operant conditioning principles extrapolated to the theory of management. *Organizational Behaviour and Human Performance 7*: 340–58.
Kohlenberg, R. and Phillips, T. (1973) Reinforcement and rate of litter depositing. *Journal of Applied Behaviour Analysis 6*: 391–6.
Kohlenberg, R., Phillips, T. and Proctor, W. (1976) A behavioural analysis of peaking in residential electrical-energy consumers. *Journal of Applied Behaviour Analysis 9*: 13–18.
Komaki, J., Waddell, U.M. and Pearce, M.G. (1977) The applied behaviour analysis approach and individual employees: improving performance in two small businesses. *Organizational Behaviour and Human Performance 19*: 337–52.
Latham, G. and Kinne, S. (1974) Improving job performance through training in goal setting. *Journal of Applied Psychology 59*: 187–91.
Luthans, F. and Kreitner, R. (1975) *Organizational Behaviour Modification* Glenview, Ill.: Scott, Foresman.
McGregor, D. (1960) *The Human side of Enterprise*. New York: McGraw-Hill.
McGregor, D. (1966) *Leadership and Motiviation*. Cambridge, Mass.: MIT Press.
Mawhinney, T.C. (1975) Operant terms and concepts in the description of individual work behaviour: some problems of interpretation, application and evaluation. *Journal of Applied Psychology 60*: 704–12.
Mawhinney, T.C. (1979) Intrinsic and extrinsic work motivation: perspectives from behaviourism. *Organizational Behavior and Human Performance 24*: 411–40.
Nord, W. (1969) Beyond the teaching machine: the neglected area of operant conditioning in the theory and practice of management. *Organizational Behaviour and Human Performance 4*: 375–401.

128 Applications of conditioning theory

Oates, D. (1973) A cafeteria approach to compensation. *International Management 28*: 14–17.

Osipow, S.H. (1972) Success and preference: a replication and extension. *Journal of Applied Psychology 56*: 179–80.

Osipow, S.H. and Scheid, A.B. (1971) The effect of manipulated success ratios on task preference. *Journal of Vocational Behaviour 1*: 93–8.

Palmer, M.H., Lloyd, M.E. and Lloyd, K.E. (1977) An experimental analysis of electricity conservation procedures. *Journal of Applied Behaviour Analysis 10*: 665–71.

Pedalino, E. and Gamboa, V.U. (1974) Behaviour modification and absenteeism: intervention in one industrial setting. *Journal of Applied Psychology 59*: 694–8.

Powers, R.B., Osbourne, J.G. and Anderson, E.G. (1973) Positive reinforcement of litter removal in the natural environment. *Journal of Applied Behaviour Analysis 6*: 579–86.

Reitz, H.J. (1971) Managerial attitudes and perceived contingencies between performance and organizational response. *Academy of Management Proceedings*: 227–38.

Schneier, C.E. (1974) Behaviour modification in management: a review and critique. *Academy of Management Journal 17*: 528–48.

Scott, W.E. (1976) The effects of extrinsic rewards on 'intrinsic motivation': a critique. *Organizational Behaviour and Human Performance 15*: 117–29.

Skinner, B.F. (1953) *Science and Human Behaviour*. New York: Macmillan.

Skinner, B.F. (1969) *Contingencies of Reinforcement: A Theoretical Analysis*. New York: Appleton-Century-Crofts.

Skinner, B.F. (1971) *Beyond Freedom and Dignity*. New York: Alfred A. Knopf.

Stephens, T.A. and Burroughs, W.A. (1978) An application of operant conditioning to absenteeism in a hospital setting. *Journal of Applied Psychology 63*: 518–21.

Thoreson, C.E. and Mahoney, M.J. (1974) *Behavioural Self-Control*. New York: Holt, Rinehart & Winston.

Vroom, V.H. (1964) *Work and Motivation*. New York: Wiley.

Wheeler, H. (1973) *Beyond the Punitive Society*. London: Wildwood House.

Where Skinner's theories work (1972) *Business Week*: 64–6.

Whyte, W.F. (1972) Skinnerian theory in organizations. *Psychology Today 5*: 66–8.

Willems, E.P. (1974) Behavioural technology and behavioural ecology. *Journal of Applied Behaviour Analysis 7*: 151–65.

Witmer, J.F. and Geller, E.S. (1976) Facilitating paper recycling: effects of prompts, raffles and contests. *Journal of Applied Behaviour Analysis 9*: 315–22.

Yukl, G.A. and Latham, G.P. (1975) Consequences of reinforcement schedules and incentive magnitudes for employees performance: problems encountered in an industrial setting. *Journal of Applied Psychology 60*: 294–8.

6 Pavlovian principles and behaviour therapy

Glyn Thomas and Mark O'Callaghan

In the early years of the present century, J.B. Watson claimed that human behaviour was nothing more than long sequences of conditioned reflexes. Fifty years on, W.F. Brewer (1974) felt able to argue that there was no convincing evidence for classical conditioning in adult humans.

The present chapter attempts to trace the fluctuating fortunes of Pavlovian (classical) conditioning as a model for analysis and treatment in clinical settings (behaviour therapy). Firstly, we provide a brief historical survey of clinical applications of Pavlovian conditioning. Secondly, taking the treatment of fear and anxiety as an illustration, we evaluate the clinical success of these applications. Finally, we attempt to relate current practices of behaviour therapy to recent theories of Pavlovian conditioning.

Historical survey

Experimentally, Pavlovian conditioning is achieved by pairing two stimuli without regard to the subject's behaviour. We can illustrate this procedure with Watson and Rayner's (1920) classic study of conditioned fear in a human infant (Little Albert). At the time of the study, Albert was eleven months old. Earlier, when he was presented with a white rat he showed no sign of fear. After seven pairings of the rat (conditioned stimulus) with a distressingly loud noise (unconditioned stimulus), Albert showed clear signs of fear when the white rat was presented alone. Watson and Rayner (1920) interpreted this result as a clear demonstration of the process by which fears of specific objects (phobias) are learned in everyday circumstances.

Experiments which have attempted to repeat Watson and Rayner's demonstration have met with varying success. Whatever the status of its empirical support Watson and Rayner's study has become an influential legend in the history of clinical psychology; that the development of emotional responses can be represented in terms of Pavlovian principles.

Unfortunately, Watson and Rayner had insufficient time to attempt to cure little Albert's conditioned phobia, but they made several suggestions for possible treatments based on Pavlovian principles. It was, however, left to Mary Cover Jones (1924a; 1924b) to demonstrate that conditioning could be used to treat phobias. Of her many cases, that of Peter will serve as our illustration. Peter's naturally acquired fears resembled those artificially generated in Little Albert. He was afraid of rats, rabbits and, indeed, any small furry object. The conditioning part of his treatment consisted of feeding him in the presence of a rabbit, initially presented at a distance but gradually brought closer to him. The rationale of the treatment was that the rabbit would acquire association with the pleasant stimulus of food (unconditioned stimulus) which would eliminate the pre-existing response of fear, a process known as counter-conditioning (cf. Pavlov, 1927).

The most enduring and widespread applications of these principles have been those generated by J. Wolpe. Wolpe (1958) followed Mary Cover Jones' procedure by attempting to eliminate fear by associating feared stimuli with some activity or stimulus that was presumed to be pleasant. Wolpe considered that food, sexual activity, relaxation or, in the case of children, playing with attractive toys might all be used for the purpose of counter-conditioning. In practice, relaxation has been most commonly used with adult patients.

The method of treatment devised by Wolpe (now termed systematic desensitization) involves three stages: relaxation training (Jacobson, 1938), construction of a list of hierarchy of feared items (anxiety hierarchies) and systematically pairing relaxation with items from the hierarchies. The treatment always begins with items low in the hierarchies which initially elicit only mild fear; more threatening material from higher up the hierarchies is only introduced when fear to the earlier items has been eliminated. Fear stimuli can either be presented *in vivo*, in representational form (e.g. pictures) or the patient can be asked to imagine the items while in the relaxed state.

Early reports of the success of systematic desensitization created a receptive climate for further applications of Pavlovian principles.

Conditioning treatments for bedwetting (nocturnal enuresis) in children pre-dated Wolpe's systematic desensitization by a number of years. For example, Mowrer and Mowrer (1938) developed an apparently successful apparatus which sounded an alarm when the child began to urinate. In terms of Pavlovian principles, the alarm can be seen as an unconditioned stimulus which wakens the child. The wakening response becomes conditioned to the internal stimuli (e.g. bladder distension) which in the natural course of events precede urination and are therefore paired with the sounding of the alarm. Despite its demonstrated superiority over alternative forms of treatment, the conditioning method was only slowly adopted by clinicians. Several authors, for example O'Leary and Wilson (1975), and Ullman and Krasner (1975), have commented that early clinical resistance to the conditioning method may have stemmed in large part from the then prevailing psychodynamic interpretations of enuresis.

Aversion therapy is probably the form of behaviour therapy based on Pavlovian principles most widely known to the general public; publicized in an extravagant and imaginary form in films such as *A Clockwork Orange*. The reality is rather less dramatic. Voegtlin (1940), and Lemere and Voegtlin (1950) performed one of the earliest large-scale applications of aversion therapy in their treatment of alcoholics. Alcoholic patients were presented with a variety of drinks after they had been dosed with emetic drugs which produced intense nausea. In conditioning terms, the taste, sight and smell of the alcoholic drinks (e.g. whisky) were the conditioned stimuli which were paired with the sensations of nausea (unconditioned stimuli) induced by the drugs. Lemere and Voegtlin (1950) ran no controls, but their follow-up data suggest that the treatment did help to increase abstinence.

Aversion therapy has also been used to modify sexual reactions in the treatment of homosexuals and patients with troublesome sexual interests such as fetishism (see O'Leary and Wilson, 1975, for a

132 Applications of conditioning theory

review). Frequently, the simple Pavlovian operation of pairing the target stimuli with an aversive unconditioned stimulus has been elaborated by the addition of an instrumental avoidance component (see Feldman and MacCulloch, 1971). With such an added component, the client or patient can avoid shock by performing a simple response (e.g. pressing a button) during the target stimulus.

Another procedure aimed at modifying sexual reactions (called orgasmic reconditioning), was developed by Marquis (1970) and revised by Keller and Goldstein (1978). Orgasmic reconditioning was developed specifically for the treatment of sexual deviance – patients who hold normal heterosexual contacts unexciting, but who are strongly aroused by unusual and often troublesome activities such as sado-masochism. The aim of orgasmic reconditioning is to transfer sexual arousal from the deviant stimuli to normal heterosexual stimuli. In the Keller and Goldstein version of orgasmic reconditioning, the patient is instructed to imagine normal heterosexual stimuli (conditioned stimuli) for a few seconds and then to generate sexual arousal (unconditioned stimulus) by quickly switching to a 'deviant' fantasy or by masturbating. In Pavlovian terms the repeated pairing of heterosexual stimuli with sexual arousal should eventually result in the conditioning of sexual arousal to the heterosexual stimuli.

Appraisal of conditioning treatments: treatment of fear and anxiety

The use of Pavlovian principles in behaviour therapy, though widespread, has seldom been free of controversy. We have chosen to illustrate some of these controversies by examining in detail just one area of application, the treatment of fear and anxiety.

In considering this clinical application of Pavlovian principles we have three claims to consider: (1) that the fears of phobic patients can be viewed as a product of natural Pavlovian conditioning contingencies, (2) that fear can be successfully eliminated with treatments based on Pavlovian principles, and (3) that the effects of such treatments can be attributed to the conditioning contingencies that they embody.

With regard to the first issue, that of whether a purely Pavlovian conditioning process really does underlie the acquisition of fears and phobias, some initial support was afforded from mainly anecdotal evidence. People who complained of particular phobias did indeed point to some traumatic incident earlier on in their lives in which a previously neutral stimulus had become paired with some sort of anxiety provoking stimulus. Unfortunately, however, more rigorous attempts to investigate the role of such traumatic events in the acquisition of fear did not yield entirely encouraging results. Lazarus (1971), for example, reported only two such incidents out of 100 cases, although it could of course be argued that the subjects could merely have forgotten such incidents. Similarly, in the case of those who did report such traumatic events, it is possible that for some individuals such events did not themselves play a crucial role in the acquisition of that fear.

Clearly, this brings us to the thorny question of the identification and interpretation of data derived retrospectively; the various controversies concerning Wolpe and Rachman's (1960) reworking of Freud's (1955, 1977) story of 'Little Hans' are of interest here (cf. Conway, 1978; Eysenck, 1965). A further problem with this 'traumatic model' is that if the patient does admit to some such influence in the acquisition of fear only one such incident is usually reported. It will, however, be remembered that in the case of Little Albert several pairings were necessary to effect learning. It has been suggested that if the initial trauma is sufficiently intense then only one trial may be necessary for conditioned fear to be acquired.

Unfortunately, there are cases in which people report certain severely disabling phobias, although the likelihood of these having arisen from one pairing is unlikely; such is the case with snake phobics. The likelihood of an urban housewife, for example, who has lived her whole life in the city, even meeting a snake, much less in anxiety provoking circumstances, is very remote indeed. Yet the number of people displaying such fears would appear relatively large. Indeed, the number (and range) of phobic objects is surprisingly small. Given that any previously neutral stimulus could become paired to an anxiety provoking object it might be expected that a wide variety of feared stimuli would result. It is generally found, however, that phobic objects are not randomly distributed. Fears of small animals or of social situations constitute the great majority of phobias.

It has been argued from this finding that some stimuli cannot be conditioned easily into becoming phobic objects. It has been suggested that in the case of Little Albert, children may normally show some fear of small furry animals and that if some other object were

134 Applications of conditioning theory

used, conditioning would not have taken place so easily. It can be noted here that Valentine (1930) attempted to engender a conditioned fear to both a small furry creature (a hairy caterpillar) as well as an inanimate object (a pair of opera glasses); success was only achieved with the former, although theoretically both should be possible. A final criticism that has been made is that in Pavlovian conditioning (and especially with single-trial learning) repeated exposure to the conditioned stimulus alone should eventually lead to the extinction of the conditioned fear response. However, it is precisely the fact that phobias *are* so resistant that leads to people seeking help. Clearly, then, the role of Pavlovian conditioning in the acquisition of fears and phobias is by no means simple and we can do no better than cite Davison and Neale's (1974) conclusion:

> The fact that fear was acquired by Little Albert in this study can *not* be taken as evidence that *all* fears and phobias are acquired through [Pavlovian] conditioning. Rather, the study demonstrates only the possibility that some fears *may* be acquired in this particular way. (p. 127; original italics).

As with many new therapies, initial reports of systematic desensitization were somewhat overgenerous in their claims of its efficacy in the treatment of anxiety related problems. Wolpe even suggested that some 90 per cent of all neurotic conditions could be successfully treated by this procedure in a mean of eleven sessions. However, as is axiomatic in clinical research, the reported effectiveness of a new therapy delines as the scientific rigour of the studies increases; such would appear to be the case with systematic desensitization. Early studies were largely anecdotal case reports; as in the case of Wolpe's own work. Clearly, if the application of laboratory based therapeutic procedures was to gain respectability then there should not be just a carry-over of the theories developed from experimental work but also of some of its scientific rigour as well. Anecdotal case reports are deficient in two main respects. Firstly, there is no control group to serve as a basis of comparison. Secondly, the evaluation of success is often entirely subjective, so that experimenter error can creep in and bias the conclusion. Paul (1966, 1967) carried out one of the first studies which overcame these objections. Systematic desensitization as a treatment for fear of public speaking was compared with an alternative therapy (insight therapy) and a placebo control (a fake treatment designed to appear credible). Objective measures (actual performance and physiological responses) were used to check the subjects' self-reports of improvement. The results indicated that systematic desensitization was significantly more effective than either insight therapy or the placebo control in reducing fear; a result which was also confirmed at a two-year follow-up.

The final issue relating to systematic desensitization in this section is concerned with whether or not Pavlovian conditioning does actually account for therapeutic improvement. Whilst there has been some general agreement by reviewers of the literature that systematic desensitization is an effective treatment, there is a wide divergence of opinion about why it works. To some extent this reflects the controversy about how fears and phobias are acquired. It also arose from attempts to identify which elements of systematic desensitization are necessary and sufficient for therapeutic success.

It will be remembered that Wolpe's original formulation for this particular procedure involved a number of stages. First of all there was the relaxation stage; secondly, there was the pairing of the feared stimulus with relaxation and, finally there was a progression through gradually increasing levels of problem difficulty. A number of studies have looked at these three elements to find out if all were necessary, or if only one or two were sufficient for treatment success. With regard to the first element, the idea underlying Wolpe's original suggestion was that anxiety needed to be reduced at the physiological level by a physiologically antagonistic state, for example, relaxation. You will recall with regard to Mary Cover Jones that there was a suggestion that the eating of sweets or eating behaviour in general was antagonistic to anxiety. Wolpe called this particular process 'reciprocal inhibition'. Davison (1968) carried out one extremely important experiment in regard to systematic desensitization and the identification of which elements were necessary and sufficient for treatment success. In Davison's experiment four groups were run. One group received the usual systematic desensitization treatment. The second condition was pseudo-desensitization in which relaxation was paired with imagined snake-irrelevant stimuli. The third group, known as the exposure group, was asked to imagine graded, snake stimuli without relaxation. The fourth condition was designed to control for the effects of having fear assessed before and then following treatment. The results demonstrated that only systematic desensitization led to significant relief of fear. Davison concluded that systematic desensitization was effective because it involved counter-conditioning; that is, the relaxation tended to counter-condition the anxiety provoking stimuli. Lang (1969) in a review of a number of studies noted that they had 'produced data which on the whole favor the use of relaxation in desensitisation' (p. 174), and hence, the notion that the success of systematic desensitization depends on counter-conditioning.

Nevertheless, systematic desensitization is a complex package, and there are good grounds for supposing that one, or more, of the separate elements (e.g. simple exposure to *fear* stimuli) may sometimes reduce fear. This supposition is supported by Gillan and Rachman (1974) who found little difference between the clinical effectiveness of conventional systematic desensitization and the same treatment *without* the relaxation component (i.e. simple exposure to fear stimuli).

Simple exposure, of course, can be construed as Pavlovian extinction, and we have just seen how it could contribute to the success of systematic desensitization. In addition, extinction induced by prolonged exposure forms the rationale for a therapy now commonly known as 'flooding'. In flooding, anxiety provoking stimuli are continuously presented to the subject until fear subsides. Flooding has often been found to be as effective as systematic desensitization in the treatment of phobias.

Given that the presentation of fear stimuli without negative consequences can lead to the reduction of fear, it is difficult to see why this should not occur in the natural environment. The most commonly accepted explanation is that phobic patients do not, in fact, experience this *prolonged* exposure in natural circumstances, indeed, they often go to great lengths to avoid any contact with phobic stimuli (for further information the reader is referred to the two-process theory of the conservation of anxiety: Solomon and Wynne, 1954).

Another view of systematic desensitization is that its success may be mediated by cognitive processes; in particular, the modification of expectations (Kazdin and Wilcoxon, 1976). For example, when patients are led to believe that a treatment will be successful they may often respond appropriately (a placebo effect). Kazdin and Wilcoxon argued that many of the investigations of systematic desensitization had not used sufficiently convincing control treatments to eliminate the possibility that the success of systematic desensitization was due to placebo effects. Typically, experiments on this question have consisted of two groups. The first is composed of subjects who were told that the treatment would be successful, and the second were either not told anything or given negative expectations. Unfortunately, however, contradictory and often inconsistent results have been obtained. Borkovec (1973) reviewed nineteen experiments with analogue subjects. It was noted that the experiments which failed to demonstrate this effect all had subjects who were presumed to be at a high anxiety level, whilst the successful experiments all had subjects who were at a low anxiety level. It seems that expectancy manipulation via instructions is only really effective with mild anxiety such as that typically exhibited by analogue subjects, but are of little help for clinical populations with more severe anxiety (cf. Mathews, 1978).

Thus, as can be clearly seen from this selective review of systematic desensitization, the simple Pavlovian paradigm provides a less than satisfactory account of the acquisition and treatment of fear. One possible conclusion is that processes other than Pavlovian conditioning are involved. There is good reason to believe, for example, that modelling may be important in both the development and treatment of fear. Indeed, Mary Cover Jones (1924a, 1924b) found that observing other children playing fearlessly with phobic objects helped anxious children overcome their fears. Bandura (1969, 1977) has been a vigorous and influential exponent of this social learning approach.

An additional possibility is that the formulations of Pavlovian conditioning employed by early behaviour therapists were too simplistic. More complex formulations have since been developed. Many of these derive from extensive research into Pavlovian conditioning in the laboratory. Unfortunately, many of these formulations, by the time they percolate into the field of clinical or applied psychology, are somewhat out of date. Furthermore, the experimental rigour of the laboratory has not always been transferred to clinical practice. The next section of this presentation is aimed at reviewing some of these contemporary issues in Pavlovian conditioning as carried out in the laboratory.

Theoretical interpretations of Pavlovian conditioning

The theories of Pavlovian conditioning adopted by most early behaviour therapists were breathtakingly simple and straightforward. One position derived from the work of Pavlov was that associations were formed between stimuli: in a sense the CS came to be a substitute for the UCS, and the CR a miniature version of the UCR. The preceding discussion leads inevitably to the conclusion that the application of this simple interpretation of Pavlovian principles in the treatment of fear and anxiety lacks convincing empirical support. Despite the modest success of therapies derived from Pavlovian principles there are just too many inconsistencies to inspire confidence in the adequacy of this model of human behaviour.

To make matters worse, many learning theorists have even questioned the status of Pavlovian conditioning as a distinct form of learning. The main threat to Pavlovian conditioning has come from its powerful neighbour – operant conditioning. Pavlovian conditioning involves the pairing of two stimuli without regard to the subject's behaviour. Operant conditioning involves the delivery of a reinforcing stimulus contingent on the subject's behaviour. The experimental operations in the two kinds of conditioning procedure are, therefore, quite distinct; but it does not necessarily follow that they represent different conditioning processes.

Indeed the many similarities between the effects of Pavlovian and operant contingencies encourage the view that there is only one underlying process. There is a surprising degree of congruence in the events occurring in the demonstrations of the two conditioning procedures. There are obvious parallels between the CS and discriminative stimuli, also between the UCS and the operant reinforcer, and the occurrence of the responses measured as an index of learning. The phenomena of acquisition, extinction after the withdrawal of reinforcement, spontaneous recovery, generalization and discrimination are all common to both kinds of conditioning procedure. It is scarcely surprising then, that many early theorists (e.g. Hull and Guthrie) blurred any distinction they may have felt tempted to draw between operant and Pavlovian procedures: they refer to both simply as 'conditioning'.

Notwithstanding these similarities, a number of other early theorists (e.g. Skinner and Mowrer) believed that there were sufficient differences between the conditioning procedures and their effects to justify designating Pavlovian and operant conditioning as representatives of different learning processes. Skinner, for example, argued that operant and Pavlovian procedures were effective with different classes of behaviour; operant conditioning working only with voluntary behaviours, and Pavlovian conditioning only being effective in modifying involuntary reflexes. Some support from physiology was claimed for this distinction on the grounds that control of involuntary behaviour was mediated by a different branch of the nervous system than that involved in the control of voluntary behaviour. In particular, it was claimed that involuntary behaviour which could be conditioned with Pavlovian procedures was controlled by the autonomic nervous system. The belief that autonomic responses could not be modified by operant conditioning procedures became, then, the foundation stone of two-process theories of conditioning.

Throughout the history of learning theory two- or one-process views of conditioning have swung in and out of fashion, turn and turn about in a rather confusing way. Smith (1954) attempted to restore a one-process view of conditioning by arguing that operant conditioning represented the only real learning process. Pavlovian conditioning, he claimed, was simply an artefact.

The kernel of Smith's argument was that autonomic responses, apparently produced by Pavlovian conditioning, were in fact innate accompaniments of voluntary responses, engendered by operant contingencies. Smith's argument was advanced in a somewhat different direction by a series of studies by N.E. Miller and associates. These studies challenged the traditional assumption that autonomic responses could not be modified with operant procedures. Miller's experiments demonstrated changes in autonomic responding, such as heart rate, as a result of operant contingencies when subjects were paralised with curare. Curare was used in an attempt to eliminate the possibility of operant procedures affecting autonomic responding indirectly through the conditioning of voluntary responses, as Smith had suggested. As a result of these studies the possibility that all conditioning could be explained in terms of operant contingencies became increasingly attractive.

The ascendancy of operant procedures as a sole embodiment of true conditioning was all too brief, however. Miller's experiments on operant conditioning of autonomic behaviour proved very difficult to replicate in other laboratories. Indeed, Miller himself later reported that he was unable to repeat his earlier work (Miller and Dworkin, 1974). What is more, phenomena which had previously been regarded without question as demonstrations of operant procedures now began to appear more and more like Pavlovian conditioning.

Traditionally, basic research into operant conditioning has proceeded by the selection of an arbitrary response in some convenient laboratory animal, and modifying it by applying rewards and punishments. The greatest part of basic operant conditioning research has in fact involved bar-pressing in rats or key-pecking in pigeons.

This revolution began with a demonstration by Brown and Jenkins (1968) that key-pecking, the operant response *sans pareil*, could be established and maintained with Pavlovian procedures. The essential feature of Brown and Jenkins's study was the pairing of an illuminated response key with the presentation of food. The almost invariable result of this pairing was the establishment of pecking to the key. Without question Brown and Jenkins used a Pavlovian procedure. Nevertheless, so strong was the established set to view key-pecking in pigeons in the context of operant conditioning, that Brown and Jenkins described their procedure merely as a convenient method for shaping-up responses for an operant conditioning experiment; hence their designation of it as *auto-shaping*.

The importance of the Pavlovian pairing operation in the auto-shaping procedure, rather than the consequences of responding, was clearly established by Williams and Williams (1969). In a modified version of Brown and Jenkins's procedure, packs to the illuminated key resulted in the omission of food on that trial. The main finding was that pecking was established and maintained. Clearly it is difficult to view this result as a product of operant conditioning since the consequences of responding were a *loss* of positive reinforcement. Williams and Williams concluded, therefore, that the occasional pairings of the key-light with food were sufficient to generate pecking regardless of the consequences of responding.

We can say, at least, that the foundation of Pavlovian conditioning as a basis for behaviour therapy is secured in the laboratory. There is a distinct effect of the pairing procedure. Granting this, however, we still have the question of how the effects of that pairing procedure are to be interpreted. There are at least two possibilities. One is that the conditioned stimulus becomes associated with the unconditioned stimulus with which it is paired. This is perhaps the most natural interpretation to place upon the procedure since the pairing of two stimuli is the operation carried out by the experimenter. Another possibility, however, is that the CS becomes linked with the response which the UCS elicits. We can designate these two alternatives as S-S (stimulus-stimulus) learning and S-R (stimulus-response) learning respectively. If we transpose this analysis to the example of 'Little Albert', we arrive at the following alternative interpretations. The first is that when the rat was paired with the loud noise, Albert formed an association between the rat and the noise itself. The other possibility is that Albert formed an association between the rat and the fear produced by the noise. There could well be implications for the treatment of Little Albert depending upon which interpretation is correct. If the association is between the rat and the noise, then the existence of fear of the rat depends on continued fear of the noise. Should the noise lose its fear-eliciting properties, then there would be no reason to expect the rat to continue to elicit fear. On the other hand, if Albert formed an association between the rat and fear, we might expect that the rat would continue to elicit fear quite independently of whether the noise was still a fear-eliciting UCS. Rescorla (1973) has attempted an experimental analysis of these possibilities with animal subjects. His conclusion was that first-order conditioning primarily involves SS associations. In contrast, second-order conditioning (conditioning based on a previously established conditioned reflex rather than on an unconditioned reflex) appeared to involve SR associations.

Second-order conditioning is of special importance since many theorists have invoked it as an important factor in human behaviour. In particular, if phobias are indeed a product of Pavlovian conditioning it is likely that some phobias are a result of second-order conditioning. We have seen that clinical phobias are very persistent and Rescorla's work suggests that second-order conditioning is relatively independent of changes in the status or aversiveness of either the UCS or the first order CS subsequent to conditioning. This result could account for the persistence of conditioned fear even when the phobic stimulus has not been closely associated with an aversive stimulus for a long period of time.

The different processes apparently involved in first- and second-order conditioning could also be an important consideration in the selection of behaviour therapy techniques to alleviate phobias. Techniques such as flooding, which involve the elicitation of fear

142 Applications of conditioning theory

during therapy, might well interfere with the S-S associations of phobias based on first-order conditioning; but might even reinforce the S-R (stimulus-fear) associations of a phobia based on second-order conditioning. Occasional reports that some phobic patients can get worse when treated with flooding are certainly consistent with this analysis (e.g. Barrett, 1969).

Another important question concerns the necessary conditions for learning to occur with the Pavlovian pairing operation. The traditional view was that simple contiguity, pairing the CS and UCS, was both necessary and sufficient for learning to occur. In clinical settings this contiguity assumption has clearly been found to be inadequate. There have been just too many instances of the pairing of a CS with a UCS occurring without subsequent learning for this simple model to be correct (see previous section). Furthermore, in the laboratory there have been a number of important demonstrations that pairing alone is not sufficient for learning to occur.

One of the most influential demonstrations was Kamin's blocking experiment. Kamin (1969) showed that a stimulus could be paired with a UCS many times and not develop a conditioned response. The crucial factor blocking conditioning appeared to be the prior conditioning of another stimulus to that UCS. Specifically, if a tone were repeatedly paired with shock then the tone would become a conditioned stimulus and elicit a fear response. If then a second CS was added to the tone, so that further trials consisted of tone-light pairings with shock then the light, although paired repeatedly with shock, would not elicit a conditioned response.

In a rather different sort of study, Rescorla (1966) showed that pairing a tone with shock would also fail to result in conditioning if the shock were also presented often enough independently of the tone. The crucial feature of both these demonstrations appears to be that the CS had in some sense to predict the UCS for conditioning to occur. In the Kamin experiment, the previous conditioning of another CS meant that the introduction of the second CS provided no further information to the subject about the occurrence of the UCS, and conditioning failed to occur. In the Rescorla example, presenting the tone with shock on some occasions and presenting the shock without the tone on other occasions meant that the tone was not a reliable predictor of shock, and again conditioning failed to occur.

Pairing, then, is clearly not a sufficient condition for learning to occur with the Pavlovian procedures. This conclusion may be relevant to the clinical observation that simple pairing of a stimulus with a frightening event does not always lead to fear conditioning. In some sense the CS has to be correlated with, or predictive of, the UCS. There may also be implications of the UCS predictiveness for conditioning therapies. Systematic desensitization, for example, attempts to alleviate fear by conditioning the phobic stimulus to a pleasant (fear inhibiting) activity or stumulus. The established procedure in systematic desensitization involves simple pairing of the phobic stimuli with the pleasant UCS, without necessarily arranging the predictive relationship which appears to be crucial for successful conditioning. It would certainly be of interest to determine whether varying CS-UCS predictiveness had any effect on the success of systematic desensitization.

Once the importance of predictiveness for conditioning became recognized, the view that Pavlovian conditioning should be interpreted in cognitive terms became increasingly attractive (but see Rescorla and Wagner, 1972). Arguments for the role of cognition in Pavlovian conditioning, particularly in human behaviour, have relied heavily on the power of instructions to modify conditioned responding. Brewer (1974), for example, reviewed much of the then available literature and concluded that cognitivie processes indexed by awareness or manipulated by instructions, could account for virtually all Pavlovian conditioning phenomena. We should note, however, that Brewer's conclusion that Pavlovian conditioning does not exist is certainly a mistake. The evidence that he reviewed merely throws light on how Pavlovian conditioning should be interpreted, not on whether it exists as a phenomenon. The sorts of evidence reviewed by Brewer involve showing that cognitive manipulations (for example, telling subjects that the UCS will no longer follow the CS) are often just as effective as conventional extinction procedures (repeated presentations of the CS alone), in eliminating a conditioned response. While it is extremely likely that cognitive factors such as those cited by Brewer are indeed very much involved in any Pavlovian conditioning of human subjects, we should also note there is evidence that cognitive manipulations can sometimes be ineffective (see Hugdahl and Öhman, 1977).

The exceptions identified by Hugdahl and Öhman involve what

they classify as fear relevant stimuli, This brings us to a very influential idea which emerged from some studies of 'taste aversion learning' (e.g. Garcia and Koelling, 1966). Garcia and Koelling found that aversion to a taste CS could be conditioned readily with nausea, but not with electric shock. Correspondingly, aversion to a light CS could be readily conditioned with shock, but not with nausea. This pair of findings has widely been interpreted to show that animals are prepared to associate internal events like nausea with other internal events such as taste and are similarly prepared to associate external events like light with other external events such as shocks. Conversely, animals are not prepared, or contra-prepared, to associate internal events with external events.

Seligman (1971) has developed this idea of 'preparedness' and applied it to the conditioning of fear in human subjects in clinical settings. Specifically, Seligman argues that there are certain stimuli to which we are particularly prone to learn to become afraid. Such stimuli or items may have become 'prepared stimuli' through evolution. They are often, Seligman argues, things like heights or insects or snakes, which might have posed genuine threats to primitive man. Preparedness explains why conditioning often appears to proceed rapidly in everyday circumstances where people acquire phobias or conditioned fears of particular conditions. Lack of preparedness also explains why many things which must often be paired with pain or distress (such as hot stoves and electrical fittings) do not readily become conditioned elicitors of fear. The previously cited study by Hugdahl and Öhman (1977) lends some support to the preparedness hypothesis. Hugdahl and Öhman found that in human subjects fear conditioned to fear-relevant stimuli (pictures of snakes and spiders) was unaffected by instructions ('There will be no more shocks'). However, fear conditioned to fear-irrelevant stimuli (pictures of circles and triangles) was completely abolished by such instructions. Conversely, instructions threatening shocks potentiated fear to fear-relevant stimuli, but not to fear-irrelevant stimuli. While the preparedness notion is indeed particularly attractive for the explanation of conditioning of fear and anxiety it must be conceded that clinical, as opposed to laboratory, evidence in support of this notion is as yet rather scarce. We must also note that there is as yet no good evidence to regard preparedness as a quality which is acquired through evolution; it is equally conceivable that preparedness is something which emerges during an individual's development.

Pavlovian principles and behaviour therapy 145

Conclusions

In this chapter we have tried to demonstrate how the limitations of a rather simple model of conditioning have led to doubts about the applicability of Pavlovian conditioning to clinical problems. With regard to systematic desensitization, perhaps the best known application of Pavlovian principles to behaviour therapy, we have seen how much of the clinical data remains unexplained. Pavlovian contingencies, for example, do not always lead to fear conditioning, and phobias are apparently often acquired without the natural Pavlovian contingencies which a strict application of the model requires. Similarly, whilst some of the effects of systematic desensitization can be attributed to Pavlovian conditioning, other factors can be invoked to account for some of its success. In these circumstances, clinicians have increasingly resorted to cognitive explanations. This is not to deny that Pavlovian conditioning may be involved in the acquisition and treatment of fears, but that the Pavlovian process itself may be cognitively mediated.

This 'cognitivization' of systematic desensitization is paralleled in theoretical developments in laboratory research. Again, cognitive interpretations are increasingly favoured. Despite the attraction of such explanations, it is still apparent that significant change often seems to be effected only by direct experience (for example, counter-conditioning) rather than by cognitive manipulations (for example, through instructions). The preparedness notion may account for many of the discrepancies between the available data and the simple Pavlovian conditioning model. Furthermore, recent findings concerning the conditions under which learning will occur (correlation rather than contiguity of CS and UCS) and on the nature of associations formed (S-S in first-order conditioning, S-R in second-order conditioning), may also be relevant to the clinical applications of Pavlovian conditioning. Thus, at the very least, clinicians should recognize that antiquated, over simplified models of Pavlovian conditioning are scarcely likely to be successful in complex clinical problems if they have been found wanting in the simplified conditions of the laboratory. Although we have examined just one area of application, that of fear and anxiety, many of the considerations that we have examined also apply to the other applications of Pavlovian conditioning.

We will cite here just a few examples. Preparedness may be highly relevant to the treatment of alcoholism with aversion therapy (Wilson and Davison, 1969). Marquis's original formulation of orgasmic reconditioning has been criticized because it apparently involved backward conditioning, a procedure which laboratory research suggests is unlikely to produce a significant conditioning (Keller and Goldstein, 1978). In several areas of application, the Pavlovian model of aetiology and treatment appears to be most successful where specific eliciting stimuli can be identified.

The available evidence prompts two conclusions. Firstly, Pavlovian conditioning is not at all the simple process that early behaviour therapists took it to be, but modern theoretical models of Pavlovian conditioning can be consistent with a significant portion of the data on certain clinical problems. Secondly, it is inconceivable that Pavlovian conditioning is the only factor which is involved in the development and treatment of such problems.

References

Bandura, A. (1969) *Principles of Behavior Modification*. New York: Holt, Rhinehart & Winston.
Bandura, A. (1977) *Social Learning Theory*. Englewood Cliffs, N.J.: Prentice Hall.
Barrett, C.L. (1969) Systematic desensitization *versus* implosive therapy. *Journal of Abnormal Psychology* 74: 587–92.
Borkovec, T. D. (1972) Effects of expectancy on the outcome of systematic desensitization and implosive treatments for analogue anxiety. *Behavior Therapy* 3: 29–40.
Borkovec, T. D. (1973) The role of expectancy and physiological feedback in fear research: a review with special reference to subject characteristics. *Behavior Therapy* 4: 491–505.
Brewer, W. F. (1974) There is no convincing evidence for operant or classical conditioning in adult humans. In W. B. Werner and D. S. Palermo (eds) *Cognition and the Symbolic Processes*. New York: Halsted Press.
Brown, P. L. and Jenkins, H. M. (1968) Auto-shaping of the pigeon's key peck. *Journal of the Experimental Analysis of Behavior* 11: 1–8.
Conway, A.V. (1978) Little Hans: misrepresentation of the evidence? *Bulletin of the British Psychological Society* 31: 285–7.
Davison, G. C. (1968) Systematic desensitization as a counterconditioning process. *Journal of Abnormal Psychology* 73: 91–9.
Davison, G. C. and Neale, J. M. (1974) *Abnormal Psychology: An Experimental-Clinical Approach*. New York: John Wiley.
Eysenck, H. J. (1965) Little Hans or Little Albert. In *Fact and Fiction in Psychology*. Harmondsworth: Penguin.
Feldman, M. P. and MacCulloch, M. J. (1971) *Homosexual Behaviour. Therapy and Assessment*. Oxford: Pergamon Press.

Freud, S. (1955) Analysis of a phobia in a five-year old boy, 1909. In *Collected works of Sigmund Freud*, vol. IV. London: Hogarth Press.
Freud, S. (1977) *Case Histories 1. 'Dora' and 'Little Hans'*. Pelican Freud Library, vol. 8. Harmondsworth: Penguin Press.
Garcia, J. and Koelling, R. A. (1966) Relation of cue to consequence in avoidance learning. *Psychonomic Science 4*: 123–4.
Gillan, P. and Rachman, S. (1974) An experimental investigation of desensitization in phobic patients. *British Journal of Psychiatry 124*: 392–401.
Hugdahl, K. and Öhman, A. (1977) Effects of instruction on acquisition and extinction of electrodermal responses to fear-relevant stimuli. *Journal of Experimental Psychology: Human Learning and Memory 3*: 608–18.
Jacobson, E. (1938) *Progressive Relaxation*. Chicago: University of Chicago Press.
Jones, M.C. (1924a) The elimination of children's fears. *Journal of Experimental Psychology 7*: 383–90.
Jones, M. C. (1924b) A laboratory study of fear: the case of Peter. *Journal of Genetic Psychology 31*: 308–15.
Kamin, L. J. (1969) Predictability, surprise, attention and conditioning. In B. A. Campbell and R. M. Church (eds) *Punishment and Aversive Behavior*. New York: Appleton-Century-Crofts.
Kazdin, A. E. and Wilcoxon, L. A. (1976) Systematic densensitization and non-specific treatment effects: a methodological evaluation. *Psychological Bulletin 83*: 729–58.
Keller, D. J. and Goldstein, A. (1978) Orgasmic reconditioning reconsidered. *Behaviour Research and Therapy 16*: 299–301.
Lang, P.J. (1969) The mechanics of desensitization and the laboratory study of fear. In C. M. Franks (ed.) *Behavior Therapy: Appraisal and Status*. New York: McGraw-Hill.
Lazarus, A. A. (1971) *Behavior Therapy and Beyond*. New York: McGraw-Hill.
Lemere, F. and Voegtlin, W. L. (1950) An evaluation of the aversion treatment of alcoholism. *Quarterly Journal of Studies on Alcoholism 11*: 199–204.
Marquis, J. N. (1970) Orgasmic reconditioning: changing sexual object choice through controlling masturbation fantasies. *Journal of Behavior Therapy and Experimental Psychiatry 1*: 263–71.
Mathews, A. (1978) Fear-reduction research and clinical phobias. *Psychological Bulletin 85*: 390–404.
Miller, N. E. and Dworkin, B. R. (1974) Visceral learning: recent difficulties with curarized rats and significant problems for human research. In P.A. Obrist, A. H. Black, J. Brener and L. V. DiCara (eds) *Cardiovascular Psychophysiology: Current Issues in Response Mechanisms, Biofeedback, and Methodology*. Chicago: Aldine Press.
Mowrer, O. H. and Mowrer, W. A. (1938) Enuresis: a method for its study and treatment. *American Journal of Orthopsychiatry 8*: 436–47.
O'Leary, K. D. and Wilson, G. T. (1975) *Behavior Therapy: Application and*

Outcome. Englewood Cliffs, N.J.: Prentice Hall.
Paul, G. L. (1966) *Insight vs. Desensitization in Psychotherapy*. Stanford, California: Stanford University Press.
Paul, G. L. (1967) Insight versus desensitization in psychotherapy two years after termination. *Journal of Consulting Psychology 31*: 333–48.
Pavlov, I. P. (1927) *Conditioned Reflexes*. Oxford: Oxford University Press.
Rescorla, R. A. (1966) Predictability and number of pairings in Pavlovian fear conditioning. *Psyhonomic Science 4*: 383–4.
Rescorla, R. A. (1973) Second-order conditioning: implications for theories of learning. In F. J. McGuigan and D. B. Lumsden (eds), *Contemporary Approaches to Conditioning and Learning*. Washington, D.C.: Winston.
Rescorla, R. A. and Wagner, A. R. (1972) A theory of Pavlovian conditioning: variations in the effectiveness of reinforcement and non-reinforcement. In A. H. Black and W. F. Prokasy (eds) *Classical Conditioning II: Current Research and Theory*. New York: Appleton-Century-Crofts.
Seligman, M. E. P. (1971) Phobias and preparedness. *Behavior Therapy 2*: 307–20.
Smith, K. (1954) Conditioning as an artifact. *Psychological Review 61*: 217–25.
Solomon, R. L. and Wynne, L. C. (1954) Traumatic avoidance learning: the principles of anxiety conservation and partial irreversibility. *Psychological Review 61*: 353–85.
Ullmann, L.P. and Krasner, L. (1975) *A Psychological Approach to Abnormal Behavior*. Englewood Cliffs, N.J.: Prentice Hall.
Valentine, C. W. (1930) The innate bases of fear. *Journal of Genetic Psychology 37*: 394–419.
Voegtlin, W. L. (1940) The treatment of alcoholism by establishing a conditioned reflex. *American Journal of Medical Science 199*: 802–10.
Watson, J. B. and Rayner, R. (1920) Conditioned emotional reactions. *Journal of Experimental Psychology 3*: 1–14.
Williams, D. R. and Williams, H. (1969) Auto-maintenance in the pigeon: sustained pecking despite contingent non-reinforcement. *Journal of the Experimental Analysis of Behavior 12*: 511–20.
Wilson, G. T. and Davison, G. C. (1969) Aversion techniques in behavior therapy: some theoretical and methodological considerations. *Journal of Consulting and Clinical Psychology 33*: 327–29.
Wolpe, J. (1958) *Psychotherapy by Reciprocal Inhibition*. Stanford, California: Stanford University Press.
Wolpe, J. (1969) *The Practice of Behavior Therapy*. New York: Pergamon.
Wolpe, J. and Rachman, S. (1960) Psychoanalytic 'evidence': a critique based on Freud's case of Little Hans. *Journal of Nervous and Mental Diseases 131*: 135–48.

7 Establishing behaviour; the constructional approach

Chris Cullen, John Hattersley and Laurence Tennant

Introduction

What is the main contribution of the experimental analysis of behaviour to our dealing with the 'real world'? In a very broad sense, it lies in our ability to establish behavioural repertoires that were either not previously extant, or were not present in a particular setting. Constructing new behavioural repertoires in animals first drew B.F. Skinner to the attention of the public at large. He became famous as the psychologist who could teach pigeons to play ping-pong (Skinner, 1962) and moreover *he could do it in the presence of an audience*. Most other learning theorists (or animal trainers) would only exhibit the *results* of such training, not the training process itself. It is this ability to establish behaviour which is so important in education – where teaching is the *raison d'être*. It is probably no accident that Skinner has generally seen himself as an educator rather than, say, a behaviour modifier, at least as indicated by his published work.

Consider now the most usual formulation of a problem facing the clinician, be he or she social worker, psychiatrist, psychologist or whatever. It is often to *remove* something. This may be couched in many ways – behavioural (reduce the frequency of hand-washing for an obsessive client) or other (reduce the anxiety of an agoraphobic) – but the basic issue is usually how to eliminate some pattern of behaviour. Goldiamond (1974) has drawn attention to the fact that practitioners are often asked to be pathological (i.e. to eliminate suffering), while our basic research background ought logically to be informing us on how to be constructional (i.e. to build repertoires). Is it possible to utilize the highly successful procedures developed in the laboratory and in education while at the same time fulfilling our obligations to produce a successful clinical outcome? Goldiamond believes that it is, and has a substantial body of clinical research to support his case.

What is a constructional approach?

Basically, two paradigms may be identified. One is the constructional orientation which is defined by Goldiamond (1974) as:

> an orientation whose solution to problems is the construction of repertoires (or their reinstatement or transfer to new situations) rather than the elimination of repertoires. (p.14)

This is contrasted with a pathological orientation which:

> focuses on the alleviation or elimination of distress through a variety of means ... Such approaches often consider the problem in terms of a pathology which, regardless of how it was established, or developed, or is maintained, is to be eliminated. (p.14)

Each approach may have a similar target – that of allowing the client ultimately to leave therapy. What is done in each case, however, may be completely different. A simple example will illustrate the difference between the two.

The client presents his/her complaint as one of compulsive hand-washing. A pathological approach to this problem might take many forms, all designed to eliminate, or to reduce the frequency of, the 'troublesome' response – i.e. hand-washing. Tranquillizers might be given to reduce (putatively causal) anxiety; psychotherapy might be entered into in order to resolve (putatively causal) conflicts; or a behaviour therapist might institute an extinction procedure by advising the family to give no attention when the client either washes, or refers to washing, his hands.

A constructional orientation would procede rather differently, asking the client 'what is it that you want to be able to do which will result in you being able to leave therapy?' It is important to understand that the answer to this question may well be different for different clients. It will depend, amongst other things, on what repertoire the person already has, and what consequences are important for him/her.

To understand how a constructional orientation would deal with clinical problems, one must consider the model on which it is based, namely the educational one of programmed instruction, which itself derives directly from the operant laboratory (Skinner, 1968). First, however, it is essential to point out that the constructional approach is not being offered as a *replacement* for traditional approaches. It is offered as an *alternative* which is more obviously based on the research background known as the experimental analysis of behaviour than are pathological approaches. As Goldiamond (1974) notes, 'the issue is not the superiority of one model over the other, nor of acceptance or rejection of one at the expense of the other' (p. 25). Indeed:

> in many cases solutions to a problem through direct elimination can be simple, more convenient, and more economical than solutions through constructional outcomes which pre-empt the distress. *The pathological orientation is not being rejected out of hand.* (p. 68, original italics).

In programmed instruction there are four questions to answer and these form the basis of therapy with a constructional orientation. They are:

(1) What are the outcomes to be achieved?
(2) What can the client already do?
(3) How do we move from the current to the desired repertoire?
(4) How do we maintain the outcome in the long term?

A brief discussion of each of these steps will further illustrate the contrast between constructional and pathological modes of operating.

(1) *Outcomes* As noted above, in one respect at least, constructional and pathological approaches are similar in that they both aim ultimately to allow the client to leave therapy; but the constructional approach is to do so by directly establishing repertoires, whereas the pathological approach, if it does establish repertoires, does so indirectly. For example, the problem may be 'teacher distress' – that is, a teacher is having difficulty controlling a classroom full of young children.

152 Applications of conditioning theory

An outcome for the pathological model might be to eliminate out-of-seat behaviour using any of a variety of procedures. An outcome for the constructional model might instead be to institute teaching procedures to establish literacy, numeracy and so on, so that there would be good reason for the children to be at their desks. Increasing in-seat behaviour would, in this case, be a consequence of establishing additional repertoires. Targets would be specified as an answer to the questions 'In what way will you (he/she) behave differently if the intervention is successful?'; 'What would we see you (him/her) do?' Marholin and Steinman (1977) have demonstrated, for example, that disruptive behaviour will decrease when reinforcement is given for solving maths problems while Ayllon and Roberts (1974) eliminated discipline problems by strengthening reading performance. There is an argument that discipline problems *must* be eliminated before academic performance can be improved, but Ferritor, Buchholdt, Hamblin and Smith (1972) showed that this may not often be the case, and that the relationship between disruption and academic performance was not simple, as is often implied. They advocated designing particular contingencies for particular desired behaviours.

(2) *Current repertoire* Where the required outcomes differ, so does the data base. In particular, the presenting symptom is seen as a *useful* operant (although one that has a high cost or other side effects) in a constructional model. The fact that school children typically do interact with each other ought to be seen as a useful asset for teaching them to be literate and numerate and teaching programmes should be designed to utilize this. A pathological approach may result in this pattern being seen as troublesome and something to be eliminated.

(3) *Change procedures* The means of achieving change and of measuring progress will be different for the two orientations. To eliminate out-of-seat behaviour, it may only be necessary to punish it using a time-out procedure, whereas to establish academic skills (which is presumably the reason for the teacher and pupils meeting) one has to draw upon the technology of educational practice, hopefully utilizing the successful model from the operant laboratory (Skinner, 1968).

Establishing behaviour

(4) *Maintaining consequences* In-seat behaviour established only by punishing out-of-seat behaviour will have to be maintained indefinitely by the presence of that contingency unless new desirable behaviours arise by chance or can then be established. It is precisely here that one can see the problems with a purely pathological approach. By contrast, an academic repertoire will be maintained by numerous social consequences – some of which may be those which maintained the initial running around – i.e. teacher attention, peer contact and so on (but see Tennant et al. (1978)).

This brief discussion illustrates some important differences between the constructional and pathological orientations, but it does no more than hint at some of the subtleties. For a comprehensive, scholarly and elegant review, the reader is referred to Goldiamond (1974).

Why be constructional?

It is clear that eliminative approaches have been effective in the past, and may well be acceptable and effective for transient personal problems of short duration, so why is the constructional orientation offered as a model of choice? There are three good reasons. The first is that a constructional orientation, one where alternatives are increased rather than decreased, is in accord with basic principles of human rights. Goldiamond (1974) discusses this issue at great length, arguing that the United States Constitution offers the best safeguards for 'at risk' populations against coercion and ill-treatment, and that a constructional model is consistent with mutual contracting and limitations of power, and with the other ethical obligations of the United States Constitution.

In countries without a written constitution, such as the United Kingdom, the relationship may be less clear, but it is still present. It is *eliminative* procedures which have caused concern generally, not those procedures designed to increase repertoires. Winnett and Winkler (1972), for example, criticized behaviour modification in the classroom as teaching children to 'be still, be quiet, be docile'. While this may be an over generalization (O'Leary, 1972) it is probably true that there is some substance in the allegation. Where there has been concern over procedures which are ostensibly designed to establish repertoires (such as token economies), it is clear, too, that there are aspects of these procedures which effectively *reduce* alternatives (cf. Goldiamond, 1975).

A second reason for adopting a constructional model is that we ought to be 'better' at increasing repertoires than at decreasing them, at least judging by the literature. A brief glance at the 1978 issues of the *Journal of the Experimental Analysis of Behaviour* indicates that approximately 75 per cent of the papers may be described as constructional, i.e. concerned with establishing or increasing repertoires. Since 'basic' research and 'applied' research are sometimes concerned with different questions (Baer, 1977), we checked also the 1978 issues of the *Journal of Applied Behaviour Analysis*. Here, nearly 80 per cent of the papers were concerned with establishing or increasing repertoires.

On the face of it, then, our basic research is largely concerned with a constructional orientation, and if this is what informs our practice (cf. Baer, Wolf and Risley, 1968) then our practice ought to be largely constructional. There is a third reason, which in a sense is both a logical point and an empirical observation. The adoption of a purely pathological approach leaves to chance the constructional aspect. Success in a pathological formulation *can* only be part of the story, the remainder being unaccounted for. Behaviour is a continuous phenomenon and thus the elimination, suppression, or reduction of some part of a repertoire is necessarily coincident with an increase in some other part. The 'wise' therapist specifies, aims for, and establishes these other behaviours (and is thereby constructional). By contrast the actual observed outcome (i.e. what behaviour occurs as opposed to what does not) in a pathological orientation cannot be specified with any degree of confidence.

A constructional model in practice

There are clearly both constructional and pathological modes of operating in all of present-day clinical practice. Sometimes a particular group of problems may be dealt with either exclusively pathologically or exclusively constructionally, or sometimes by a combination of the two. Let us examine one area where therapists could potentially be either constructional of pathological. Our aim in so doing is to:

(a) illustrate further the important differences between constructional and pathological approaches,

(b) demonstrate the hold that pathological modes of operating have on our therapeutic procedures and theories, and
(c) show how a constructional mode of operating can have an important contribution to make, particularly when it implies a different set of therapeutic steps.

The area we have chosen is the problem of excessive consumption of alcohol. The same exercise might be performed in other areas of clinical psychology, such as self-control problems (obesity, stuttering, etc.), social skills training and so on. The interested reader is encouraged to do such an exercise.

Alcoholism[1]

From the way in which the problem is defined – in terms of a behavioural excess – the field is ripe for a pathological approach. Indeed, this was the case up until 1962 when D.L. Davies reported that 7 of 93 cases had returned to normal drinking after a period of abstinence. Prior to this, the Alcoholics Anonymous model was the accepted one, and this is quite clearly pathological. 'Once an alcoholic, always an alcoholic' is the maxim, and the only solution is the pathological one of complete abstinence (Alcoholics Anonymous, 1955). Something of a furore followed Davies's (1962) claim, the main concern seeming to be that here was a licence for abstinent alcohol addicts to start drinking again (cf Heather and Robertson, 1981).

The more reasoned reaction was to re-examine the question 'can alcoholics acquire a controlled drinking pattern?' Here now is a question which lends itself to a constructional orientation, and there have been numerous reports that the answer is in the affirmative.

Among the most cited of the reports to inculcate controlled drinking is the Patton State Hospital Programme (Sobell and Sobell, 1973a; 1973b; 1976). They reasoned that alcohol drinking is an operant maintained by consequences such as its sedative effect, disinhibiting function, and the fact that it allows avoidance of participation in otherwise undesirable situations. Further, while such 'stress-related' contingencies are often important in maintaining alcohol consumption, there are likely to be other effective contingency relationships, probably different ones for each individual alcoholic (Sobell, Sobell and Sheahan, 1976).

Faced with a problem stated in constructional terms 'any effective

156 Applications of conditioning theory

form of therapy' they assert 'must consider the kinds of behaviour which our society reinforces' (Sobell and Sobell, 1973b, p. 53) – a clear constructional solution. In a simulated cocktail bar and a simulated home environment, they set out to establish a number of responses, such as ordering mixed drinks, refusing drinks after a fixed limit, and other alternative responses to excessive drinking, tailored for each client individually. Interestingly, bearing in mind our earlier comments on the overlapping of constructional and pathological orientations, there was also an eliminative procedure built in. 'Inappropriate drinking behaviours (respective to treatment goal) were punished by electric shocks delivered on a variable ratio two avoidance schedule' (Sobell and Sobell, 1973b, p. 56). This particular part of the programme will be discussed again later.

One-year (Sobell and Sobell, 1973a) and two-year (Sobell and Sobell, 1976) outcomes have been reported and results have been very encouraging. Even after two years:

> using both drinking measures and adjunctive measures of outcome . . . hospitalised male alcoholic Ss who received the programme of individualised behaviour therapy with a treatment goal of controlled drinking functioned significantly better . . . than did their respective control Ss who received only conventional treatment oriented towards abstinence (Sobell and Sobell, 1976, p.210).

Here we have, then, a constructional approach (albeit one apparently involving a pathological component) which is demonstrably superior, for some people, than a purely pathological model.

Another widely cited report is that of Hunt and Azrin (1973). Their procedure was to increase dramatically the number of available repertoires for alcoholics by a 'community reinforcement' programme. They reasoned that many alcoholics have fewer alternative behaviours other than drinking available to them since they may have no job, few friends, little opportunity for recreation and so on. The programme aimed to help clients to achieve a satisfying, steady job; to solve legal and financial problems; to re-establish harmonious family relationships; to provide access to an enlarged social community via provision of telephone and transportation, and so on.

The outcome of this study was extremely encouraging. Experimental subjects spent considerably less time drinking, more time in

Establishing behaviour   157

employment, more time at home and less time institutionalized than did a comparable control group.

But, the *rationale* for the Hunt and Azrin (1973) project was essentially pathological! Although the whole procedure was constructional, the reinforcement density was increased since:

> individuals are deterred from drinking because of the interference that drinking produces with other sources of satisfaction... and deterrents will be maximised if the postponed reinforcers are of maximum quality, frequency, varied in nature and regularly occurring (Hunt and Azrin, 1973, p.92).

It becomes clear that as Goldiamond indicated there is not a simple they would lose the benefits they had gained if they started drinking again. It is also worth remembering that even one of the main outcomes of the Hunt and Azrin (1973) project was expressed in pathological terms – i.e. abstinence from drinking.

It becomes clear that as Goldiamond indicated there is not a simple dichotomy of pathological versus constructional therapies. One successful programme with constructionally stated outcomes has a clearly pathological component (Sobell's) while another successful programme has clearly constructional procedures, but a pathologically stated outcome and rationale (Hunt and Azrin). However, a more careful look at what actually happened in these two programmes reveals the relevance of a constructional orientation.

Taking the Hunt and Azrin (1973) project first, it seems clear that the 'time-out from positive reinforcement' element, which apparently was the basis of the procedure, did not figure in the day-to-day running of the programme at all. As the authors acknowledge, 'time-out did not occur in many cases since drinking never occurred' (pp.100–1). This would seem to remove the need for a pathological interpretation of the success of this programme. The authors, however, tied as they are to the pathological model, insist that, 'the patients all stated that time-out would occur if they did take a drink and this knowledge of the consequences seemed to be a deterrent' (p.101).

It is unusual for such an account in terms of unobserved and unidentified variables such as 'knowledge of consequences' to be offered by behavioural researchers. It is our contention that a simpler and more parsimonious account might be that the construction of alternative repertoires was a major factor in the success, rather than the possibility of eliminative procedures which did not occur. (Although if the punishment contingency came into effect it might, of course, in combination with the alternative sets strengthen the therapeutic effect.)

What then, of the Sobells' procedure? Strickler, Bigelow, Lawrence and Liebson (1976) have pointed out that most of the subjects in the Sobells' study avoided shocks during treatment sessions and that 'the changes could be attributed to positive reinforcement for moderation rather than shock for excessive patterns of drinking' (p. 280). In other words, the impressive results of the Sobells' study might be attributed to the constructional rather than the pathological elements of their model.

To demonstrate that this contention is reasonable, Strickler et al. (1976) carried out a thoroughly constructional programme. They argued that there has been a lack of agreement on the definition of what repertoires constitute 'controlled drinking' and that many of the dependent variables have been 'proscriptive' or in our terms pathological (e.g. *avoidance* of excessive drinking and maintenance of blood alcohol *below* certain levels).

They report an 'instructional, practical and positively-oriented approach' to the 'teaching of proper and acceptable moderate drinking habits'. In other words, a constructional approach to alcoholism. While their programme did not specifically use a programmed instruction format, the procedure and rationale are obviously constructional, as we are using the term here. They demonstrated that two out of three subjects could achieve moderation without the use of aversive contingencies.

The three programmes reviewed here suggest that a constructional orientation *can* be effective, and also that there is a strong tendency for us to persist with a pathological mode of explanation even where there is evidence that it is not the effective element. As Goldiamond (1974) points out, 'the pathological orientation has ... profoundly affected our social institutions, the activity and training of relevant professionals, and the related scientific cultures and traditions' (p.19).

Conclusion

We have argued that our current clinical practices are often pathological, whereas the basic laboratory research on which we are generally supposed to have modelled these practices is largely constructional. It is possible to be constructional in clinical practice (cf. Hattersley et al. 1979; Schwartz and Goldiamond, 1975), so what might be the result of a more general acceptance of such an approach? Firstly, there would be a change in the balance of clinical interventions from being usually pathological to being more often constructional. Of course there will be many occasions when a pathological or eliminative approach is desirable or even necessary, but the emphasis would be on increasing alternatives for our clients.

We could also argue that society in general might be served better if constructional modes of operating were the norm. Some 50 years ago an experiment was set up in Britain by two remarkable doctors, Innes H. Pearse and her husband George Scott Williamson. They wanted to get away from viewing medicine simply as the removal of disease, and to recognize health as the establishment of happy personal relationships, a conducive living and working environment and good nutrition (Pearse, 1979).

They founded a centre in London which had these aims, and although their own account of the approach is laden with what we might today term 'pseudo-science', the centre was a great success. We can now recognize, of course, the constructional orientation of a centre whose aim was to establish health rather than eliminate disease. Unfortunately, with the advent of the British National Health Service, a curative model was adopted, so we may never known if the Peckham approach could have become a long-term success.

The planning of societies which do not rely exclusively on eliminative measures is also, of course, one of the crusades of B.F. Skinner (cf. Skinner, 1948; 1976), and an aim towards which he has devoted his career. That career started with the study of laboratory rats under controlled and progressively more complex conditions. It led Skinner inexorably towards a constructional approach, although we do not know if he would wish to use the term. It is our contention that pathological approaches are not based on the bulk of basic research, and moreover they have not often been notably successful in achieving dramatic change. Perhaps we ought to turn to approaches derived more directly from basic research, and these would be constructional.

Applications of conditioning theory

Note

1 We are grateful to Clive Eastman for help with this section.

References

Alcoholics Anonymous (1955) *Alcoholics Anonymous: The Story of How Many Thousands of Men and Women Have Recovered from Alcoholism.* New York: A.A. Publishing.

Ayllon, T. and Roberts, M.D. (1974) Eliminating discipline problems by strengthening academic performance. *Journal of Applied Behaviour Analysis* 7: 71–8.

Baer, D.M. (1977) Perhaps it would be better not to know everything. *Journal of Applied Behaviour Analysis* 10: 167–72.

Baer, D.M., Wolf, M.M. and Risley, T.R. (1968) Some current dimensions of applied behaviour analysis. *Journal of Applied Behavior Analysis* 1: 91–7.

Davies, D.L. (1962) Normal drinking in recovered alcohol addicts. *Quarterly Journal of Studies on Alcohol* 23: 49–55.

Ferritor, D.E., Buckholdt, D., Hamblin, R.L. and Smith, L. (1972) The non-effects of contingent reinforcement for attending behaviour on work accomplished. *Journal of Applied Behaviour Analysis* 5: 7–17.

Goldiamond, I. (1974) Toward a constructional approach to social problems. Ethical and constitutional issues raised by applied behaviour analysis. *Behaviourism* 2: 1–84.

Goldiamond, I. (1975) Alternative sets as a framework for behavioural formulations and research. *Behaviourism* 3: 49–86.

Hattersley, J., Brewster, L., Cullen, C. and Tennant, L. (1979) A constructional approach to social problems. *Social Work Today* 10 (40): 10–12.

Heather, N. and Robertson, I. (1981) *Controlled Drinking.* London: Methuen.

Hunt, G.M. and Azrin, N.H. (1973) A community-reinforcement approach to alcoholism. *Behaviour Research and Therapy* 11: 91–104.

Marholin, D. and Steinman, W.M. (1977) Stimulus control in the classroom as a function of the behaviour reinforced. *Journal of Applied Behaviour Analysis* 10: 465–78.

O'Leary, K.D. (1972) Behaviour modification in the classroom: a rejoinder to Winett and Winkler. *Journal of Applied Behaviour Analysis* 5: 505–11.

Pearse, I.H. (1979) *The Quality of Life: The Peckham Approach to Human Ethology.* Edinburgh: Scottish Academic Press.

Schwartz, A. and Goldiamond, I. (1975) *Social Casework: A Behavioural Approach.* New York: Columbia University Press.

Skinner, B.F. (1948) (re-issued 1976) *Walden Two.* New York: Macmillan.

Skinner, B.F. (1962) Two 'synthetic social relations'. *Journal of the Experimental Analysis of Behaviour* 5: 531–3.

Skinner, B.F. (1968) *The Technology of Teaching.* Englewood Cliffs, N.J.: Prentice Hall.

Skinner, B.F. (1976) Human behaviour and democracy. Reprinted in B.F. Skinner (1978) *Reflections on Behaviourism and Society*. Englewood Cliffs, N.J.: Prentice Hall.
Sobell, M.B. and Sobell, L.C. (1973a) Alcoholics treated by individualised behaviour therapy: one year treatment outcome. *Behaviour Research and Therapy 11*: 599–618.
Sobell, M.B. and Sobell, L.C. (1973b) Individualised behaviour therapy for alcoholics. *Behaviour therapy 4*: 49–72.
Sobell, M.B. and Sobell, L.C. (1976) Second year treatment outcome of alcoholics treated by individualised behaviour therapy: results. *Behaviour Research and Therapy 14*: 195–215.
Sobell, M.B., Sobell, L.C. and Sheahan, D.B. (1976) Functional analysis of drinking problems as an aid in developing individual treatment strategies. *Addictive Behaviours 1*: 127–32.
Strickler, D., Bigelow, G., Lawrence, C. and Liebson, I. (1976) Moderate drinking as an alternative to alcohol abuse: a non-aversive procedure. *Behaviour Research and Therapy 14*: 279–88.
Tennant, L., Hattersley, J. and Cullen, C. (1978) Some comments on the punishment relationship and its relevance to normalisation for developmentally retarded people. *Mental Retardation 16*: 42–4.
Winnett, R.A. and Winkler, R.C. (1972) Current behaviour modification in the classroom: be still, be quiet, be docile. *Journal of Applied Behaviour Analysis 5*: 499–504.

8 Self-instructional training and cognitive behaviour modification: a behavioural analysis[1]

C.F. Lowe and P.J. Higson

> The important properties of verbal behavior which remain to be studied concern special arrangements of responses. Part of the behavior of an organism becomes in turn one of the variables controlling another part. There are at least two systems of responses, one based upon the other. The upper level can only be understood in terms of its relations to the lower. The notion of an inner self is an effort to represent that fact that when behavior is compounded in this way, the upper system seems to guide or alter the lower. But the controlling system is itself also behavior. . . .
> The speaker is the organism which engages in or executes verbal behavior. He is also a locus – a place in which a number of variables come together in a unique confluence to yield an equally unique achievement. (Skinner, 1957, p. 313)

Over the past decade one of the most significant developments in clinical psychology has been the emergence of a new 'movement', which has come to be known as 'cognitive behaviour modification' (CBM). It is a development which has been widely acclaimed (e.g. Foreyt and Rathjen, 1978; Kendall and Hollon, 1979; Mahoney, 1974), widely condemned (e.g. Greenspoon and Lamal, 1978; Ledwidge, 1978; Observer, 1977; Wolpe, 1978), and has at the very least, attracted the attention of most psychologists interested in the application of learning principles to human behaviour (cf.

Lowe, 1979). Both the theory and the practice of the movement, and indeed its very name, cognitive behaviour modification, have proved controversial.

'Cognitive behaviour modification' as a term covers a wide variety of research and clinical activities which have in common a concern with psychological events, processes or behaviours which are not publicly observable. Such 'private events' include, for example, imagining and covert speech, activities which are frequently labelled 'cognitive' (Catania, 1979). The current debate, which has been energetically pursued, has seen advocates of the 'new' approach argue that (i) understanding and control of private events (or 'cognitions') is of great importance for clinical psychology, and (ii) behaviourism rejects the study of private events. On this basis they have concluded either that behaviourism should be abandoned or that it should be fundamentally revised to take into account the cognitive aspects of human functioning (Bandura, 1977; Kendall and Hollon, 1979; Locke, 1979; Mahoney, 1974; Meichenbaum, 1977a; Wilson, 1978).

Many of the behaviourists who have responded to this critique have adopted, either explicitly or implicitly, the position of methodological behaviourism, which accepts that private events are not a proper subject of scientific study since they are not directly observable and hence, it is claimed, do not meet the prerequisite of objective identifiability. The main concern of this group has been to reject the argument that private events play a significant role in the determination of human behaviour or that they can be manipulated to achieve therapeutic aims. Not surprisingly, these authors have been less than enthusiastic about the achievements and prospects of the 'cognitive' therapies (Greenspoon and Lamal, 1978; Ledwidge, 1978; 1979; Rachlin, 1977; Wolpe, 1978).

How do the existing clinical data bear upon this issue of the validity and usefulness of cognitive behaviour modification? There are a number of therapies which come under this rubric, including, for example, rational emotive therapy (Ellis, 1962), self-instructional training (Meichenbaum, 1977a), cognitive therapy (Beck, 1976), coping-skills training (Goldfried, 1971; Kazdin, 1974), and problem-solving therapy (D'Zurilla and Goldfried, 1971). An assessment of all these approaches is beyond the scope of the present paper. It will focus instead on one of the most successful and influential of the 'cognitive' therapies, namely self-instructional training (cf. Mahoney, 1974). What distinguishes this approach from much of traditional behaviour modification is that, whereas the latter concentrates upon direct control of overt motor behaviour, in self-instructional training the aim is to influence events at a covert level which in turn will have a controlling effect on overt behaviour; specifically, the subjects are taught a series of corrective self-instructional statements which are to be repeated covertly and used by them to regulate their own behaviour.

This approach to therapy has been promoted and developed in the west chiefly by Donald Meichenbaum and his associates. Interestingly, from the point of view of the present volume, Meichenbaum's use of verbal 'self-control' procedures did not spring directly from his acquaintance with the ideas and practice of operant conditioning. Serendipity appears to have played a crucial role. While engaged in a research project which involved operant conditioning of 'healthy talk' in schizophrenic subjects, Meichenbaum noticed that some of those patients who had been effectively trained to emit 'healthy talk' would often repeat spontaneously the experimental instruction 'give healthy talk, be coherent and relevant' and that this self-instruction appeared to help the subject to perform appropriately. The possible virtues of explicit training in self-instruction became apparent. When Meichenbaum and Goodman set out to devise their first self-instructional programme, for use with 'impulsive' children, their source of inspiration and information was, again, not the operant literature but the work of Soviet psychologists, particularly Vygotsky (1934) and Luria (1961). The Soviet research had suggested a three-stage sequence in the development of self-regulation in children, whereby (i) initially the speech of others, usually parents, controls a child's behaviour; (ii) at a later stage children learn to use their own overt speech to control their behaviour; and (iii) yet later, this controlling monologue becomes covert and 'private speech' has developed. Preliminary studies (Meichenbaum, 1971; Meichenbaum and Goodman, 1969) had suggested that impulsive behaviour in children was a function of inadequate development of private speech (see Zivin, 1979, for a detailed discussion of the nature of private speech). So the way was open for Meichenbaum and Goodman (1971) to devise a programme of self-instruction based upon the Soviet model. Their procedure will be described here in some detail as it has served as the prototype for most subsequent studies of self-instructional training.

Self-instructional training

The subjects in their first experiment were seven to nine-year-old children classified as 'impulsive' or as having related behavioural problems. All were pre-tested on a Porteous maze test (Porteous, 1955), a matching familiar figures (MFF) test[2] (Kagan, 1966), and performance sub-tests of the Weschler Intelligence Scale for Children (WISC). One group of subjects then received self-instructional training on a variety of different tasks; training consisted of the following sequence of steps:

(a) The experimenter/therapist performed a task while talking aloud to himself; the child watched this performance.
(b) The child performed the same task while the experimenter gave instructions how to do so.
(c) The child performed the task while instructing him/herself aloud.
(d) The child whispered the instructions during task performance.
(e) The child performed the task and used only covert self-instructions.

The self-instructions which the experimenter modelled and which the child was taught to use included the following elements: (i) questions about the nature of the task; (ii) answers to these questions in the form of verbal rehearsal and planning; (iii) self-instructions to control specific behaviours; (iv) 'self-reinforcing' statements. An example of such self-instructions taught for a task which required the copying of line patterns was:

> Okay, what is it I have to do? You want me to copy the picture with the different lines. I have to go slow and be careful. Okay, draw the line down, down, good; then to the right, that's it; now down some more and to the left. Good, I'm doing fine so far. Remember go slow. Now back up again. No, I was supposed to go down. That's okay. Just erase the line carefully . . . Good. Even if I make an error I can go on slowly and carefully. Okay, I have to go down now. Finished. I did it. (Meichenbaum and Goodman, 1971, p. 8)

The remaining two groups acted, respectively, as an attention-placebo group receiving similar experimenter attention and exposure to test materials, and an assessment group which received only the pre-test, post-test and follow-up assessments. Relative to the attention and no-treatment groups, the subjects in the self-instruction group showed considerable improvements in performance on many of the tests. These improvements were shown in a number of tests on which no direct training had been given, and thus provided evidence for 'generalization' of treatment effects. The improved performance was also evident at a one-month follow-up. In addition, the authors found that 60 per cent of the self-instructionally trained children talked to themselves spontaneously during post-test sessions.

This study shows why the self-instructional approach has proved to be attractive to many clinical psychologists. It offered the promise of successfully dealing with some of the most intractable of clinical issues, namely, the maintenance and generalization of treatment effects (cf. Baer, Wolf and Risley, 1968; Keeley, Shemberg and Carbonell, 1976). An additional merit of self-instructional training for researchers was that, like all good approaches to behaviour modification, it offered not only effective therapy but a distinctive *analysis* of behavioural problems. In the case of the Meichenbaum and Goodman study, for example, impulsive behaviour was considered in relation to a model of how self-control develops in 'normal' children (Luria, 1961). From this standpoint, impulsive behaviour could be seen as a secondary effect of a more general dificit in private speech.

How well has the early promise of the Meichenbaum and Goodman (1971) study been fulfilled and how effective has self-instructional training proved with different subject populations? If it is a successful treatment method, what are the essential features of the complex procedure which determine its effectiveness? Finally, there is the central theoretical question: are the mechanisms through which these effects are achieved 'cognitive' or behavioural? The remainder of the present paper will address itself to these questions.

Empirical studies of self-instructional training

The theraputic applications of self-instructional behaviour cover a wide variety of behaviour problems and clinical populations, for example, children with impulsive/aggressive behaviours, mentally handicapped children, depressed adults, overweight adults, brain-damaged and schizophrenic patients (cf. Meichenbaum, 1977a;

1977b; 1979). Two kinds of research strategy have frequently been employed to evaluate the effectiveness of such therapy. The first is the comparative-outcome disign (cf. Kazdin and Wilson, 1978), such as that used by Meichenbaum and Goodman (1971, Exp. 1), which typically involves a comparison of three groups of matched subjects: one group receives self-instructional training on one or more tasks; one is a placebo-practice group that receives the same exposure to the training tasks and similar experimenter contact but no self-instructional training; and finally, there is an assessment group which receives only the pre-test, post-test and follow-up assessments on the tasks. The second experimental strategy is the dismantling treatment design in which an attempt is made to separate the self-instructional training package into its different components and then evaluate the relative efficacy of each component separately or in combination with other components. Each component may be withheld from some clients and presented to others or presented in varying degrees across clients. Both of these experimental strategies are illustrated in the following sections which consider the evidence for the efficacy of self-instructional training with two clinical populations: (i) children with problem behaviours of impulsivity and aggression, and (ii) adult schizophrenic patients.

Children with impulsive and aggressive behaviours

Following Meichenbaum and Goodman's (1971) lead some of the most detailed studies of self-instructional training have been conducted with children who have impulsive behaviour problems and, like the earlier study, the efficacy of this procedure in producing improvements in subjects' task performance has been demonstrated with some consistency. However, the degree of generalization of these improvements to non-trained tasks has differed markedly in different studies. For example, although Meichenbaum and Goodman (1971, Exp.1) observed generalization of improvement in training-task performance to performance on other psychometric tests, they failed to find any evidence of generalization in the children's classroom behaviour. Essentially similar results were reported by Douglas et al. (1976) whose training programme resembled that of Meichenbaum and Goodman, except that some of the training was conducted by the children's teachers and parents. Compared to an assessment-only control group, the children who received self-instructional training improved on a variety of verbal and motor tasks such as listening, spelling and oral comprehension; while these improvements in task performance generalized to similar non-trained tasks, there was no evidence of generalization to the children's classroom behaviour.

On the other hand, there have been a number of studies which found that improvements in training-task performance *did* generalize to classroom behavior. Bornstein and Quevillon (1976) used a self-instructional training programme to alter the impulsive behaviour of three children enrolled in a Head Start programme. They employed a multiple-baseline design across subjects and a training programme like that of Meichenbaum and Goodman (1971), with two modifications: firstly, the programme included the contingent presentation of sweets for correct responses during training and, secondly, during training the sujects were asked to imagine that it was their teacher and not the experimenter who was instructing them. Self-instructional training, on a variety of tasks selected from different IQ tests, resulted in marked improvements not only on these tasks but also in appropriate classroom behaviour such as paying attention, working appropriately, etc. Similar results were reported in a study by Kendall and Finch (1978), who found that, in comparison with an attention-placebo control group, the subjects who received self-instructional training showed significant improvement in performance on the MFF tests both at post-test and three-month follow-up. Furthermore, these treatment effects generalized to the children's classroom behaviour as measured by a teacher's rating scale of impulsivity; other measures, however, including self-reports made by the children, fialed to demonstrate generalization.

Self-instructional training has also been used as a treatment for aggressive behaviour. Camp et al. (1977) used a 'think aloud' programme of self-instructional training with a group of young 'overly aggressive' boys, who were taught to develop answers to four basic questions: 'What is my problem?', 'What is my plan?', 'Am I using my plan?', and 'How did I do?'. It was found that, in comparison with two assessment-only control groups of either boys with similar aggressive behaviours or 'normal' boys, the performance of the training-group subjects improved significantly on some, but not all, of the behavioural measures, e.g. Porteus Maze, the MFF test, WISC performance – IQ scale and reading achieve-

Self-instructional training 169

ment. Moreover, these improvements in task performance generalized to the boys' classroom behaviours as measured by teachers' ratings.

Some studies have compared self-instructional training with other forms of therapeutic intervention. For example, Neilsons and Israel (1978) compared self-instructional training with a conventional programme of token-reinforcement in changing the classroom behaviour of 7–13-year-old 'problem-behaviour' children. They found that while the token programme was immediately successful in producing changes in behaviour, these were not maintained once the token system was withdrawn. The self-instructional training, on the other hand, produced a greater reduction in disruptive classroom behaviour and, a greater improvement in academic performance over the follow-up period. Similarly, Bugental, Whalen and Henker (1977) found that self-instructional training was more effective than contingent social reinforcement in producing improvements in children's performance on the Porteus maze test.

A number of attempts have been made to dismantle the self-instructional training 'package' and to examine the relative effectiveness of the different components. For example, Meichenbaum and Goodman (1971, Exp. 2) compared the effects of having subjects either just observe the experimenter modelling the self-instructions, or not only observe the model but also explicitly rehearse the self-instructions. They found that while both of these treatments produced a significant increase in latencies on MFF performance compared with a control group, only the modelling-plus-rehearsal group showed a decrease in errors. They concluded that while the experimenter's modelling of the self-instructions was required to produce self-regulation in impulsive children it was not sufficient in itself. The key component of the training procedure was the combining of modelling with the rehearsal of the self-instructions.

Nelson and Birkimer (1978) compared a self-instructional programme which included a 'self-reinforcement' component (e.g. the statement 'Good, I've done well') with a programme which omitted this component. They found that the programme which included the 'self-reinforcement' component was more effective than the programme which did not, and was also more effective than control conditions, in improving the performance of impulsive children on the MFF test.

A study by Nelson (1976) examined the relative success of (i) a self-instructional training programme, (ii) a response-cost procedure which involved reward loss following mistakes, and (iii) a combination of (i) and (ii), in changing impulsive behaviour. Nelson found that the two self-instructional programmes (with and without the response-cost contingency) produced similar improvements in children's performance on the MFF test, while the response-cost procedure alone had little effect.

The foregoing studies demonstrate the success of self-instructional methods in altering the behaviour of impulsive and aggressive children (but see Friedling and O'Leary (1979) for a failure to find positive effects). Whether generalization of treatment effects occurred varied from study to study and from behaviour to behaviour. The research on self-instructional training with adult schizophrenic subjects presents a similar picture.

Schizophrenic patients

It is perhaps, ironic that the clinical population which inspired Meichenbaum's research on self-instructional training, namely, schizophrenics, is the population which has yielded some of the most equivocal data on the efficacy of self-instructional training. Meichenbaum and Cameron (1973) conducted two experiments with hospitalized schizophrenics. In their first experiment they investigated the effectiveness of self-instructional training in changing performance on two tasks, i.e. digit-symbol substitution (M. Brown, 1969) and digit-recall tests. They found that, compared to a practice group and an assessment-only group, self-instructional training produced significant improvements in performance on both tests. Having achieved these initial positive results, they then investigated, in a second experiment, the therapeutic efficacy of extended training on a variety of tasks and behaviours. The self-instructional training progressed from having subjects use their private speech in an overt manner on simple tasks through stages in which the subjects learned to monitor both their own and others' behaviour in order to emit task-relevant self-instructions. An example of the type of self-instructions employed comes from the training procedure for one of the items on a similarities test, one of several tasks used in training; the experimenter modelled the following verbal self-instructions which the subject subsequently used,

Self-instructional training 171

initially overtly, then covertly:

> I have to figure out how a fly and a tree are alike. A fly and a tree? (pause). A fly is small and a tree is big. I got it, the fly can carry germs to the tree ... (pause). No that doesn't make sense. That doesn't tell me how they are alike. I have to see how they are alike. Go slowly and think this one out. Don't just say the first thing that comes to mind. (Pause while the model thinks.) I want to give the best answer I can. Let me imagine in my mind the objects ... fly, tree ... out in the sunshine. They both need sunlight to live. That is it they are both living things. Good I figured it out. If I take my time and just think about how the two objects are alike, I can do it. (Meichenbaum and Cameron, 1973, p.525).

Meichenbaum and Cameron found that in comparison with a yoked practice group, who received equivalent exposure to the practice materials and experimenter attention, the performance of the subjects in the self-instructional-training group improved significantly on four dependent variable measures. These included a proverb interpretation test and a standardized interview which were employed to determine the extent of subjects' bizarre speech; subjects were given explicit training on these tasks. The remaining two dependent measures – responses to the Holzman inkblot test and digit recall under distraction conditions – were not included in training; the improvements on these tests thus represent generalization of training effects. These improvements were maintained at a three-week follow-up.

These findings were supported by the results of two case studies. Meyers, Mercatoris and Sirota (1976) employed a self-instructional procedure similar to that of Meichenbaum and Cameron, with a 47-year-old hospitalized chronic schizophrenic. By the end of training inappropriate psychotic speech had decreased from 65 per cent to 8 per cent and this decrease was largely maintained at a six-month follow-up. Higson (1978) found that self-instructional training was effective in reducing a schizophrenic patient's frequent repetition of people's names from an average of 100 to 5 times per 15-minute session.

In contrast with these findings a study by Margolis and Shemberg (1976), using a larger number of subjects, failed to replicate the findings of Meichenbaum and Cameron's (1973) first experiment.

In addition, Margolis and Shemberg cite a study by Gresen (1974) which attempted to replicate Meichenbaum and Cameron's second experiment and likewise failed to produce confirmative results. There were, however, procedural differences between the Margolis and Shemberg (1976) and the Meichenbaum and Cameron (1973) studies. Firstly, Meichenbaum and Cameron used a mixed group of acute and chronic schizophrenic patients, whereas Margolis and Shemberg selected their subjects on the basis of their scores on the Ullmann and Giovannani (1964) scale, to yield two groups of 'process' and 'reactive' schizophrenics; these groups were further subdivided into training and control groups. Secondly, in Margolis and Shemberg's study the individual subjects in the control group were explicitly yoked to the experimental group subjects in equating the number of trials on a task. Finally, Margolis and Shemberg divided their self-instructional training period into two half-hour sessions, whereas Meichenbaum and Cameron conducted all the training in a single one-hour training session. In view of the equivocal nature of the data, however, Margolis and Shemberg (1976) and Meichenbaum (1977b) have concluded that the efficacy of self-instruction with schizophrenics remains to be demonstrated with different populations of schizophrenics and across a wide variety of tasks.

In view of these contradictory findings a series of studies has recently been conducted by the present authors (Lowe et al. 1979) in order to evaluate self-instructional training with chronic schizophrenics. The role of self-instructional training in fostering generalization of behaviour change was also investigated. In the first experiment two tasks were used. The training task was a 'number-concept' test, similar to that employed by Bem (1967) to investigate verbal self-control in children. Over a series of trials, subjects were presented with a row of lights, a number of which were briefly illuminated; four seconds after the lights had been turned off they were given the instruction 'Press now' following which they were required to press a lever for the appropriate number of times matching the number of lights which had been displayed. A second task was employed to test for generalization of treatment effects; this was a delayed-matching-to-sample test which involved matching of geometric shapes (cf. Sidman, 1969). After pre-testing on both tasks the eight subjects were randomly allocated to either a training or an attention-placebo control group. Training on the

Self-instructional training 173

number-concept task consisted of the experimenter modelling self-instructions, which the subject was taught to repeat, in the following sequence:

(i) counting aloud in the presence of lights,
(ii) counting aloud in the absence of the lights,
(iii) counting faded to covert level in the absence of the lights,
(iv) in the absence of the lights, counting gradually faded to covert level with simultaneous lever-pressing.

Training was conducted in two phases. All subjects were tested on both experimental tasks before training began and following each training phase. Control subjects received the same experimenter time and number of practice trials as the maximum received by any of the experimental group.

Figure 8.1 shows that self-instructional training produced marked and significant improvements in the performance of all four subjects in the experimental group; the behaviour of the controls showed little change throughout the experiment. On the delayed-matching-to-sample test, however, neither of the two groups showed any effects of treatment. The beneficial effects of self-instructional training did not generalize.

The question of generalization was directly addressed in a second experiment. Eight tasks were employed, all of which involved the bridging of a temporal gap between stimulus and response, e.g. delayed-matching-to-sample, digit recall, delayed recall of words. Subjects in the experimental group received self-instructional training on two of the tasks; the training programme was similar to that used in the first experiment but, in addition, after subjects had been trained on the first task they were taught to instruct themselves to apply the same instructional technique to subsequent tasks. The results replicated those of Experiment 1 in that performance of the self-instructional group on the two training tasks improved markedly, while control subjects' performance showed no improvement. In addition, however, training effects generalized to some, though not all, of the other tasks. The extent of generalization appeared to be directly related to the extent to which simple specific self-instructional techniques learned on training tasks could be directly used in the generalization tasks.

A further assault upon the problem of generalization was conducted in a third experiment. The design was similar to that used in

174   Applications of conditioning theory

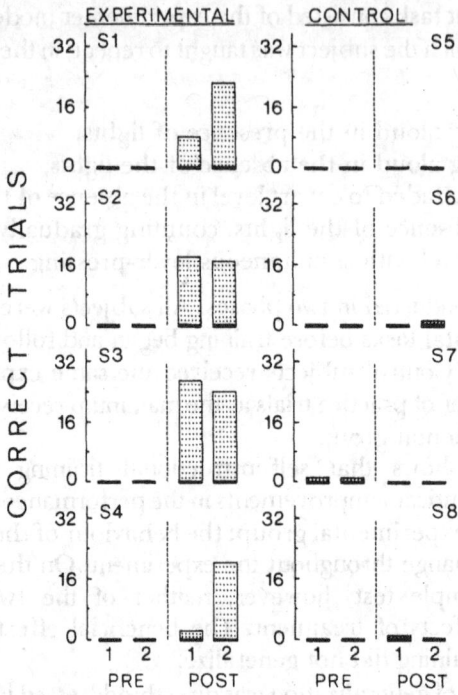

Fig. 8.1   Shows the total number of correct trials for each subject in the experimental group (left side) and the control group (right side) on the number-concept task. The data are from the two pre-tests (PRE 1, 2), conducted prior to training, and from the post-tests (POST 1, 2), which followed each of the two training phases. Each test phase consisted of 32 trials.

Experiment 2 but, apart from standard self-instruction and control groups, a third group was taught additional general problem-solving self-instructions along lines suggested by D'Zurilla and Goldfried (1971), emphasizing problem definition, generation of alternatives, hypothesis testing, etc. A variety of psychometric tasks were employed, e.g. Ravens progressive matrices, Weschler Adult Intelligence Scale sub-tests, and the MFF test; training was given on four of these tests and generalization assessed on three. Both the self-instruction groups showed improvements in performance on the training tasks relative to controls, but none of the groups showed significant improvements on the tests of generalization.

Self-instructional training 175

Taken together these three experiments consistently demonstrated the effectiveness of self-instructional training in improving the performance of different groups of long-stay, chronic schizophrenic patients (perhaps the most difficult of schizophrenic subpopulations to train, cf. Margolis and Shemberg, 1976), on a wide variety of tasks. These results confirm the original findings of Meichenbaum and Cameron (1973) and suggest that Margolis and Shemberg's (1976) negative findings may have been the result of procedural aspects, such as insufficient training time or a training programme not adequately tailored to the requirements of the patients concerned (see pp.176-7). Given the complexity of the self-instructional procedure, however, along with the variation in tasks and subject populations from study to study, it is difficult to assess what are the critical determinants of treatment efficacy. This is particularly true of treatment generalization. It occurs with some behaviours in some studies. How it occurs, and how it can be enhanced, remains to be systematically investigated.

Summary of empirical studies

Despite the dearth of adequate systematic research and the many procedural differences between studies, both in the structure of the self-instructional training programme and in the dependent variable measures used, three main themes are discernible in the foregoing research. Firstly, self-instructional training can, with different clinical populations, and with a variety of tasks, produce marked improvements in subjects' performance, both in comparison with control conditions and with other therapeutic approaches (Neilsons and Israel, 1978; Bugental, Whalen and Henker, 1977). However, the therapeutic relevance of self-instructional training needs to be further demonstrated as frequently its effectiveness has only been shown in relation to arbitrarily selected experimental tasks. There is also a need to determine whether treatment gains are successfully maintained over time. Secondly, the few studies which have so far attempted to dismantle the self-instructional training 'package' suggest that two factors are important in maximizing changes in the subjects' performance. One is the behavioural rehearsal of the self-instructions by the subject (Meichenbaum and Goodman, 1971, Exp. 2), and the other is the inclusion of a 'self-reinforcement' component in the training programme (Nelson and

Birkimer, 1978). Thirdly, while generalization of treatment effects has been demonstrated, it has varied greatly betwen different studies and remains a problematic issue.

The degree of maintenance and generalization of behaviour change following any form of therapeutic intervention is obviously of primary importance in the evaluation of that therapy. Traditional approaches to behaviour modification have all too often failed to deal with this problem effectively (Baer, Wolf and Risley, 1968; Keeley et al., 1976). In the area of self-instructional training, several authors have recently addressed themselves to these issues (cf. Brown and Campione, 1978; Meichenbaum and Asarnow, 1979), and there is a growing recognition, as Baer, Wolf and Risley (1968) suggest, that generalization has to be programmed rather than hoped for or expected. That is, teaching subjects maintenance and generalization skills should form an integral part of any self-instructional training procedure. In programming for generalization the following strategies have been suggested and warrant further investigation. Firstly, the self-instructional training programme should be conducted in a variety of settings and with a variety of experimenters (cf. Brown and Campione, 1978). Secondly, a thorough task-analysis of all the experimental tests used (including those employed to assess generalization) would seem desirable in an attempt to identify the component behaviours involved in the performance of each of the tasks (cf. Meichenbaum and Asarnow, 1979). Thirdly, the training programme should include self-instructions explicitly aimed at facilitating generalization (cf. Bornstein and Quevillon, 1976; Lowe et al., 1979, Exp. 2). This might be achieved by teaching subjects general or 'metacognitive' self-instructional skills, in addition to task-specific self-instructions (Meichenbaum and Asarnow, 1979; and see pp. 181–3). These programming strategies are in contrast with those of most studies where the experimental tasks have been arbitrarily selected, the subjects have been taught self-instructions specific only to the training tasks, and the training programme has been implemented by one or possibly a few experimenters in a single setting. Given such procedures, it is surprising that so many studies have been able to demonstrate generalization of behaviour change following self-instructional training.

Finally, few studies have taken into account or attempted to describe the subjects' existing covert and overt behavioural repertoires before implementing an often complex programme of self-instructional training, thereby making it difficult to identify or evaluate the relative efficacy of the different components of the programme. For example, it may be that in some instances self-instructional training actually interferes with existing appropriate covert self-regulatory behaviours (cf. Higa, Tharp and Calkins, 1978). A detailed analysis of each individual client's existing behavioural repertoires, and their relationships both with each other and with environmental events, would form the basis for the design of individualized programmes of self-instruction in both experimental and therapeutic contexts. The use of a research strategy which uses group comparisons, however, is likely to hinder rather than aid this endeavour. In this respect, a single-subject research design should prove more useful (cf. Bornstein and Quevillon, 1976; Kazdin and Wilson, 1978), and should be a more sensitive measure of the effectiveness of self-instructional training in changing subjects' behaviour.

Self-instruction and behaviour analysis

Does the recognition of the effectiveness of private speech in controlling behaviour pose serious problems for behaviourism? Many of the cognitive 'revolutionaries' argue that this is indeed the case, hence the term *'cognitive behaviour modification'* to indicate that mere 'behaviour modification' is no longer an adequate strategy for clinical psychology. Clearly, if private events are important determinants of overt behaviour but are ignored in behavioural analyses then this is a serious, perhaps fundamental, deficiency in behaviourism. The point is made by Mahoney as follows:

> Watson and Skinner have been among the more outspoken proponents of a non-mediational approach to human behaviour. In brief, their arguments have included assertions that (a) science can only deal with publicly observable events and (b) inferential accounts of behavior are to be avoided because they are unparsimonious. (Mahoney, 1977, p. 9)

Views essentially similar to that of Mahoney have been expressed by most participants in the CBM debate (e.g. Kendall and Hollon, 1979; Ledwidge, 1978; Locke, 1979; Strupp, 1979; Wilson, 1978; Wolpe, 1978).

178 Applications of conditioning theory

But is this an accurate representation of Skinner? Since 1945 his approach to matters such as private speech, thinking, imagining and dreaming, has been carefully detailed in a number of books and papers. A cursory reading of any of these sources (e.g. Skinner, 1945; 1953; 1957; 1963; 1974) shows that Mahoney and other critics with a similar viewpoint have entirely misconstrued the Skinnerian position; indeed, Skinner has been quite 'turned on his head'. The Skinnerian thesis consistently has been that: (i) inference is *essential* to any scientific endeavour, and (ii) a science of behaviour, like other physical sciences, *must* deal with events which are not directly observable. Just two quotations should suffice:

> The present analysis ... continues to deal with the private event, even if only as an inference. It does not substitute the verbal report from which the inference is made for the event itself. The verbal report is a response to the private event and may be used as a source of information about it. (Skinner, 1953, p. 282)

> A science of behavior must consider the place of private stimuli. ... The question then is this: What is inside the skin, and how do we know about it? The answer is, I believe, the heart of radical behaviorism. (Skinner, 1974, pp. 211–12)

It is not a little ironic that a theoretical position which, in contradistinction to methodological behaviourism, has established its identity largely on the basis of its recognition of private events, should now be criticized for ruling them out of court!

There remains, however, the question of why such misconceptions about radical behaviourism are apparently so widespread. Part of the explanation may be found in the activities of behaviourists themselves. For unhappily, despite the clear theoretical lead given by Skinner, radical behaviourists have generally been reluctant to investigate the role of private events in human behaviour. Thus, for example, whereas Vygotsky's (1934) ideas inspired a great deal of valuable Soviet research on the way in which self-directed speech is established and interacts with other behaviour, Skinner's writings (1945; 1963), which in many respects closely resemble those of Vygotsky, have not been empirically investigated to anything like the same degree. Hence, basic operant research has not provided the empirical support or the theoretical impetus for developments in clinical psychology such as that of self-instructional training, Instead, many operant researchers have focused upon animal behaviour and simplistic extensions of the animal model to human behaviour (see Lowe, 1979, for a critique of such approaches); and some have gone to considerable lengths to deny the importance of uniquely human variables. An example of this is Rachlin's assertion, by the way of criticism of the 'cognitive' approach, that 'It makes little sense that verbal behaviour should cause other behaviour' (Rachlin, 1977, p. 662). This is clearly at odds with much of experimental psychology, both operant and non-operant (e.g. Bem, 1967; Goss, 1961; Hunter, 1917; Lowe, 1979; McLeish and Martin, 1975; Sokolov, 1972) and directly contradicts Skinnerian theory: 'Any actual formulation of the relationship between a response and its consequences (perhaps simply the observation "Whenever I respond in this way such and such an event follows") may of course function as a prior controlling stimulus' (Skinner, 1969, p. 147).

The relationship between speech and other behaviour appears to pose problems for writers on both sides of the CBM debate. According to one view, overt behaviour is controlled by environmental factors and no role is assigned to covert behaviour such as inner speech (Ledwidge, 1978; 1979; Rachlin, 1977; Wolpe, 1978). On the other hand, there is the neo-Kantian approach, which adopts as its guide Castenada's (1972) declaration that 'The world is such-and-such or so-and-so only because we tell ourselves that is the way it is' (see, for example, Mahoney, 1974; Meichenbaum, 1977a). An alternative account, more dialectical in character, to both these views is that proposed by psychologists such as Skinner (1963), Vygotsky (1934), Luria (1961) and Sokolov (1972). This might be summarized as follows: In the lifetime of the 'normal' individual: (i) the world exists prior to his being able to talk, (ii) the world, that is his particular social environment, establishes the skill of his being able to talk about the world and himself, and (iii) being able to speak about his interactions with the environment has a profound effect on the way he behaves; his actions and the consequences of these actions determine what he says to himself.

Recent research on human operant performance provides empirical support for this latter theoretical position and for the self-instructional approach to therapy. A series of studies by one of the present authors (Lowe, 1979; Lowe, Harzem and Bagshaw, 1978; Lowe, Harzem and Hughes, 1978; Harzem, Lowe and Bagshaw, 1978) has shown that in situations where contingencies of reinforcement are arranged for human responding, the effects of the reinforcer are profoundly affected by subjects' covert verbal behaviours and formulations of the contingencies, such behaviours being in turn a function of prior environmental histories. The main conclusion to be derived from this research is that in any experimental or theraputic situation human subjects will normally talk to themselves and that what they say will effect their behaviour: *almost all behaviour modification thus involves changing subjects' private events.* This is achieved by the therapist either knowingly, as in the case of self-instructional training or unwittingly, as in many behaviour modification studies where no explicit attempt is made to take into account the role of self-directed speech. What the subject says to himself may be affected by a great many factors, for example: (i) physical features of the therapeutic/experimental environment, e.g. apparatus features, (ii) previous reinforcement history, (iii) observation of the behaviour of others (modelling), and (iv) therapist/experimenter instructions (Lowe, 1979). It could not but enhance the effectiveness of behavioural therapy if these relationships were to be recognized and directly manipulated (cf. Ayllon and Azrin, 1964; Kazdin, 1973; Risley, 1977). This is at least partly achieved by the self-instructional approach and related 'cognitive' therapies (e.g. Ellis, 1962; Beck, 1976; Spivack and Shure, 1974).

At the same time, a behavioural analysis must benefit the practice of CBM. An emphasis upon the behavioural nature of private speech and the ways in which, like any other behaviour, it is affected by antecedents and consequences should result in a better understanding of the functional relationships involved, and, hence lead to better techniques of control. For example, in the course of describing their procedure for establishing self-instructional behaviour in schizophrenics, Meichenbaum and Cameron (1973) give the following advice:

> A word of *caution* is in order concerning the implementation of such SI (self-instructional) training with schizophrenics, as well as other clinical populations. It is important to ensure that the subject does not say the self-statements in a relatively mechanical, rote or automatic fashion without the accompanying meaning and reflection. What is needed is modelling and practice in synthesizing and internalizing the meaning of one's self-statements. (p. 526)

Self-instructional training 181

Those who have attempted to teach self-instructions will recognize the difficulty described here, but how does one see to it that clients engage in 'synthesizing and internalizing the meaning' of self-statements? A behavioural approach to this problem would be to ensure that the clients' statements functioned as effective discriminative stimuli for specific behaviours. Thus, rather than simply reinforcing the clients' 'saying the right things', only the appropriate verbal behaviour (S^D)-other behaviour relationship would be followed by reinforcement. Evidence that such a procedure is effective comes from recent behavioural research on verbal-nonverbal correspondence and 'self-control'. A number of studies (Israel and O'Leary, 1973; Karoly and Dirks, 1977; Risley, 1977; Rogers-Warren and Baer, 1976) have shown that when children are required to describe how they will behave or how they have behaved and reinforcers are only given when their verbal reports correctly match their nonverbal behaviours, then the incidence of those reports and of the actual behaviours greatly increases; reinforcing the verbal reports alone markedly increases their frequency but has little effect on the behaviours to which they refer.

Another area in which a behavioural analysis should be helpful is that of 'metacognition'. Metacognition has been described variously as knowing about knowing (Brown, 1978), being aware of one's own cognitive machinery and the way that machinery operates (Meichenbaum and Asarnow, 1979), and the processes involved in strategy invention, the 'executive' functions of cognition (Belmont and Butterfield, 1977). In behavioural terms, much of this might be described as talking to oneself about one's own imaginal and verbal behaviours. If one were to take, for example, a subject who receives self-instructional training on three different tasks, when subsequently he encounters a task, either one of the training tasks or a novel one, how does he determine which self-instructional strategy will be appropriate? Talking to himself about which self-instructions he should use would be an instance of 'metacognition', a process which is described in the quotation by Skinner which prefaced this chapter. And it should, of course, be possible to directly train this kind of behaviour using self-instructional procedures. In the context of the present example this would involve teaching the client a series of general self-instructions which would set the occasion for further appropriate specific self-instructions and subsequently overt behaviour. This is shown schematically in Figure 8.2. The interesting situation is one where a new task (here specified as D) is encountered. If the subject is taught to examine his available self-instructional skills and to match a particular skill of skills (here specified as some combination of self-instructions used for tasks B and C) with the new task, then the basis for *generalization* of treatment effects will have been established. But just as it is necessary to reinforce a correspondence between specific self-instructions and behaviour it may also be necessary to explicitly reinforce the appropriate use of 'executive' self-instructions (cf. Borkowski and Cavanaugh, 1978).

The clinical psychologist should have a great deal to gain from the integration of behavioural and CBM approaches; not least of the benefits should be a better understanding of behavioural relationships and more effective therapy. Moreover, in so far as the 'new' therapy is involved with the development of subjects' self-control, this may create a different public image and, perhaps more importantly, a different self-image on the part of the clinicians, of what is being done in behavioural therapy; that they are helping clients to control their behaviour should do much to dispel the authoritarian incubus of traditional 'behaviour modification'.

Conclusion

The central theme of the present paper is that for radical behaviourists to study the role of private events in controlling behaviour is not to step outside their conceptual boundaries but rather to fulfil the obligations of their theoretical position. Several CBM studies and recent human operant research point to the importance of such an investigation. It is certainly within the scope of a behavioural analysis.

Clearly, from a behavioural perspective and in the light of the foregoing account, the term 'cogntive behaviour modification' poses problems. If the term 'cognitive' refers to the occurrence of behaviours which are not publicly observable, such as private speech, then all behaviour modification with humans who have developed language is cognitive to a greater of lesser degree. If, on the other hand, 'cognition' refers to some non-behavioural event, a hypothetical construct of the type discussed by Skinner (1950), then it has no place in a radical behaviourist analysis.[3] In either event, the implication that there are two kinds of behaviour modification, one

Self-instructional training

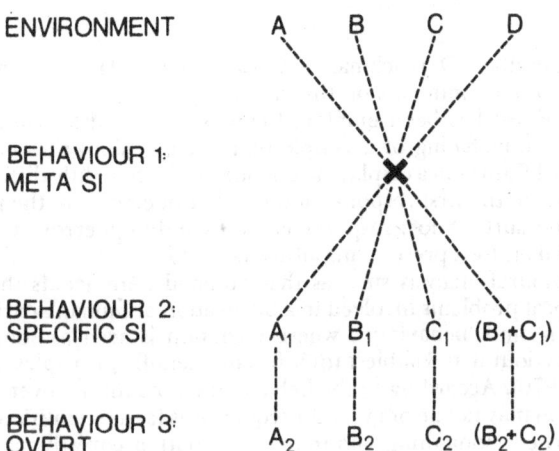

Fig. 8.2 Schematization of the behavioural organization involved in 'metacognition', where A,B,C,D represent four different tasks. Self-instructional training has been given on tasks A,B,C; task D is novel. A_1, B_1, C_1 and $(B_1 + C_1)$ represent appropriate self-instructions for tasks A,B,C,D respectively. A_2, B_2, C_2 and $(B_2 + C_2)$ represent overt behaviours controlled by A_1, B_1, C_1 and $(B_1 + C_1)$. See text for further details.

cognitive an the other non-cognitive, can only lead to conceptual confusion.

If, however, the label 'cognitive behaviour modification' is used, as it is by many, to refer to the group of therapies which, in terms of therapeutic procedure, explicitly acknowledge the role of private events in controlling behaviour, then by dint of usage the term has some meaning, and may, despite sound theoretical objections, remain in use.

Paivio (1975), discussing the dangers of a fascination with cognition, has warned of being led down the garden path of introspection and mysticism forever and has suggested that only a 'tough-minded behaviourist can afford to entertain the seductress'. One might go further and suggest that with his growing maturity it is time the behaviourist made an honest woman of his cognitive companion; a formal union is timely and it would, perhaps, be the more fruitful if her name were changed to his.[4]

Notes

1 We wish to thank D. Blackman, A.C. Catania, P.N. Hineline and T.R. Miles for their comments on this chapter.
2 The MFF test has been employed extensively in CBM studies and involves the matching of a sample figure (e.g. a ship) with one of a number of figures in a display, all but one of which slightly differ from it. Latency to the first response and number of errors are the performance measures. Short response latencies and high error scores are usually taken to represent 'impulsive behaviour'.
3 A behavioural analysis such as that outlined here avoids the epistemological problems involved in a bifurcation of human activity into 'cognition' and 'behaviour', where cognition is seen as something non-behavioural and subject to different scientific principles (cf. Ullmann, 1970). According to the behavioural account the overt-covert distinction may not be of great consequence as far as scientific analysis is concerned. Something said to oneself aloud or covertly may be of equal effectiveness in controlling behaviour.
4 The behavioural, though not the malt, chauvinism here is entirely intentional.

References

Ayllon, T. and Azrin, N.T. (1964) Reinforcement and instructions with mental patients. *Journal of the Experimental Analysis of Behavior 7*: 327–31.
Baer, D., Wolf. M. and Risley, T. (1968) Some current dimensions of applied behavior analysis. *Journal of Applied Behavior Analysis 1*: 91–7.
Bandura, A. (1977) Self-efficacy: towards a unifying theory of behavior change. *Pyschological Review 89*: 191–215.
Beck, A. (1976) *Cognitive Therapy and Emotional Disorders*. New York: International Universities Press.
Belmont, J. and Butterfield, E. (1977) The instructional approach to developmental cognitive research. In R. Kail and J. Hagen (eds) *Perspectives on the Development of Memory and Cognition*. Hillsdale, N.J.: Lawrence Erlbaum.
Bem, S.L. (1967) Verbal self-control: the establishment of effective self-instruction. *Journal of Experimental Psychology 74*: 485–91.
Borkowski, J. and Cavanaugh, J. (1978) Maintenance and generalization of skills and strategies by the retarded. In N. Ellis (ed.) *Handbook of Mental Deficiency: Psychological Theory and Research*. Hillsdale, N.J.: Lawrence Erlbaum.
Bornstein, P. and Quevillon, R. (1976) The effects of a self-instructional package on overactive preschool boys. *Journal of Applied Behavior Analysis 9*: 179–88.
Brown, A. (1978) Development, schooling and the acquisition of knowledge about knowledge. In R. Anderson, R. Spiro and W. Montague

(eds) *Schooling and the Acquisition of Knowledge*. Hillsdale, N.J.: Lawrence Erlbaum.
Brown, A. and Campione, J. (1978) Permissible inference from the outcome of training studies in cognitive development research. *Quarterly Newsletter of the Institute for Comparative Human Development 2*: 46–53.
Brown, M. (1969) A set of eight parallel forms of the digit-symbol test. Unpublished set of tests. University of Waterloo, Ontario.
Bugental, D., Whalen, C. and Henker, B. (1977) Causal attributions of hyperactive children and motivational assumptions of two behavior-change approaches: evidence for an interactionist position. *Child Development 48*: 874–84.
Camp, B., Blom, G., Hebert, F. and Van Doorninck, W. (1977) 'Think aloud': a program for developing self-control in young aggressive boys. *Journal of Abnormal Child Psychology 5*: 157–69.
Castaneda, C. (1972) *A Separate Reality: Further Conversations with Don Juan*. New York: Pocket Books.
Catania, A.C. (1979) *Learning*. Englewood Cliffs, N.J.: Prentice Hall.
Douglas, V., Parry, P., Marton, P. and Garson, C. (1976) Assessment of a cognitive training program for hyperactive children. *Journal of Abnormal Child Psychology 4*: 389–410.
D'Zurilla, T. and Goldfried, M. (1971) Problem solving and behavior modification. *Journal of Abnormal Psychology 78*: 107–26.
Ellis, A. (1962) *Reason and Emotion in Psychotherapy*. New York: Lyle Stuart Press.
Foreyt, J. and Rathjen, D. (1978) *Cognitive Behavior Therapy: Research and Application*. New York: Plenum Press.
Friedling, C. and O'Leary, S.G. (1979) Effects of self-instructional training on second- and third-grade hyperactive children: a failure to replicate. *Journal of Applied Behavior Analysis 12*: 211–19.
Goldfried, M. (1971) Systematic desensitization as training in self-control. *Journal of Consulting and Clinical Psychology 37*: 228–34.
Goss, A.E. (1961) Early behaviorism and verbal mediating responses. *American Psychologist 16*: 285–98.
Greenspoon, J. and Lamal, P. (1978) Cognitive behavior modification – who needs it? *Psychological Record 28*: 343–57.
Gresen, R. (1974) The effects of instruction and reinforcement versus a multifaceted self-control procedure on the modification and generalization of behavior in schizophrenics. Unpublished doctoral dissertation. Bowling Green State University.
Harzem, P., Lowe, C.F. and Bagshaw, M. (1978) Verbal control in human operant behavior. *Psychological Record 28*: 405–23.
Higa, W.R., Tharp, R.G. and Calkins, R.P. (1978) Developmental verbal control of behavior: implications for self-instructional training. *Journal of Experimental Child Psychology 26*: 489–97.
Higson, P.J. (1978) The role of self-instruction in changing an inappropriate verbal response: a single case study. Unpublished manuscript. North Wales Hospital, Great Britain.

Hunter, W.S. (1917) Delayed reaction in a child. *Psychological Review* 24: 74–87.
Israel, A.C., and O'Leary, K.D. (1973) Developing correspondence between children's words and deeds. *Child Development* 44: 575–81.
Kagan, J. (1966) Reflection-impulsivity: the generality and dynamics of conceptual tempo. *Journal of Abnormal Psychology* 71: 17–24.
Karoly, P. and Dirks, M.J. (1977) Developing self-control in pre-school children through correspondence training. *Behavior Therapy* 8: 398–405.
Kazdin, A.E. (1973) The failure of some patients to respond to token programs. *Journal of Behavior Therapy and Experimental Psychiatry* 4: 7–14.
Kazdin, A.E. (1974) The effect of model identity and fear relevant similarity on covert modelling. *Behavior Therapy* 5: 624–36.
Kazdin, A.E. and Wilson, G.T. (1978) *Evaluation of Behavior Therapy: Issues, Evidence and Research Strategies*. Cambridge Mass.: Ballinger.
Keeley, S., Shemberg, K. and Carbonell J. (1976) Operant clinical intervention: behavior management or beyond? Where are the data? *Behavior Therapy* 7: 292–305.
Kendall, P.C. and Finch, A. (1978) A cognitive-behavioral treatment for impulsivity: a group comparison study. *Journal of Consulting and Clinical Psychology* 46: 110–18.
Kendall, P.C. and Hollon, S.D. (1979) Cognitive-behavioral interventions: overview and current status. In P.C. Kendall and S.D. Hollon (eds) *Cognitive-Behavioral Interventions: Theory, Research and Procedures*. New York: Academic Press.
Ledwidge, B. (1978) Cognitive-behavior modification: a step in the wrong direction? *Psychological Bulletin* 85: 353–75.
Ledwidge, B. (1979) Cognitive behavior modification: a rejoinder to Locke and Meichenbaum. *Cognitive Therapy and Research* 3: 133–9.
Locke, E.A. (1979) Behavior modification is not cognitive and other myths: a reply to Ledwidge. *Cognitive Therapy and Research* 3: 119–25.
Lowe, C.F. (1979) Determinants of human operant behaviour. In M.D. Zeiler and P. Harzem (eds) *Advances in Analysis of Behaviour, Vol. 1: Reinforcement and the Organisation of Behaviour*. Chichester, England: Wiley.
Lowe, C.F., Harzem, P. and Bagshaw, M. (1978) Species differences in temporal control of behavior II: human performance. *Journal of the Experimental Analysis of Behavior* 29: 351–61.
Lowe, C.F., Harzem, P. and Hughes, S. (1978) Determinants of operant behavior in humans: some differences from animals. *Journal of Experimental Psychology* 30: 373–86.
Lowe, C.F., Higson, P.J., Bentall, R.P. and Dean, P. (1979) Self-instructional training in schizophrenics: specific and generalized effectiveness. Paper presented at the Ninth European Congress of Behaviour Therapy, Paris.
Luria, A. (1961) *The Role of Speech in the Regulation of Normal and Abnormal Behaviors*. New York: Liveright.

McLeish, J. and Martin, J. (1975) Verbal behavior: a review and experimental analysis. *Journal of General Psychology* 93: 3–66.

Mahoney, M.J. (1974) *Cognition and Behavior Modification*. Cambridge, Mass.: Ballinger.

Mahoney, M.J. (1977) Reflections on the cognitive-learning trend in psychotherapy. *American Psychologist* 32: 5–13.

Margolis, R.B. and Shemberg, K.M. (1976) Cognitive self-instruction in process and reactive schizophrenics: a failure to replicate. *Behavior Therapy* 7: 668–71.

Meichenbaum, D. (1971) The nature and modification of impulsive children. Paper presented at meeting of the Society for Research in Child Development, Minneapolis.

Meichenbaum, D. (1977a) *Cognitive Behavior Modification: An Integrative Approach*. New York: Plenum Press.

Meichenbaum, D. (1977b) *Cognitive Behavior Modification Newsletter*. Number 3. University of Waterloo, Ontario.

Meichenbaum, D. (1979) *Cognitive Behavior Modification Newsletter*, Number 4. University of Waterloo, Ontario.

Meichenbaum, D. and Asarnow, J. (1979) Cognitive-behavior modification and metacognitive development: implications for the classroom. In P.C. Kendall and S.D. Hollon (eds) *Cognitive-Behavioral Interventions: Theory, Research and Procedures*. New York: Academic Press.

Meichenbaum, D. and Cameron, R. (1973) Training schizophrenics to talk to themselves: a means of developing attentional controls. *Behavior Therapy* 4: 515–34.

Meichenbaum, D. and Goodman, J. (1969) Reflection-impulsivity and verbal control of motor behavior. *Child Development* 40: 785–97.

Meichenbaum, D. and Goodman, J. (1971) Training impulsive children to talk to themselves: a means of developing self-control. *Journal of Abnormal Psychology* 77: 115–26.

Meyers, A., Mercatoris, M. and Sirota, A. (1976) Use of covert self-instruction for the elimination of psychotic speech. *Journal of Consulting and Clinical Psychology* 44: 480–3.

Neilsons, T. and Israel, A. (1978) Towards maintenance and generalization of behavior change: teaching children self-regulation and self-instructional skills. Unpublished manuscript. SUNY at Albany.

Nelson, W.M. (1976) Cognitive-behavioral strategies in modifying an impulsive cognitive style. Unpublished doctoral dissertation. Virginia Commonwealth University.

Nelson, W.J. and Birkimer, J. (1978) Role of instruction and self-reinforcement in the modification of impulsivity. *Journal of Consulting and Clinical Psychology* 46: 183.

Observer (1977) Concerning cognitive reversions in psychology. *Psychological Record* 27: 351–4.

Paivio, A. (1975) Neomentalism. *Canadian Journal of Psychology* 29: 263–91.

Porteus, S.D. (1955) *The Maze Test: Recent Advances*. Palo-Alto, California: Pacific Books.

Rachlin, H. (1977) A review of M. Mahoney's cognition and behavior modification. *Journal of Applied Behavior Analysis 10*: 369–74.

Risley, T.R. (1977) The social context of self-control. In R.B. Stuart (ed.) *Behavioral Self-Management: Strategies, Techniques and Outcomes*. New York: Brunner/Mazel.

Rogers-Warren, A.R. and Baer, D.M. (1976) Correspondence between saying and doing: teaching children to share and praise. *Journal of Applied Behavior Analysis 9*: 335–54.

Sidman, M. (1969) Generalization gradients and stimulus control in delayed matching-to-sample. *Journal of the Experimental Analysis of Behavior 12*: 745–57.

Skinner, B.F. (1945) The operational analysis of psychological terms. *Psychological Review 52*: 270–7.

Skinner, B.F. (1950) Are theories of learning necessary? *Psychological Review 57*: 193–216.

Skinner, B.F. (1953) *Science and Human Behavior*. New York: Macmillan.

Skinner, B.F. (1957) *Verbal Behavior*. New York: Appleton-Century-Crofts.

Skinner, B.F. (1963) Behaviorism at fifty. *Science 134*: 566–602.

Skinner, B.F. (1969) *Contingencies of Reinforcement: A Theoretical Analysis*. New York: Appleton-Century-Crofts.

Skinner, B.F. (1974) *About Behaviorism*. New York: Knopf.

Sokolov, A.N. (1972) *Inner Speech and Thought*. New York: Plenum Press.

Spivack, G. and Shure, M. (1974) *Social Adjustment of Young Children: A Cognitive Approach to Solving Real-Life Problems*. San Francisco: Jossey-Bass.

Strupp, H.H. (1979) Psychotherapy research and practice: an overview. In S.L. Garfield and A.E. Bergin (eds) *Handbook of Psychotherapy and Behavior Change: An Empirical Analysis* (second edn). New York: Wiley.

Ullmann, L.P. (1970) On cognitions and behavior therapy. *Behavior Therapy 1*: 201–4.

Ullmann, L.P. and Giovannani, J.M. (1964) The development of a self-report measure of the process-reactive continuum. *Journal of Nervous and Mental Disease 138*: 38–43.

Vygotsky, L. (1934) *Thought and Language*. Moscow: Sovgiz; New York: Wiley, 1962.

Wilson, T. (1978) Cognitive behavior therapy: paradigm shift or passing phase. In J. Foreyt and D. Rathjen (eds) *Cognitive Behavior Therapy: Research and Application*. New York: Plenum Press.

Wolpe, J. (1978) Cognition and causation in human behavior and its therapy. *American Psychologist 33*: 437–46.

Zivin, G. (1979) *The Development of Self-regulation Through Private Speech*. New York: Wiley.

9 Conditioning principles, behaviourism and behaviour therapy

Graham Davey

Most general text books on psychotherapy currently contain a sizable section on behaviour therapy techniques. Because of this fact there must be no doubting the popularity of these techniques in dealing with problems of a clinical and psychopathological nature. In addition to cataloguing the plethora of different techniques that are now subsumed under the headings of behaviour therapy and behaviour modification, these texts also take pains to outline the roots of these techniques. The general written consensus of opinion is that these origins can be traced independently to the writings of Eysenck and Wolpe in the 1950s, that their techniques were developed from established principles of learning and conditioning, and the ideology of their approach to psychopathology and therapy owed much to the tenets of behaviourism. There is certainly no doubting these factors as being catalysts in the development of modern behaviour therapy, but what is not immediately available from such a statement is a description of the process by which these rather diffuse conceptual notions became translated into the sophisticated and often successful techniques that the modern clinician has at his disposal. One could quite reasonably ask such questions as 'why use conditioning principles?', 'what are the established principles of conditioning?', 'do we know that behaviour therapies work simply because they contain conditioning principles?' and so on. All of these questions relate to the validity of the process of extrapolation that is required when one moves from theory to practical technique. In this chapter we shall analyse some of the important features of this extrapolation process, firstly, in an attempt to uncover some of the important theoretical relationships between conditioning theory and modern behaviour therapy, and secondly, to contrast modern-day behaviour therapy with one of its traditional philosophical bases – behaviourism.

Why use conditioning principles in applied psychology?

Perhaps the first question to ask concerns the potential value of conditioning principles to anything other than animal learning. In effect, why choose conditioning theory to form the basis of an approach to applied human psychology? In respect to this question it might be instructive to trace the origins of behaviour therapy and pinpoint some of the events from which it subsequently developed. Krasner (1971) has outlined a number of these historical factors, some of the more important of which are:

(1) the early conditioning studies of J.B. Watson and his subsequent influence on experimental psychology;
(2) the field of instrumental conditioning, including in particular a report by Lindsley, Skinner and Solomon (1953) on conditioned bar-pulling in psychotics;
(3) Wolpe's development of reciprocal inhibition techniques based on the classical conditioning research of Pavlov and Hull;
(4) the work of Eysenck and his collegues at the Maudsley Hospital, England, working within a Hullian framework;
(5) Dollard and Miller's (1950) attempts to interpret psychoanalysis into learning theory terms.
(6) the development of behavioural and social learning alternatives to the traditional medical model of psychopathy; and
(7) the failure of psychodynamic and psychoanalytic psychotherapies as indicated by internal dissatisfaction and widespread external critique.

In effect, these historical influences can be distilled to form just three good reasons why conditioning theory was to provide a basis for the new psychotherapy. Firstly, the writings of behaviourists J.B. Watson and later B.F. Skinner (1953) were to stress a belief in the continuity of psychological mechanisms between non-human

Conditioning, behaviourism and therapy 191

animals and man. If conditioning principles had been established with animals then – since man was only quantitatively rather than qualitatively different from animals in his learning abilities – these principles should apply to humans. Secondly, there was a growing dissatisfaction in the late 1940s and early 1950s with the medical or disease model of psychopathology. This was gradually being replaced by a 'faulty learning' account which stressed the need to treat symptoms as *bona fide* behavioural problems rather than mere symptoms of some underlying cause. Thirdly, the growing belief in the greater efficiency and usefulness of concepts derived from experimental psychology. In particular, that branch of experimental psychology which rested on the rubric of behaviourism was most favoured, primarily because the principles of behaviour derived from behaviouristic analyses readily suggested therapeutic action and had greater predictive power than their contemporary psychodynamic counterparts.

Functional analyses: controlling variables vs. underlying mechanisms

We have briefly discussed some of the justifications commonly given for adopting conditioning theory as a basis for an approach to psychotherapy, but let us be quite clear about one thing – these justifications tell us very litte about *how* conditioning principles have been utilized in applied psychology, or about the current state of behaviour therapy. London (1972) has expressed the view that behaviour therapy is simply a commitment to the notion that all psychological problems require a functional analysis; that is, an analysis in terms of the interrelationships between environmental and behavioural events. This is a commitment to an ideology or philosophy of behaviour rather than to the importance of conditioning principles *per se*. In contrast, if we look back to the therapies conceived by Wolpe and Eysenck in the 1950s they rested crucially on very particular animal conditioning paradigms (e.g. systematic desensitization, see pp. 130–1). Why has this change in emphasis over the years from a very direct kind of extrapolation to a broadranging philosophy occurred? There is certainly no doubt that behaviour therapists currently value the importance of functional analysis; many instances of this can be found in this volume. Three reasons for the change immediately spring to mind. Firstly, there has been sporadic discovery of evidence that many principles of

192   Applications of conditioning theory

conditioning derived from animal studies could not be extrapolated so simply to formalistically comparable human learning situations (cf. Erwin, 1978; Buchwald and Young, 1969; Lowe, 1979). Secondly, cognitive behaviour modification techniques have been developed which, although generally successful, do not fit easily into traditional animal behavioural models. And thirdly, there have been recent changes in emphasis in animal learning research away from the inductive approach to research characterized by the cataloguing of controlling variables (Skinner, 1950; Ferster and Skinner, 1957), to a more deductive approach emphasizing the need to describe the mechanisms underlying learning. The first two reasons will be discussed in later sections of this chapter, but let us consider the third reason now.

There are many levels at which explanation of a behavioural phenomenon can occur and the radical behaviourists have, following Skinner, tended to emphasize the importance of identifying the variables (usually environmental) which control behaviour. For instance, using this method of explanation I could explain the behaviour of my car in terms of the use of the accelerator, foot brake, steering wheel, etc.; these are all variables which control the speed and direction of my car and enable me to predict speed and direction should I manipulate them. Alternatively, I could explain the behaviour of my car by describing the detailed workings of the engine; that is, in describing the workings of the carburettor, pistons, gear-box, and the interrelations between them I am also explaining how the car comes to behave in the way it does. This latter explanation is akin to one in terms of underlying mechanisms. Now, if you want to drive the car ('change its behaviour in a predictable fashion') you need only to possess knowledge of the controlling variables; it does not particularly matter how the engine mediates the relationship between controlling variables and behaviour. It is this latter rationale that appeals to the behaviour therapist. Without needing to know the workings of the 'black box' the therapist can produce predictable changes in behaviour by making modifications to the external variables he/she has identified as controlling the behaviour (this is a functional analysis). Consistent with one of the reasons for adopting conditioning theory for therapeutic means we find that certain controlling relationships are common to many animals, including man. Perhaps the most notable controlling relationship is the one between behaviour and its conse-

Conditioning, behaviourism and therapy 193

quences (operant reinforcement). This is a relationship which controls behaviour in both the laboratory rat and the psychiatric patient; *but* this is where the similarity ends. This does not imply that operant reinforcement has its effects via a similar underlying mechanism in the two organisms. For instance, although most makes of cars go faster when the accelerator is pressed, stop when the brake is applied, etc. (i.e. possess similar controlling relationships) the details of the way these relationships are mediated (the engine) may be quite different in different makes of cars. Now, learning about the consequences of one's behaviour is extremely important for survival's sake, so it does not seem unreasonable to suppose that different organisms have evolved different systems for this purpose. For instance, operant reinforcement in the rat may have its characteristic effect by stamping in relatively reflexive stimulus-response relationships. In humans, however, it may have the same effect on behaviour by being both a source of information and an incentive which regulates behaviour (Bandura, 1969). If this supposition is true (as some theorists and research suggest, cf. Bolles, 1972; Bitterman, 1965; Shuttleworth, 1972; Razran, 1971; Bandura, 1969; Moore, 1973) it has an important implication for the relationship between animal learning and behavioural therapy. As research in animal learning concentrates more and more on identifying the mechanisms *underlying* conditioning it will become less and less relevant to a technology of human behaviour modification. This has appeared to be the recent drift of things, with animal research tending more towards the development of techniques for identifying the details of underlying associative mechanisms whilst leaving the behaviour therapist not so much with principles of conditioning applicable to man as a general theoretical commitment to a functional analysis. Nevertheless, having said, as London (1972) does, that the behaviour therapist is characterized solely by his commitment to a functional analysis, this is not quite enough. A functional analysis must be supplemented by at least some general principles of behaviour change. For instance, if I know that event A controls behaviour B, how do I go about manipulating this relationship in order to change behaviour B in the way I desire? It is here that we return to a discussion of conditioning principles.

Applications of conditioning theory

What principles does conditioning theory have to offer and what grounds are there for applying them?

In applying conditioning principles to therapy there should ideally be three steps. Firstly, establishing the validity of conditioning principles – normally in non-human animals. Secondly, ensuring that these principles also apply to human behaviour. And thirdly, adapting the principles to the practicalities of the applied situation and moulding them into a viable therapeutic technique. As we outlined in the previous section, for a functional analysis to be of any efficacy it has to be combined with certain principles of behaviour change. Therefore, what principles have been considered important to a technology of behaviour change? Let us briefly review the opinions of a number of writers and comment on them.

Many writers, including Sherman and Baer (1969) stress the importance of principles derived from operant conditioning; these include (1) the importance of response consequences (the principles of operant reinforcement and punishment), (2) extinction, and (3) the principles of stimulus control as reflected in the processes of discrimination and generalization. Rachman and Eysenck (1966), whilst admitting that there is no general consensus as to a specific set of principles, claim that behaviour therapists would not disagree with statements of the following kind: (1) 'reinforced pairings of CS (conditioned stimulus) and UCS (unconditioned stimulus) under appropriate conditions produce conditioning', (2) 'intermittent reinforcement slows down subsequent extinction', (3) 'nonreinforcement produces extinction', and (4) 'different schedules of reinforcement produce predictably different response rates' (1966, pp. 165–6). There are two kinds of difference between the views of Sherman and Baer, and Rachman and Eysenck. Firstly, the former appeal solely to the importance of operant conditioning while the latter also emphasize Pavlovian principles; and secondly, the former are content to list particular *phenomena* as the basis of behaviour therapy while the latter pinpoint explicit laws or principles. The lack of a consensus between behaviour therapists as to the important conditioning notions underlying behaviour therapy and psychopathology is so great that it has led Buchwald and Young (1969) to comment:

> learning theory is so open that it allows Eysenck (1960) to suggest that classical conditioning is the paradigm for symptom

formation, while Ullman and Krasner (1965) emphasise operant conditioning, and Dollard and Miller (1950) couch their discussion in terms of conflict, repression, anxiety and defense, all within the framework of learning theory.

Now, the fact of the matter is that pinning down the principles of conditioning relevant to behaviour therapy is difficult because literally any phenomenon from conditioning (human and animal) can be taken as a basis for therapy if the therapist feels it might be relevant. The extrapolation might be made on the basis of a 'lawful' statement extracted from the conditioning phenomenon (à la Rachman and Eysenck), or it may be made simply on the basis of metaphor or analogy. For instance, it is noted that rats cease pressing levers if given intense electric shocks following each lever-press. This leads the therapist to extract the principle 'electric shocks immediately following a behaviour eliminate that behaviour'. He/she then attempts to eliminate self-injurious behaviour in an autistic child using this principle. Alternatively, he/she observes that unavoidable electric shocks given to a dog produce a lethargic dog who is eventually unable to learn to avoid shocks (learned helplessness). He decides that this is very similar on a formalistic level to certain types of human depression, and hence decides to construct therapeutic techniques for depression based on conditioning procedures which help to alleviate the helpless dog's inability to learn. The first example of application was based on an experimentally observed principle but generalized across behaviours and across species, the second based on analogy and the therapist's own intuitions. Yet if both techniques work, in that they fulfil the therapists objectives, then they are both considered to be therapies derived from learning theory. With this in mind, it is not the 'openness' of learning theory that contributes to the lack of consensus as to the principles underlying behaviour therapy, as Buchwald and Young suggest, but the lack of any rules governing extrapolation from conditioning phenomenon to therapy. As can be seen in the second example the therapy is based on no particular principles at all, so it is no wonder it is sometimes difficult to elaborate the conditioning principles underlying behaviour therapy.

Now, although it could be claimed that some behaviouristic analyses of psychopathic behaviour and the subsequent therapies derived from these analyses are primarily analogues of animal paridigms (e.g. experimental neuroses in animals and its application to human neuroses; learned helplessness in animals and its application to human depression), there is still a majority of therapies which are soundly based on conditioning principles. The most prominent principles involve the contingency relationships derived from classical conditioning and operant conditioning respectively. In classical conditioning a conditioned stimulus (CS) is followed by an unconditioned stimulus (UCS). Any response that occurs naturally to the UCS (the unconditioned response, UCR), eventually becomes elicited by the CS (it is then called a conditioned response, CR). These principles form the basis of a number of therapies, but primarily those which are intended to treat emotional or phobic problems (e.g. such techniques as systematic desensitization, massing, flooding, implosion therapy, counter-conditioning, etc; see Chapter 6). In operant conditioning the frequency of a behaviour is influenced by its consequences. If the behaviour has reinforcing or rewarding consequences it increases in frequency, if it has punishing or aversive consequences it decreases in frequency. These principles form the basis of numerous therapies aimed at removing undesirable or maladaptive behaviours, creating new behaviour repertoires in behaviour deficient individuals, and treating socially oriented behaviours in group situations (e.g. the token economy, response shaping, modelling, contingency contracting, time-out, behavioural self-control, etc.; see Davey, 1981, Chapter 14; Mikulas, 1978; Bootzin, 1975; Sandler and Davidson, 1973; and Chapters 2, 3 and 4 in this volume for reviews of these and other techniques). Given that we can identify the principles underlying a therapy, and these principles are well established in the animal literature, what grounds does the behaviour therapist have for assuming that these principles work with humans? This is certainly a bone of contention because many of the opponents of behaviourism rest their case on the belief that principles like that of operant reinforcement do not apply to humans (e.g. Chomsky, 1959; Koestler, 1967). In effect, we now need to find evidence relating to step number two in the idealized sequence outlined at the beginning of this section: that is, what experimental evidence is there that supports the claim that conditioning principles applicable to animals also apply directly to humans? Much experimental evidence is not particularly favourable to simple extrapolation. For instance: (1) there is some evidence that classical conditioning fails to occur in human subjects unless the subject is aware of, and able to verbalize, the contingencies involved (Razran, 1955; Dawson and Biferno, 1973; Öhman, Ellström and Björkstrand, 1976); (2) a number of writers have encountered great difficulty in extinguishing a simple learned operant in human subjects under experimental conditions (e.g. Buchwald, 1959; Bijou and Baer, 1966); (3) human operant performance on schedules of reinforcement often differs markedly from the reliably characteristic patterns of responding emitted by non-human animals. Human performance is often characterized by persistent high-rate responding and an insensitivity to changes in schedule contingencies (e.g. Weiner, 1964; 1965; 1969; Lowe, 1979; Davey, 1981, Chapter 13).

As Erwin (1978) points out, it is evidence such as this which puts in doubt a learning theory rationale for behaviour therapy, and even suggests that behaviour therapies might work for reasons other than the fact that they contain conditioning principles. Indeed, the anomalies between animal and human conditioning that we have just noted contradict three of the four statements outlined by Rachman and Eysenck (1969) as suitable learning theory bases of behaviour therapy: in human subjects reinforced pairings of CS and UCS do *not* always produce conditioning, non-reinforcement does *not* always produce extinction, and different schedules of reinforcement do *not* always produce predictable rates of responding.

However, this evidence can be viewed in one of two ways. It may be taken as evidence that certain conditioning principles simply do not apply to humans. Alternatively, it may suggest that although conditioning principles do apply to humans we need *supplementary* principles in order to explain what we observe. It is this latter statement which is worth exploring. For instance, experiments of conditioning in human subjects differ in two important ways from their animal counterparts: the human subject has linguistic capabilities which allow him to instruct himself; and he is not only in a conditioning experiment, he is also in a social setting where social variables – such as his interactions with the experimenter – may influence his performance. Both of these factors have been shown to exert a profound influence even on phenomena as simple as those in human schedule performance. For example, on a fixed-interval schedule of reinforcement, animals pause after each reward and then slowly accelerate their responding up to the next reinforcement. However, human fixed-interval performance usually falls into one of two categories: consistent high-rate responding which is both unnecessary and fatiguing (cf. Weiner, 1965), or stable low-rate responding with just a few responses being given when reinforcement becomes available. These anomalous, unanimal-like behaviours can be traced to the cueing effect of self-instructive behaviours. In the case of high-rate responding, the subject may see the experimenter as an authority figure whose wishes must be complied with (e.g. Milgram, 1974). Thus, when the subject sees the word 'respond' in the pre-experimental instructions, he does just that by instructing himself to respond (e.g. Lippman and Meyer, 1967; Kaufman, Baron and Kopp, 1966; Weiner, 1962). Pre-experimental instructions seem to provide the subject with a rich source of inappropriate self-instructing cues, and it is interesting to note that when subjects are given no instructions but are simply 'shaped-up' to respond using successive approximations to the required response, the patterning of schedule behaviour is favourably comparable with that of animals (Matthews et al., 1977). In other cases social factors may directly influence the performance and overshadow schedule contingencies. Bijou and Baer (1966, p. 722) report a classic example of this where a young child continued responding for some considerable time during extinction. When asked why he continued responding, he replied 'You didn't tell me I could stop'! Other self-instructive behaviours can produce low levels of responding — these include counting in order to span the temporal interval between reinforcers. Once again, when these internal cues are experimentally eliminated, the subsequent schedule performance is practically identical to that produced by non-human animals (e.g. Laties and Weiss, 1963; Lowe, Harzem and Hughes, 1978; Lowe, Harzem and Bagshaw, 1978).

The moral here seems to be that in many human conditioning experiments social and linguistic factors produce self-instructive behaviours which control behaviour. However, underneath the effects of these self-instructive behaviours at least some kinds of human conditioning performances can be compared with those of animals, and are consistent with conditioning principles derived from animal experiments. Although there seems to have been a failure in laboratory studies of conditioning to appreciate the contingencies which produce self-instructive behaviour, this has not been so in applied psychology where writers have emphasized the importance of self-instructions as being powerful determinants of behaviour (e.g. Thoresen and Mahoney, 1974; Meichenbaum,

1977). Self-instructive behaviour can often result in behaviour maladaptive to a particular situation (e.g. the agoraphobic will pronounce 'I can't go out of the house otherwise I will become dizzy and faint'), or behaviour which is simply over-persistent and inappropriate to the immediate contingencies (as in the case of the high-rate human fixed-interval performer who responds because 'the instructions told me to respond'). This emphasis on internal as well as external cues in the control of behaviour is one of the characteristics of social learning theory. Let us argue through the logic of this approach: (1) environmental contingencies can influence our external behaviour in a way predicted by conditioning theory, (2) environmental contingencies – including the contingencies involved in social interactions – can also generate 'internal' behaviours, e.g. cognitions, perceptions, and internal verbal responses (Skinner, 1963) in a manner consistent with conditioning theory, (3) some of these internal responses are self-instructive behaviours which act as cues which control external behaviours, (4) thus, behaviours may be emitted in the absence of any environmental contingencies which might have been assumed to maintain them.

This kind of analysis has three particular implications for conditioning theory and its relation to behaviour therapy. Firstly, conditioning principles derived from animals do not *seem* to apply to humans when they are extrapolated directly to experimental studies of human conditioning. However, if one appreciates the influence of contingencies which generate self-instructive behaviours this dilemma may be resolved. In cases where these self-instructive behaviours have been experimentally eliminated, the subsequent performance is observed to be consistent with animal conditioning performance. Secondly, a knowledge of the fact that contingencies related to social interactions and subject expectations can produce powerfully influential internal controlling cues, should provide the therapist with extra techniques when it comes to guiding and motivating his client (cf. Kanfer and Karoly, 1972). Krasner (1971) has pointed out the value of combining traditional techniques based on conditioning theory with a knowledge of social learning theory:

> It is important to emphasise that behaviour therapy involves both the technology and its social influence base. Some of the behaviour therapy investigators are clearly cognizant of this fact, but most ignore it. The behaviour therapist is a compound social reinforcing and discriminative stimulus. He is a source of mean-

ingful stimuli that alter, direct, and maintain another individual's behaviour. Viewing the therapist as a 'social reinforcement machine' means the he is *deliberately* applying behavioural principles within the relationship defined in social reinforcement terms to bring about change in another person's life situation.

Thirdly, to acknowledge that maladaptive or inappropriately persistent behaviour is controlled by internal cues such as self-instructive behaviours is not to deny a conditioning theory account of psychopathy nor to succumb to any kind of cognitive mysticism in explaining behaviour. Conditioning theory provides an adequate account of the acquisition of such behaviours (e.g. Rachlin, 1974) and an acceptance of such behaviours as simple discriminative cues for other, external behaviours suggests several possible therapeutic avenues (e.g. Thoresen and Mahoney, 1974; Meichenbaum, 1976; see also Chapter 8, this volume).

Is behaviour therapy still behaviouristic?

In 1968 Wolpe wrote the following about behaviour therapists:

> There is a widespread idea that a behaviour therapist is anybody who uses behaviour therapy techniques. The use of a technique can be quite a mechanical matter, requiring no particular intellectual orientation. What distinguishes the behaviour therapist is that, while moved to help his patient by feelings of warmth and compassion he thinks of each of them as an intricate system of neurophysiological and related mechanisms, and of their inappropriate or inadequate habits in terms of the stimulus-response relationships that these mechanisms subserve. He perceives these relationships, and bases his strategy exclusively upon his knowledge of experimentally established principles of learning against a background of physiology. He operates in this way whether the stimulus is exogenous or endogenous, simple or complex, a bodily sensation or a mental image; and whether the response is motor, autonomic or imaginal, or any combination of these. In short, a behaviour therapist is a *behaviourist* who does behaviour therapy.

There is no doubt that behaviour therapy techniques originated in the laboratories and clinics of therapists who conceived of themselves as behaviourists, whether in the traditional classical behaviourist mould of J.B. Watson or the more liberal behaviourism of Skinner's radical or analytical behaviourists. However, the number of techniques calling themselves behaviour therapies has expanded to a point where many reviewers feel they can find no general factors which they can unambiguously use to define a therapy as a behaviour therapy (e.g. Erwin, 1978; Krasner, 1971; Buchwald and Young, 1969). This being so, it leads one to suspect that even the defining tenets of behaviourism are no longer adequate for defining a therapy as a behaviour therapy, and although a therapy may in some way be based in conditioning theory (e.g. by being based on principles or mere analogy) it may no longer satisfy the rubric of behaviourism.

To answer this suspicion we must first tackle the question of what defines a behaviourist. There is little argument about the characteristics of a classical or methodological behaviourist, since these were clearly outlined in Watson's original manifestos (Watson, 1913; 1919; 1924). But it would be harsh to apply these criteria to current therapies, mainly because the climate of behaviourism was changing, even in the 1950s when behaviour therapies were being conceived. The main changes concerned the gradual acceptance of internal events as suitable subject matter for psychology – given appropriate techniques of detection and measurement; and the shift from mechanistic S-R analyses of behaviour relying on the principles of classical conditioning to a functional analysis of behaviour which emphasized the importance of operant conditioning (Skinner, 1953). This latter form of behaviourism, known as radical behaviourism, has a number of defining characteristics (see Chapter 1 above). Some of the characteristics that concern us here include: (1) the principle that behaviour should be explained in terms of the functional relationships that exist between behaviour and environment (an emphasis on *contingency* relationships between behaviour and environment); (2) operant reinforcement is the primary principle of adaptive behaviour; (3) humans and non-human animals share similar psychological features, e.g. they learn through operant reinforcement; (4) on a purely theoretical level, unobservable cognitive phenomena such as 'thinking', 'dreaming', 'awareness', 'hallucinating', etc. should first and foremost be considered as behaviours which are produced and controlled by environmenatal contingencies in the same way that external behaviours are controlled; (5) on a purely practical level, diffuse psychological phenomena, such as anxiety, fear, depression, etc. should be clearly linked to observable behaviour if they are to be experimentally manipulated (cf. Davey, 1980, pp. 394–6). These principles provide the analytical behaviourist with specific strategies for the three stages involved in therapy:

(1) The *diagnosis* rule: psychological problems should be identified only in terms of observable behaviours; diffuse psychological phenomena, such as 'anxiety', need to be operationally defined before they can be treated.

(2) The *causes* rule: the search for the causes of a behavioural problem should in the last analysis involve a functional analysis of environment-behaviour relationships and *not* a recourse to internal, mental or cognitive factors.

(3) The *intervention* rule: therapy involves the appropriate manipulation of the contingency relations between behaviour and its antecedents or consequents according to the principles of classical and operant conditioning.

The majority of behaviour therapies, including the more recently developed cognitive therapies, such as self-instruction training (see Chapter 8), covert conditioning and behavioural self-control all proclaim a *prima facie* adherence to at least some of these rules. For instance, the area of behaviour therapy which has recently come to be called cognitive behaviour therapy (Mahoney and Arnkoff, 1978) certainly claims to adhere to one of these rules. For example, in attempting to modify an individual's 'low self-esteem' this notion is 'operationalized' in terms of the client's self-descriptive verbal behaviour, e.g. statements such as 'I don't think I have a chance of getting that job I want', or 'so-and-so is a much better golfer than me' are made the targets for modification. Similarly, in covert self-control procedures, although the therapist relinquishes overt control over the contingencies, and indeed he also relinquishes the ability to monitor directly the application of the therapy, the success of this technique is still laid at the feet of operant reinforcement. If the client is being treated for alcoholism he is asked to imagine taking a drink of his favourite liquor and then he must immediately swich to imagining a scene the he finds particularly abhorrent. Although this therapy seems to violate the behaviourist's principles of direct observation and measurement it

Conditioning, behaviourism and therapy

still claims to treat problematic behaviour by recourse to reinforcement theory, albeit by proxy since it is not the target behaviour itself that is being subjected to aversive consequences, but an imagined analogue. Nevertheless, the success of this technique in treating many behavioural problems cannot be denied (Cautela and Baron, 1977).

Failing to comply with any one of the behaviourist's rules governing the three stages of therapy is at least some evidence for denying that a therapy is purely behaviouristic.[1] The fact that cognitive behaviour therapies choose to intervene at the cognitive level might strengthen the conviction that many nominally behaviouristic therapies are not in reality 'behaviouristic'. The nature of the relationship between cognitive states and overt behaviour is an important one in this context. By operationalizing low self-esteem in terms of self-critical statements uttered either overtly or covertly by the client, the therapist is making a number of assumptions which may not be valid in terms of the behaviourist's three-point strategy for therapy. It is often necessary to be aware of step number two in the therapy procedure, that is, to be aware of the role and influence of environmental-behaviour relationships. For instance, individual's low self-esteem or, in fact, *are* the client's low self-don't think I have a chance of getting that job I want' or 'so-and-so is a much better golfer than me', and then attempting to modify these cognitions assumes that the cognitions are either the *causes* of the individual's low self-esteem or, in fact, are the client's low self-esteem. However, if the client really is a bad golfer and he really does not have the skills to get the job he would like, the therapy would seem doomed to failure. A simple functional analysis would have revealed that rather than being causes of the low self-esteem the verbal statements were either secondary corollaries of the feeling of low self-esteem or at best a mediational link between the client's environmental contingencies and his low self-esteem. More efficient therapy might have been to teach the client either to value a job he had the requisite skills for, or to practise his golf a little

Despite all this, perhaps a more condemning criticism is one pointed out by Erwin (1978). Although the cognitive therapist might believe he is operationalizing a cognitive or mentalistic notion by translating it into verbal statements, this can be entirely unfounded. Firstly, *measuring* or 'operationalizing' entity A in terms of entity B (e.g. low self-esteem in terms of a set of verbal statements) does not suddenly turn entity B into the same thing as entity A or *vice versa*. For instance, many people have cognitions they have never verbalized. I may believe that I will never win the men's or women's tennis tournament at Wimbledon, but I have never previously verbalized that belief either to myself or to anyone else. Consequently, to suggest that a mentalistic concept such as 'low self-esteem' is isomorphic with a set of verbal statements does not necessarily follow. Certainly, the therapist can go ahead and modify the frequency of the emissions of these statements, but there is no logical reason to believe he is also modifying the cognition he claims to have operationalized. As Erwin (1978) points out, this strategy 'helps to foster the illusion that we are incorporating cognitive phenomena into the behaviouristic model: if *behaviour* is used in the sense behaviourists have traditionally used it (i.e. to draw a contrast between behaviour and the mind), then talk about cognitions is not translatable into talk about behaviour.'

Even more bizarre from the behaviourist viewpoint is the procedure involved in covert conditioning. Here the therapist often takes a behaviour which is observable and measurable (e.g. the alcoholic consuming a whisky) and transforms it into one which is neither observable nor measurable (the alcoholic *imagining* he is drinking). Similarly, although the therapist claims he has instructed the client to set up a contingent relationship between the image and a particular consequence, he has no proof that this contingency has been arranged (unless, as is the case in some situations, the images can be monitored using particular physiological measures such as heart-rate and GSR changes). Furthermore, nor does the therapist have any theoretical reason for supposing that modifying a cognition will generalize to the overt behaviour that the cognition represents, and indeed, there is much evidence to suggest that behaviourally based therapies are more successful than their cognitive or imaginal counterparts (e.g. Bandura, 1977; Rachman and Hodgson, 1979; Sherman, 1972).

As one looks at these and other behaviour therapy techniques which contain similar 'cognitive' elements, it becomes clear that each violates at least one of the behaviourist's three rules for therapy. But, alternatively most claim to possess at least one. The two examples quoted so far either bypass one of the behaviourist's 'rules for therapy' or violate one of the rules by introducing assumptions which are not directly derivable from the behaviourist's rule.

Nevertheless, they do claim to adhere to the third rule by basing their intervention on conditioning principles directly derived from operant and classical conditioning. However, other behaviour therapies can be found which adhere stringently to the first two stages but violate the third. That is, they operationalize the client's problem in behavioural terms, analyse the functional relationships which maintain the problem behaviour but intervene using principles which are by no means directly derived from conditioning theory. Azrin (1977) has pointed out that more and more behaviour therapies – whilst adhering to the spirit of the behaviourist philosophy – have developed their own principles of therapeutic intervention:

> Learning theory has . . . developed other emergent principles such as behavioural contracting, generalized imitation, desensitization and behavioural rehearsal, all of which represent far more than the laboratory-derived reinforcement concepts. Such emergent principles need not be interpreted as a failure of the reinforcement schema, but as an indication of the emergent identity of the learning therapies.

It is worth stressing Azrin's point that although it is not possible to derive these principles directly fron animal studies of operant and classical conditioning they do not testify to the inadequacy of conditioning principles, but represent an extension of these principles to fit the practical needs of behaviour therapy as an area of research in its own right.

The conclusion that must be drawn from this discussion is that many therapies labelled as behaviour therapies have grown away from the fundamental tenets of behaviourism. They are called behaviour therapies because they claim to adhere to at least one of the behaviourist's three-stage programme for therapy. Whilst from the behaviourist's point of view it is perhaps not such a heresy to omit one of the stages (for instance, many early behaviour modification techniques often bypassed stage two and treated behavioural symptoms directly without regard to the environmental contingencies supporting them; cf. Wolpe, 1977) some therapies, such as covert conditioning and self-instructional training, do stretch the rules a little by making assumptions which cannot be directly derived from the rules.

In summary, a therapy is often called a behaviour therapy if it

206 Applications of conditioning theory

claims a *prima facie* adherence to one of the behaviourist's three-stage rules for therapy. However, it should only be considered behaviourist in a strong sense if it adheres strictly to all three. To claim that problems which are basically cognitive in their conception can be treated behaviourally by 'operationalizing' the cognition is not necessarily a logical extension of the behaviourist philosophy nor is it necessarily valid from a therapeutic point of view.

Why do behaviour therapies work? – the heuristic value of conditioning theory

The implicit assumption made by the behaviour therapist who incorporates conditioning principles into his technique is that the therapy works *because of* the conditioning principles. Yet the truth of the matter is that we are far from understanding the mechanisms that underlie many of the successful behaviour therapies. If this is the case, conditioning theory may provide us, not with principles of behaviour change that apply to both animals and man, but with heuristic hunches that form the basis of a therapy that simply looks as though it is a conditioning therapy. To take a simple example, during the systematic desensitization procedure for treatment of phobias, the therapist claims at a theoretical level to be attempting to form an association between a particular response (relaxation) and the phobic stimulus (the CS). Now, for an association to be formed in a classical conditioning procedure the CS must bear some kind of contingency relationship to events it becomes associated with (Rescorla, 1967). However, since the therapist attempts to maintain a *continuous* state of relaxation in the client there is in reality no predictive contingency present at all. Under analogous laboratory conditions an animal would probably show little, if any, conditioning, yet systematic desensitization is one of the most successful of all the behaviour therapies! Further studies have suggested that relaxation may not be necessary at all in order to reduce phobia-induced anxiety (e.g. Lazarus, 1965; Paul, 1969; Rachman, 1968), and there seems to be a good deal of social reinforcement involved in successful systematic desensitization treatment, a factor which is not explicitly stated in the therapy (Leitenberg et al., 1968; Wagner and Cauthen, 1968). Thus, not only do we not know what mechanisms underlie the success of this therapy (Sloane, 1975) but also we might reasonably assume that it is not related to the conditioning principle on which it was originally based.

Another technique which violates the strict notion of contingency (which is extremely important in both classical and operant conditioning theories) is that of behavioural self-control. According to this technique a client attempts to control a particular behaviour by presenting himself with certain consequences following incidents of that behaviour. For example, a client wishing to diet may be told by the therapist to set up a self-punishment procedure whereby the client tears up a £1 note following every instance of unscheduled snacking. The procedure is simply based on the principle of operant punishment, except that the client delivers his/her own punishing stimulus (Thoresen and Mahoney, 1974). But how strictly does this therapy adhere to the principles in its animal analogue? If a rat is being punished with mild electric shock for every instance of lever-pressing, the lever-press *causes* the shock; that is, there is an explicit and rigid contingency between response and consequence. In the case of self-control, however, there is no such causal relationship and hence no contingency (Goldiamond, 1976). The rat cannot avoid the consequence, the dieting client can – by simply deciding not to tear-up the £1 note. In effect, what the therapist does in self-control treatment is to persuade the client that one behaviour (snacking) should be followed immediately by another behaviour (tearing up a £1 note). It may be that the temporal relationship between these two behaviours is quite unnecessary for successful therapy. For instance, convincing the client that he/she can be helped is often a major factor in producing a successful outcome to the therapy (Locke, 1971) and tearing up the £1 note may simply continue to motivate this conviction. The therapist's ability to convince the client of success (a social reinforcing factor) may be independently maintaining the dieting behaviour *and* the behaviour of tearing up £1 notes. If this is so, the correlation between behaviour and consequence may be superfluous.

Let us look at this from a slightly different angle. How, for instance, would we go about teaching a non-human animal to operate a self-reinforcement programme? Mahoney and Bandura (1972) have attempted this by setting up a self-reinforcement programme for a pigeon. The main problem here is to ensure that the hungry pigeon samples a freely available food source only after performing a particular response (pecking a key). Mahoney and Bandura succeeded in this task by initially punishing (by withdrawal of food) any food sampling that was not preceded by the appropriate response. Now, there are two types of controlling relationship here. There is the self-reinforcing relatioship between key-peck and food, and there is the externally imposed relationship between violations of the self-reinforcement contingency and food withdrawal. This two-tier relationship between self-control and external control is quite important, because in the last analysis all instances of self-control can be subsumed by external control contingencies (Kanfer and Karoly, 1972). In all probability key-pecking was not controlled by the key peck-food relationship avoided externally programmed food withdrawal. In effect 'peck the key' then 'eat food' was a behaviour sequence generated and probably maintained by the fact that this behaviour 'chain' avoided shock. It is true that the self-rewarding behaviour continued for hundreds of trials after the punishment contingency had been withdrawn, but probably testifies to the well-known fact that, when hungry, pigeons have an innate tendency to peck at stimuli correlated with food (e.g. response keys).

The anology with human self-control therapies can be easily represented. The therapist may tell the client who is a compulsive cigarette smoker that he must tear up a £1 note after each cigarette which exceeds his daily limit. Whether the client complies with this sequence of behaviours might very well depend on how motivated he/she is to reduce his/her cigarette smoking, and this can be assessed in terms of the external contingencies bearing upon that behaviour. For instance, the client who has lung cancer is exposed to eminently punishing long-term contingencies if he/she continues smoking; others may wish to give up smoking because of the immediately socially punishing consequences of what others see as an undesirable or dirty habit. In effect, if the therapist can emphasize these external controlling factors and perhaps help to bring long-term consequences into the effective present, the self-control 'contingency' he/she has asked the client to instigate may be therapeutically unnecessary; any reduction in cigarette smoking may be a direct result of the perceived contingency between continued smoking and external consequences. The behavioural chain of smoking a cigarette and then tearing up a £1 note may also be maintained by the client's belief that it will enable him/her to avoid external aversive consequences. Consistent with this kind of analysis is the fact that self-punishment programmes similar to the one described above depend a great deal for their success upon the extent to which the client expects a successful outcome, i.e. the extent to which he/she expects the self-control behaviour will avoid subsequent external aversive consequences (e.g. Weingartner, 1971). Similarly, subjects will tend to persevere with self-reward programmes only when they anticipate external social-reward for doing so (Bass, 1971). Other studies suggest that the sequencing of problem behaviour and self-presented consequence, and the nature of these consequences, may be irrelevant to successful therapy. For instance, using behavioural consequences which are not necessarily reinforcing or punishing (e.g. turning on a kitchen tap or answering the telephone) have produced successful therapeutic outcomes (Lawson and May, 1970). Furthermore, in some instances when a self-punishing consequence is scheduled to *precede* the problem behaviour, therapy can be as successful as when the theoretically accepted ordering is used (Ashem and Donner, 1968).

What this discussion of systematic desensitization and behavioural self-control implies is that although both therapies were conceived in terms of analogies of strict conditioning principles, in practice they do not adhere to those principles. Both operant and classical conditioning require the setting up of explicit contingencies between events, and both systematic desensitization and behavioural self-control fail to meet this requirement. Yet they often succeed as therapeutic techniques despite this fault. Thus, the relationship to conditioing theory is, in strict terms, only analogous, and such therapies may work either for reasons other than the fact that they contain principles analogous to those from conditioning theory, or because conditioning principles fail to represent all of the processes involved. There are three points to be made here: (1) the conditioning principle on which a behaviour therapy was explicitly based may play only a minor role, if any, in the success of that therapy (cf. Sloane, 1975); (2) the reasons why such therapies work may still be interpreted in conditioning terms (e.g. the possible role of external controlling factors contributing to the success of self-reinforcement techniques, and the social reinforcing potential of the therapist in many others) but not in terms of the original rationale for their development; (3) some therapies, such as covert conditioning, are not in reality simple analogues of operant and classical conditioning, and a comprehensive discussion of them requires the use of notions such as 'training in physical relaxation, establishing a strong positive expectancy, and the development of goal-oriented hierarchies of performance', etc. (Thoresen and Mahoney, 1974), none of which are notions which have been derived from conditioning theory and do not fit comfortably into a conditioning theory analysis.

Summary

Earlier in this chapter an idealized sequence of steps was outlined for the application of conditioning principles for therapeutic use: (1) the principles are established in animal studies, (2) laboratory studies should ensure that these principles apply to humans, and (3) the principles are adapted into a technique to cope with the practicalities of the therapy situation. However, step (2) is often bypassed or considered irrelevant (although we have argued that there are good grounds for suggesting that basic conditioning principles do apply to humans – given that we supplement them with a knowledge of contingencies related to self-instruction and social learning). And in carrying out step (3), the conditioning principle – in order to fit the therapy technique – is often mutated to a point where it is no longer an accurate representation of the original principle. In reality the application sequence seems to resemble the following: firstly, the therapist starts with an ideological commitment to either learning theory, behaviourism, or both; secondly, he/she derives his/her technique in a metaphorical or analogous way from examples of animal conditioning; thirdly, he/she applies his/her technique to see if it works; fourthly, if it works he/she may begin to analyse *why* it works, and from this analysis derive principles of behaviour change which are not necessarily isomorphic with conditioning principles (e.g. generalized imitation, behavioural rehearsal, self-instructional training, etc.) but which represent a growing body of knowledge contributing to an understanding of human behaviour change. As London (1964) has concluded, 'However interesting, plausible and appealing a theory may be, it is technique not theories, that are actually used on people. Study of the effect of psychotherapy, therefore, is always the study of effectiveness of techniques.'

Note

1 But not definitive evidence because as we shall point out later, many eminently behaviouristic therapies omit totally – but do not violate – rule number two.

References

Ashem, B. and Donner, L. (1968) Covert sensitization with alcoholics: a controlled replication. *Behaviour Research and Therapy* 6: 7–12.
Azrin, N.H. (1977) A strategy for applied research: learning based but outcome oriented. *American Psychologist* 32: 140–9.
Bandura, A. (1969) *Principles of Behaviour Modification*. New York: Holt, Rinehart & Winston.
Bandura, A. (1977) Self-efficacy: towards a unifying theory of behaviour change. *Psychological Review* 84: 191–215.
Bass, B.A. (1971) Demand characteristics as a determinant of self-reinforcement. Unpublished doctoral dissertation: University of Tennessee.
Bijou, S.W. and Baer, D.M. (1966) Operant methods in child behaviour and development. In W.K. Honig (ed.) *Operant Behaviour: Areas of Research and Application*. New York: Appleton-Century-Crofts.
Bitterman, M.E. (1965) Phyletic differences in learning. *American Psychologist* 20: 396–410.
Bolles, R.C. (1972) Reinforcement, expectancy and learning. *Psychological Review* 79: 394–409.
Bootzin, R.R. (1975) *Behaviour Modification and Therapy*. Cambridge, Mass.: Winthrop.
Buchwald, A.M. (1959) Extinction after acquisition under different verbal reinforcement combinations. *Journal of Experimental Psychology* 57: 43–8.
Buchwald, A.M. and Young, R.D. (1969) Some comments on the foundations of behaviour therapy. In C.M. Franks (ed.) *Behaviour Therapy: Appraisal and Status*. New York: McGraw-Hill.
Cautela, J.R. and Baron, M.G. (1977) Covert conditioning: a theoretical analysis. *Behaviour Modification* 1: 351–68.
Chomsky, N. (1959) *Verbal Behaviour* by B.F. Skinner. *Language* 35: 26–58.
Davey, G.C.L. (1981) *Animal Learning and Conditioning*. London: Macmillan Press.
Dawson, M.E. and Biferno, M.A. (1973) Concurrent measurement of awareness and electrodermal classical conditioning. *Journal of Experimental Psychology* 101: 55–62.
Dollard, J. and Miller, N.E. (1950) *Personality and Psychotherapy: An Analysis in Terms of Learning, Thinking and Culture*. New York: McGraw-Hill.
Erwin, E. (1978) *Behaviour Therapy: Scientific, Philosophical and Moral Foundations*. London: Cambridge University Press.
Eysenck, H.J. (1960) *Behaviour Therapy and the Neuroses*. London: Pergamon Press.
Ferster, C.B. and Skinner, B.F. (1957) *Schedules of Reinforcement*. New York: Appleton-Century-Crofts.
Goldiamond, I. (1976) Self-reinforcement. *Journal of Applied Behaviour Analysis* 9: 509–14.
Kanfer, F. and Karoly, P. (1972). Self-control: a behaviouristic excursion into the lion's den. *Behaviour Therapy* 3: 398–416.

Kaufman, A., Baron, A. and Kopp, R.M. (1966) Some effects of instructions on human operant behaviour. *Psychonomic Monograph Supplements 1* (11): 243–50.

Koestler, A. (1967) *The Ghost in the Machine*. London: Hutchinson.

Krasner, L. (1965) The behavioural scientist and social responsibility: no place to hide. *Journal of Social Issues 21*: 9–30.

Krasner, L. (1971) Behaviour therapy. *Annual Review of Psychology 22*: 483–532.

Laties, V.G. and Weiss, B. (1963) Effects of a concurrent task on fixed-interval responding in humans. *Journal of the Experimental Analysis of Behaviour 3*: 431–6.

Lawson, D.M. and May, R.B. (1970) Three procedures for the extinction of smoking behaviour. *Psychological Record 20*: 151–7.

Lazarus, A.A. (1965) A preliminary report on the use of directed muscular activity in counter conditioning. *Behaviour Research and Therapy 2*: 301–3.

Leitenberg, H., Agras, W.S., Thompson, L.E. and Wright, D. (1968). Feedback in behaviour modification: an experimental analysis of two phobic cases. *Journal of Applied Behaviour Analysis 1*: 131–7.

Lindsley, O.R., Skinner, B.F. and Solomon, H.C. (1953) *Studies in Behaviour Therapy: Status Report 1*. Waltham, Mass: Metropolitan State Hospital.

Lippman, L.G. and Meyer, M.E. (1967) Fixed-interval performance as related to instructions and to subjects' verbalisations of the contingency. *Psychonomic Science 8*: 135–6.

Locke, E. (1971) Is behaviour therapy behaviouristic? *Psychological Bulletin 76*: 318–27.

London, P. (1964) *The Modes and Morals of Psychotherapy*. New York: Holt, Rinehart & Winston.

London, P. (1972) The end of ideology in behaviour modification. *American Psychologist 27*: 913–20.

Lowe, C.F. (1979) Determinants of human operant behaviour: temporal control. In P. Harzem and M.D. Zeiler (eds) *Reinforcement and the Organization of Behaviour*. New York: Wiley.

Lowe, C.F., Harzem, P. and Bagshaw, M. (1978) Species differences in temporal control of behaviour. II human performance. *Journal of the Experimental Analysis of Behaviour 29*: 351–61.

Lowe, C.F., Harzem, P. and Hughes, S. (1978) Determinants of operant behaviour in humans: some differences from animals. *Quarterly Journal of Experimental Psychology 30*: 373–86.

Mahoney, M.J. and Arnkoff, D. (1978) Cognitive and self-control therapies. In S.L. Garfield and A.E. Bergin (eds) *Handbook of Psychotherapy and Behaviour Change* (2nd edn). New York: Wiley.

Mahoney, M.J. and Bandura, A. (1972) Self-reinforcement in pigeons. *Learning and Motivation 3*: 293–303.

Matthews, B., Shimoff, E., Catania, A.C. and Sagvolden, T. (1977) Uninstructed human responding: sensitivity to ratio and interval contingencies. *Journal of the Experimental Analysis of Behaviour 27*: 453–67.

Meichenbaum, D. (1977) *Cognitive Behaviour Modification*. New York: Plenum.
Mikulas, W.L. (1978) *Behaviour Modification*. New York: Harper & Row.
Milgram, S. (1974) *Obedience to Authority. An Experimental View*. New York: Harper & Row.
Moore, B.R. (1973) The role of directed Pavlovian reactions in simple instrumental learning in the pigeon. In R.A. Hinde and J. Stevenson-Hinde (eds) *Constraints on Learning*. New York: Academic Pess.
Öhman, A., Ellström, P. and Björkstrand, P. (1976) Electrodermal responses and subjective estimates of UCS probability in a long interstimulus interval conditioning paradigm. *Psychophysiology 13*: 121–7.
Paul, G.L. (1969) Physiological effects of relaxation training and hypnotic suggestion. *Journal of Abnormal Psychology 74*: 425–37.
Rachlin, H. (1974) Self-control. *Behaviourism 2*: 94-107.
Rachman, S. (1968) *Phobias: Their Nature and Control*. Springfield, Illinois: Charles C. Thomas.
Rachman, S. and Eysenck, H.J. (1966) Reply to a critique and reformulation of behaviour therapy. *Psychological Bulletin 65*: 165–9.
Rachman, S. and Hodgson, R. (1979) *Obsessions and Compulsions*. Englewood Cliffs, N.J.: Prentice-Hall.
Razran, G. (1955) Partial reinforcement of salivary CRs in adult human subjects: preliminary study. *Psychological Reports 1*: 409–16.
Razran, G. (1971) *Mind in Evolution: An East-West Synthesis of Learned Behaviour and Cognition*. Boston: Houghton Mifflin.
Rescorla, R.A. (1967) Pavlovian conditioning and its proper control procedures. *Psychological Review 74*: 71–80.
Sandler, S. and Davidson, R.S. (1973) *Psychopathology: Learning Theory, Research, and Application*. New York: Harper & Row.
Sherman, A.R. (1972) Real-life exposure as a primary therapeutic factor in the desensitization treatment of fear. *Journal of Abnormal Psychology 79*: 19–28.
Sherman, J.A. and Baer, D.M. (1969) Appraisal of operant therapy techniques with children and adults. In C.M. Franks (ed.) *Behaviour Therapy: Appraisal and Status*. New York: McGraw-Hill.
Shettleworth, S.J. (1972) Constraints on learning. In D.S. Lehrman, R.A. Hinde and E. Shaw (eds) *Advances in the Study of Behaviour 4*: 1–68. New York: Academic Press.
Skinner, B.F. (1950) Are theories of learning necessary? *Psychological Review 57*: 193–216.
Skinner, B.F. (1953) *Science and Human Behaviour*. New York: Macmillan.
Skinner, B.F. (1963) Behaviourism at fifty. *Science 140*: 951–8.
Sloane, R.B. (1975) *Psychotherapy Versus Behaviour Therapy*. New York: Harvard University Press.
Thoresen, C.E. and Mahoney, M.J. (1974) *Behavioural Self-control*. New York: Holt, Rinehart & Winston.
Wagner, M.K. and Cauthen, N.R. (1968) A comparison of reciprocal inhibition and operant conditioning in the systematic desensitization

of a fear of snakes. *Behaviour Research and Therapy* 6: 225–7.
Watson, J.B. (1913) Psychology as a behaviourist views it. *Psychological Review* 20: 158–77.
Watson, J.B. (1919) *Psychology from the Standpoint of a Behaviourist.* Philadelphia: Lippincott.
Watson, J.B. (1924) *Behaviourism.* New York: Norton.
Weiner, H. (1962) Some effects of response costs upon human operant behaviour. *Journal of the Experimental Analysis of Behaviour* 5: 201–8.
Weiner, H. (1964) Conditioning history and human fixed-interval performance. *Journal of the Experimental Analysis of Behaviour* 7: 383–5.
Weiner, H. (1965) Conditioning history and maladaptive human operant performance. *Psychological Reports* 17: 935–42.
Weiner, H. (1969) Controlling human fixed-interval performance. *Journal of the Experimental Analysis of Behaviour* 12: 349–73.
Weingartner, A.H. (1971) Self-administered aversive stimulation with hallucinating hospitalized schizophrenics. *Journal of Consulting and Clinical Psychology* 36: 422–9.
Wolpe, J. (1977) Inadequate behaviour analysis: the Achilles heel of outcome research in behaviour therapy. *Journal of Behaviour Therapy and Experimental Psychiatry* 8: 1.3.

Name index

Figures in italics refer to bibliographical references

Agras, W.S., *212*
Aldis, O., 115, *126*
Allyon, T., xvi, 60, 66, 67, 69, 72, 77, 85, 94, *100*, 152, *160*, 180, *184*
Anderson, E.G., 75, *79*, 103, *128*
Arnkoff, D., 202, *212*
Asarnow, J., 176, 181, *187*
Ashem, B., 209, *211*
Azrin, N., xvi, 5, *26*, 33, *55*, 60, 74, 77, *78*, *89*, *101*, 108, *126*, 156, 157, *160*, 180, *184*, 205, *211*.

Bachman, J.A., 39, 40, *55*
Baer, D.M., 18, *26*, 29, 48, *55*, *56*, 72, *80*, 154, *160*, 166, 176, 181, *184*, *188*, 194, 197, 198, *211*, *213*
Bagshaw, M., 179, *185*, *186*, 198, *212*
Bakan, D., 7, 8, *26*
Bandura, A., xvii, *xviii*, 82, *100*, 137, *146*, 163, *184*, 193, 204, 207, *211*, *212*
Barber, B.J., 82, *100*
Barlow, D.H., 21, 22, *27*
Baron, A., 198, *212*
Baron, M.G., 203, *211*
Barrett, C.L., 142, *146*
Barrett, J.E., 39, *56*
Bass, B.A., 209, *211*
Beasley, A., 33, *56*
Beck, A., 163, 180, *184*
Becker, W.C., 67, *78*

Belmont, I., 88, *100*
Belmont, J., 181, *184*
Bem, S.L., 172, 179, *184*
Bentall, R.P., *186*
Bergin, A.E., 19, *27*
Biferno, M.A., 197, *211*
Bigelow, G., 158, *161*
Bijou, S.W., 17, 18, *26*, 29, *56*, 197, 198, *211*
Birkimer, J., 169, 176, *187*
Bitterman, M.E., 193, *211*
Björkstrard, P., 197, *213*
Blackman, D.E., xvi, 1*ff*., 2, 15, 19, 24, *26*, 84, *101*
Blom, G., *185*
Blood, M.R., 110, *126*
Blurton-Jones, N., 16, *26*
Bolles, R.C., 193, *211*
Bootzin, R.R., 196, *211*
Boren, J.J., 10, *28*
Borkovec, T.D., 137, *146*
Bornstein, P., 168, 176, 177, *184*
Borkowski, J., 182, *184*
Bradshaw, C., 6, *26*
Braukmann, C.T., 67, *79*
Brewer, W.F., 129, 143, *146*
Brewster, L., *160*
Brigham, J.A., 19, *26*, 49, *56*
Brinkman, R., *101*
Broden, M., 33, *56*
Brown, A., 176, *185*

Brown, B.S., xiv, *xviii*
Brown, M., 170, *185*
Brown, P.L., 140, *146*
Buckhalt, J.A., 44, *56*
Buckholdt, D., 152, *160*
Buckwald, A.M., 192, 194, 197, 201, *211*
Bugental, D., 169, 175, *185*
Burroughs, W.A., 115, *128*
Bushell, D., 67, 70, *78*
Butterfield, E., 181, *184*

Calkins, R.P., 177, *185*
Cameron, R., 170, 171, 175, 180, *187*
Camp, B., 168, *185*
Campione, J., 176, *185*
Carbonell, J., 166, *186*
Carmine, B.W., 67, *78*
Carpenter, F., 122, *126*
Castenada, C., 179, *185*
Catania, A.C., 19, 26, 35, 52, 56, 163, *185, 212*
Cathey, P.J., 111, *126*
Cautela, J.R., 203, *211*
Cauthen, N.R., 206, *213*
Cavanaugh, J., 182, *184*
Chadwick, B.A., 72, *78*
Chaffee, J.L., 75, *78*
Chapman, C., 75, *78*
Cherrington, D.J., 106, 123, *126*
Chomsky, N., 102, 122, *126*, 196, *211*
Cohen, D., xiii, *xviii*
Cone, J.D., 61, *79*
Conway, A.V., 133, *146*
Copeland, G., 33, *56*
Cullen, C.N., xvi, 29*ff.*, 45, 49, 50, 52, 56, 57, 82, *100*, 149*ff.*, 153, *160, 161*

Dapcich-Miura, E., 76, *78*
Davey, G.C.L., xiv, xvi, *xviii*, 102*ff.*, 108, 122, 125, 189*ff.*, 196, 197, 201, *211*
Davidson, R.S., 197, *213*
Davidson, W.S., *27*
Davies, D.L., 155, *160*
Davis, R.T., 111, *126*
Davison, G.C., 23, *27*, 134, 135, *146, 148*
Dawson, M.E., 197, *211*
Day, R.C., 72, *78*
Dean, P., *186*
De Charms, R., 111, *126*
Deci, F.L., 111, *127*

De Montes, A.I., 108, *127*
De Vries, D.L., 109, *127*
Deslauriers, B.C., 103, *127*
Dimond, S., *101*
Dirks, M.J., 181, *186*
Dolan, M.P., 81, *101*
Dollard, J., 190, 195, *211*
Dominques, B., 108, *127*
Donner, L., 209, *211*
Douglas, V., 167, *185*
Drabman, R.S., 64, *78*
Dunham, P., 112, *127*
Dworkin, B.R., 139, *147*
D'Zurilla, T., 163, 174, *185*

Eames, P., xvi, 81*ff.*, 82, *83*
Ellis, A., 163, 180, *185*
Ellström, P., 197, *213*
Engel, B.T., 20, *28*
Ervin, F.R., 85, *101*
Erwin, E., 192, 197, 201, 203, 204, *211*
Etzel, B.C., 51, 52, 53, *57*
Everett, P.B., 74, *78*, 103, *127*
Eysenck, H.J., 133, *146*, 189, 190, 191, 194, 195, 197, *211*

Feldman, M.P., 132, *146*
Ferritor, D.E., 152, *160*
Ferster, C.B., 4, 5, 17, *27*, 43, 45, 55, 56, 192, *211*
Field, J.H., 88, *101*
Finch, A.J., 168, *186*
Fixen, D.L., 64, 67, *79*
Flores, T., 74, *77*
Foit, J., *101*
Fordyce, W.E., 25, *27*
Foreyt, J., 162, *185*
Foxx, R.M., 74, *78*
Freud, S., 133, *147*
Friedling, C., 170, *185*
Freisen, D.D., 63, *78*

Gamboa, V.U., 115, *128*
Garcia, J., 144, *147*
Garfield, S.L., 19, *27*
Garson, C., *185*
Geesey, S., 63, *79*
Geller, E.S., 75, *78*, 103, *127, 128*
Gentry, W.D., 75, *80*
Gillan, P., 136, *147*
Giovannani, J.M., 172, *188*
Glowa, J.R., 39, *56*
Glynn, E.L., 64, *78*

Name index 217

Goldberg, K., 44, 56
Goldfried, M., 163, 174, *185*
Goldiamond, I., xvi, 30, 36, 40, 41, 48, 56, 57, 149, 150, 151, 153, 154, 158, 159, 207, *211*
Goldstein, A., 132, 146, *147*
Gollub, L.R., 5, *27*
Goodman, J., 164, 165, 166, 167, 168, 169, 175, *187*
Goodwin, W., *101*
Goss, A.E., 179, *185*
Green, A.H., 40, *56*
Greenberg, D.J., 63, *78*
Greenspoon, J., 162, 163, *185*
Gresen, R., *185*
Gripp, R.F., 69, *78*
Guthrie, E., 138

Hager, J.L., 6, *28*
Hake, D.F., 74, *78*
Hall, R.V., 33, *56*
Hamblin, R.L., 152, *160*
Harlow, H.F., 111, *126*
Harris, B., xiv, *xviii*
Hartlage, L.C., 69, *78*
Harzem, P., 4, 6, *28*, 179, *185*, *186*, 198, *212*
Hattersley, J., xvi, 29*ff*., 38, *56*, 149*ff*., 153, 159, *160*, *161*
Hayward, S.C., 74, *78*
Heather, N., 155, *160*
Hebert, F., *185*
Henker, B., 169, 175, *185*
Hermann, J.A., 108, *127*
Herrnstein, R.J., 40, *56*
Hersen, M., 21, 22, *27*
Herzberg, F., 104, *127*
Higa, J.R., 177, *185*
Higson, P., xvii, 24, 25, 162*ff*., 171, *185*, *186*
Hineline, P.N., 5, *27*
Hodgson, R., 204, *213*
Holland, J.G., 123, *127*
Hollon, S.D., 162, 163, 177, *186*
Hollon, T.H., 81, *101*
Holz, W.C., 5, *26*, 108, *126*
Hopkins, B.L., 55, *56*, 108, *127*
House, B.J., 82, 87, *101*
Hovell, M.R., 76, *78*
Hugdahl, K., 143, 144, *147*
Hughes, S., 179, *186*, 198, *212*
Hull, C.L., 138
Hunt, G.M., 156, 157, *160*

Hunter, W.S., 179, *186*
Hutchinson, R.R., 39, *56*

Ingram, R.E., 75, *78*
Israel, A.C., 169, 175, 181, *186*

Jablonsky, S.F., 109, *127*
Jacobsen, E., 130, *147*
Jenkins, H.M., 140, *146*
Jones, L., 52, *57*
Jones, M.C., 130, 137, *147*
Jones, R.T., 74, *78*, 82

Kagan, J., 165, *186*
Kamin, L.J., 142, *147*
Kanfer, F., 199, 208, *211*
Kaplan, S.J., 74, 77
Karoly, P., 181, *186*, 199, 208, *211*
Kaufman, A., 198, *212*
Kazdin, A.E., xvi, 19, 20, 21, *27*, 32, 33, 34, 49, *57*, 59*ff*., 60, 63, 66, 69, 70, 72, 76, *78*, *79*, 136, *147*, 163, 165, 167, 177, 180, 186
Keehn, J.D., 84, *101*
Keeley, S., 166, *186*
Kelleher, R.T., 5, *23*, 27
Keller, D.J., 132, 146, *147*
Kelly, K., 72, 77
Kelly, M.B., 34, *57*
Kendall, P.C., 162, 163, 177, *186*
Kimble, G.A., 100, *101*
Kinne, S., 124, *127*
Kirigin, K.A., 67, *78*
Knapczyk, D.R., 66, *79*
Koegel, R.L., 70, *78*
Koelling, R.A., 144, *147*
Koestler, A., xv, *xviii*, 196, *212*
Kohlenberg, R., 103, *127*
Komaki, J., 120, *127*
Kopp, R.M., 198, *212*
Krantz, D.V., 15, *27*
Krasner, L., 18, *27*, *28*, 131, *148*, 190, 195, 199, 201, *212*
Kreitner, R., 110, 117, 122, 123, *127*

Lamal, P., 162, 163, *185*
Lancaster, J., 59
Landeen, J., *101*
Lang, P.J., 136, *147*
Latham, G., 115, 124, *127*, *128*
Laties, V.G., 198, *212*
Lawrence, C., 158, *161*
Lawson, D.M., 209, *212*

218 Applications of conditioning theory

Lazarus, A.A., 133, *147*, 206, *212*
Leblanc, J.M., 53, *57*
Ledwidge, B., 162, 163, 177, 179, *186*
Legewie, H., *101*
Legewie-Bertzborn, H., 81, *101*
Legge, D., 82, *100*
Leitenberg, H., 206, *212*
Lemere, F., 131, *147*
Lentz, R.J., 65, 70, *79*
Liebson, I., 158, *161*
Lindsley, O.R., 84, *101*, 190, *212*
Lippman, L.G., 198, *212*
Lishman, W.A., 83, *101*
Lloyd, K.E., 103, *128*
Lloyd, M.E., 103, *128*
Locke, E.A., 163, 177, *186*, 207, *212*
London, P., 191, 193, 210, *212*
Lovaas, I.O., 45, *57*
Lowe, C.F. xv, 6, 24, 25, *26*, *27*, 162*ff.*, 163, 172, 176, 179, 180, *185*, *186*, 192, 197, 198, *212*
Luria, A.R., 82, *101*, 164, 166, 179, *186*
Luthans, F., 110, 111, 117, 122, 123, *127*

MacCulloch, M.J., 132, *146*
MacDonald, M.L., *27*
Mackintosh, N.J., 6, *27*
Magaro, P.A., 69, *78*
Mahoney, M.J., 124, *128*, 162, 163, 164, 177, 179, *187*, *188*, 198, 200, 202, 207, 210, *212*, *213*
Margolis, R.B., 172, 175, *187*
Marholin, D., 72, *79*, 152, *160*
Mark, V.H., 85, *101*
Marquis, J.N., 132, *147*
Martin, J., 179, *187*
Marton, P., *185*
Mathews, A., 137, *147*
Matson, J.L., 48, *57*
Matthews, B., 198, *212*
Mawhinney, T.C., 105, 112, *127*
May, R.B., 209, *212*
McDowell, J.J., 19, *27*
McGregor, D., 104, 105, 112, *127*
McKee, J.M., 67, *77*
McLeish, J., 179, *187*
McNamara, J.R., 75, *79*
Meichenbaum, D., 163, 164, 165, 166, 167, 168, 169, 170, 171, 172, 175, 176, 179, 180, 181, *187*, 198, 200, *213*
Mercatoris, M., 171, *187*

Meyer, M.E., 198, *212*
Meyers, A.W., 74, *78*, 171, *187*
Michael, S., 85, 94, *100*
Milan, M.A., 67, *77*
Milgram, S., 198, *213*
Miller, N.E., 20, *27*, 139, *147*, 190, 195, *211*
Minke, K.A., *101*
Mikulas, W.L., 196, *213*
Mittler, P., 26, *27*
Moore, B.R., 193, *213*
Montes, F., 108, *127*
Morse, W.H., 5, 23, *27*
Mowrer, O.H., 131, 138, *147*
Mowrer, W.A., 131, *147*
Murphy, G.H., 48, *57*

Neale, J.M., 134, *146*
Neilsons, T., 169, 175, *187*
Nelson, G.L., 61, *79*
Nelson, W., 169, 175, *187*
Neitzel, M.T., 25, *27*
Nord, W., 105, 108, 112, *127*
Norton, C., 81, *101*

Oakley, D.A., 86, 87, *101*
Oates, D., 111, *128*
O'Brian, F., 89, *101*
O'Callaghan, M., xvi, 129*ff.*
Öhman, A., 143, 144, *147*, 197, *213*
O'Leary, K.D., 131, *147*, 153, *160*, 181, *186*
O'Leary, S.G., 170, *185*
Ollendick, T.H., 48, *57*
Osbourne, J.G., 75, *79*, 103, *128*
Osipow, S.H., 106, *128*

Paivio, A., 183, *187*
Palmer, M.H., 103, *128*
Parry, P., *185*
Patterson, G.R., 68, 74, *79*, *80*
Paul, G.L., 65, 69, 70, *79*, 134, *148*, 206, *213*
Pavlov, I.P., xi, xii, xiv, xvii, 130, *148*
Pearce, M.G., 120, *127*
Pearse, I.H., 159, *160*
Pedalino, E., 115, *128*
Phillips., D., 72, *79*
Phillips, E.A., 64, *79*
Phillips, E.L., 64, 67, *79*
Phillips, T., 103, *127*
Pisa, A., 63, *78*
Porteus, S.D., 165, *187*

Name index

Powers, R.B., 75, 79, 103, *128*
Procter, W., 103, *127*
Pulaski, J.L., 59, *79*

Quevillon, R., 168, 176, 177, *184*

Rachlin, H., 163, 179, *188*, 200, *213*
Rachman, S., 133, 136, *147*, *148*, 194, 195, 204, 206, *213*
Rathjen, D., 162, *185*
Ray, B.A., 37, 51, 52, 53, 54, *57*
Rayner, R., 129, 130, *148*
Razran, G., 193, 197, *213*
Reitz, H.J., 106, 111, 123, *126*, *128*
Rescorla, R.A., 141, 142, 143, *148*, 206, *213*
Rincover, A., 70, *79*
Risley, T.R., 75, *78*, 154, *160*, 166, 176, 180, 181, *184*, *188*
Roberts, M.D., 67, 77, 152, *160*
Robertson, I., 155, *160*
Rogers-Warren, A.R., 181, *188*
Rosenbaum, M.S., 66, 69, *77*
Russo, D.C., 70, *79*
Rutherford, R.B., 44, *56*

Sagvolden, T., *212*
Salzingker, K., 20, *27*
Sandler, S., 196, *213*
Scheid, A.B., 106, *128*
Schilmoeller, G.L., 53, *57*
Schilmoeller, K.J., 51, 52, 53, *57*
Schnaitter, R., 36, *57*
Schneiderman, N., 20, *28*
Schneier, C.E., 108, *128*
Schoenfeld, W.N., 41, *57*
Schwartz, A., 30, *51*, 159, *160*
Schwartz, G.E., 75, *79*
Scott, W.E., 106, 112, 123, *126*
Seaver, W.B., 73, *80*
Seligman, M.E.P., 6, *28*, 144, *148*
Settlage, P.H., 111, *126*
Sheahan, D.B., 155, *161*
Shean, J.D., 69, *80*
Schemberg, K., 166, 171, 172, 175, *186*, *187*
Sherman, A.R., 204, *213*
Sherman, J.A., 48, *56*, 194, *213*
Shettleworth, S.J., 193, *213*
Shimoff, E., *212*
Shure, M., 180, *188*
Sidman, M., 10, *28*, 37, 51, 52, 53, 54, *57*, 172, *188*

Siegel, L.J., 72, *79*
Sirota, A., 171, *187*
Skinner, B.F., xiv, 2, 4, 5, 11, 14, 15, 17, 20, *27*, *28*, 33, 35, 36, 37, 40, 42, 43, 45, 55, 56, *57*, *58*, 59, *80*, 82, *101*, 102, 103, 105, 106, 107, 122, 123, 124, *128*, 138, 149, 151, 152, 159, *160*, 162, 177, 178, 179, 182, *188*, 190, 192, 199, 201, *211*, *212*, *213*
Sloane, R.B., 206, 209, *213*
Smith, K., 139, *148*
Smith, L., 152, *160*
Sobell, L.C., 155, 156, *161*
Sobell, M.B., 155, 156, *161*
Sokolov, A.N., 179, *188*
Solomon, R.L., 136, *148*, 190, *212*
Sperling, G., 82, *101*
Spivack, G., 180, *188*
Staats, A.W., 86, *101*
Stallings, J., 70, *80*
Steinman, W.M., 152, *160*
Stephens, T.A., 115, *128*
Stokes, T.F., 72, *80*
Stolz, S.B., xiv, *xviii*
Stricker, D., 158, *161*
Strupp, H.H., 177, *188*
Stuart, R.B., 68, *80*
Szabadi, E., 6, *26*, *27*

Tennant, L., xvi, 29*ff.*, *56*, 149*ff.*, 153, *160*, *161*
Terrace, H.S., 5, *28*
Tharp, R.G., 25, *28*, 177, *185*
Thomas, G., xvi, 84, *101*, 129*ff.*
Thomas, J.D., 64, *78*
Thompson, C.E., *212*
Thompson, T., 10, *28*
Thoresen, C.E., 124, *128*, 198, 200, 207, 210, *213*
Thorndike, E.L., xi, xvii
Tierney, A.J., 33, *58*
Tuso, M.A., 103, *127*
Tyron, W.W., 42, *58*

Ullman, L., 18, *27*, *28*, 131, *148*, 172, *188*, 195

Valentine, C.W., 134, *148*
Van Doorninck, W., *185*
Voegtlin, W.L., 131, *147*, *148*
Vroom, V.H., 109, *128*
Vygotsky, L., 164, 178, 179, *188*

Waddell, V.M., 120, *127*
Wagner, A.R., 143, *148*
Wagner, M.K., 206, *213*
Wall, R.T., 81, *101*
Watson, D.L., 25, *28*
Watson, J.B., xi, xii, xiii, xiv, xvii, 129, 130, *148*, 177, 190, 201, *214*
Watson, L.S., 23, *28*
Weiner, H., 197, 198, *214*
Weingartner, A.H., 209, *214*
Weiss, B., 198, *212*
Weiss, D.A., 94, *101*
Weiss, S.M., 75, *79*
Weiss, T., 20, *28*
Wesolowski, M.D., 33, *55*
Whalen, C., 169, 175, *185*
Wheeler, H., 122, *128*
Whyte, W.F., 122, *128*
Wienckowski, L.A., xiv, *xviii*
Wilcoxon, L.A., 136, *147*
Willems, E.P., 118, *128*
Williams, D.R., 140, *148*
Williams, H., 140, *148*
Williams, R.B., 75, *80*

Wilson, G.T., 131, 146, *147*, *148*, 167, 177, *186*
Wilson, T., 163, 177, *188*
Winkler, R.C. 153, *161*
Winett, R.A., 27, 153, *161*
Witmer, J.F., 103, *127*, *128*
Wolf, M.M., 29, 33, *58*, 64, 67, *79*, 154, *160*, 166, 176, *184*
Wolpe, J., 130, 133, *148*, 162, 163, 177, 179, *188*, 189, 190, 191, 200, 205, *214*
Wood, R., xvi, 81*ff.*, 82, 83, 87
Woodworth, R.S., 84, *101*
Wright, D., *212*
Wynne, L.C., 136, *148*

Yoppi, J.O., 66, *79*
Young, R.D., 192, 194, 201, *211*
Yukl, G.A., 115, *128*

Zeaman, D., 82, 87, *101*
Zeidberg, Z, 69, *80*
Zeiler, M.D., 4, 6, *28*
Zivin, G., 164, *188*

Subject index

alcoholism, 155
anxiety, 132
applied behaviour analysis, 16, 46
assessment tests: and mental handicap, 31-2
aversion therpay, 131
aversive control 39; in work organizations, 107-8
avoidance learning, 5, 41-4

behaviour modification, 16, 18-25; and brain injury, 81-100; in organizations, 102-26
behaviour therapy, xiv, 129-46; and conditioning principles, 189-209;and pavlovian principles, 129-46
behavioural medicine, 75
behavioural self-control, 124, 181, 202, 207-9
behaviourism, xi-xiii; and private events, 163 and behaviour therapy, 189-209;
blocking: in classical conditioning, 142

choice behaviour, 6
classical conditioning, 194, 196; and behaviour therapy, 129-46; cognitive interpretations, 143; theoretical interpretations, 137-145

cognitive behaviour modification, xv, 162-83, 192, 202
community reinforcement, 156
conditioning: and behaviour therapy, 189-209; principles of, ix, 113, 122; *see also* classical conditioning, operant conditioning
constraints on learning, 85-6
constructional approach, 149-59
contingency contracting, 24
convert conditioning, 204

differential reinforcement: of low-rate, 45; of high-rate, 43; of other behaviour, 44
discrimination learning, 5, 45, 50-5

experimental analysis of behaviour, 1-26, 149; *see also* radical behaviourism, applied behaviour analysis, functional analysis
experimental design: in the experimental analysis of behaviour, 6-11, 21-2; and self-instructional training, 167-8
extinction, 5, 38-9, 44-5; of a punishment contingency, 43

feedback: in work organizations, 109-10, 118-20

flooding, 141
functional analysis, 13, 17, 23, 35-6, 191-3, 201

intrinsic motivation, 111-12

mental handicap, 29-55
metacognition, 181-2
modelling, 48
motivation: and brain injury, 87-9, 96-9; intrinsic, 112; and work performance, 104-7
multiple determination, 40, 44

neocortex: and learning, 86-7

observation techniques, 30-6
operant conditioning, 2-6, 15, 20, 23, 193-4, 196
operant response, 37
operationalism, 33, 35-6, 203-4
organizational behaviour modification, 103-26; critical issues in 121-5; procedures associated with, 116-18
overcorrection, 48

pavlovian conditioning, *see* classical conditioning
phobias, 130, 133-4
positive reinforcement, 43; *see also* reinforcers, reinforcement contingencies
preparedness: and phobias, 144
private events, 13-14, 24-5, 163, 177-82
prompting, 46, 98
punishment, 44, 90-4, 107-8

radical behaviourism, 11-16, 82, 84, 210; *see also* experimental analysis of behaviour
reinforcement contingencies: in token economy, 61-3; in work organizations, 104-7, 112-16
reinforcers: self-administered, 64; in token economy, 60-1; in work organizations, 107, 109-12
response shaping, 46, 96-7

schedules of reinforcement, 4, 112-16; human performance on, 197-8
second-order conditioning, 141
selective attention, 87
self-injurious behaviour, 39-80
self-instructional training, 162-83, 198-9; and behavioural analysis, 177-82; and control of aggression, 167; empirical studies, 166-77; with schizophrenics, 170-5
social learning theory, 199
stimulus control, 49-55
stimulus fading, 47-51
systematic desensitization, 130-2, 134-7, 143, 206

time-out, 40, 48, 96, 152; and aggressive behaviour, 90-3

token economy, 59-77; and brain injury, 95-6, 98-9; in the classroom, 66-7; efficacy of, 69-70; and environment problems, 73-5, 103; and medical applications, 75-6; with mental handicap, 66; outpatient applications, 68-9; with psychiatric patients, 65; and staff training, 71-1; and transfer of training, 71-3

verbal behaviour, 179